PRAISE FOR *THE TAO OF STRATEGY*

'*The Tao of Strategy* is a tour de force of ancient wisdom and its application in the modern world, properly illustrated with examples. It bridges Western and Eastern concepts of strategy to provide surefire solutions in the business arena'

Deepak Parekh, former chairman, HDFC

'An insightful expedition into the world of Eastern philosophies like Taoism, Zen and Confucianism and its immense potential for management principles. The book examines mindfulness, equanimity and strategic intuition, often unappreciated in a fast-paced data-driven age. It shifts the focus from purely analytical approaches to strategies that balance external dynamics with inner calm and presence of mind . . . A relevant book for the future of management as the world looks eastwards for new ideas in a complex geopolitical environment'

Harsh Goenka, chairman, RPG Enterprises

'A discerning blend of Eastern philosophy and modern strategic thinking that is deeply pertinent in today's evolving global landscape. As the Global South rises as a transformative force in the world economy, the need for cultural insights in addressing existential business challenges has never been greater. [This] insightful exploration serves as a vital resource for those seeking to harness the wisdom of diverse traditions to create sustainable success in an interconnected world. This book not only enriches our understanding of strategy but also inspires a holistic approach to leadership that is inclusive, adaptable and forward-thinking . . . An essential companion for the next generation of leaders poised to make their mark on the global stage'

Amitabh Kant, G20 Sherpa, former CEO, NITI Aayog, and author

'A highly intriguing, but equally relevant, thesis for Western-trained minds. In today's turbulent and frenetic data-obsessed world, Bourgeois, Eygenson and Namasondhi rightly argue that data merely keeps one locked in the past. Business strategy is a game into the future . . . and the future is not going to be like the past. A new mindset and a panoramic perspective derived from seven Eastern philosophies (from Japan, India and China) coupled ... hard data is the Tao (the way) forward. Soft science is going to be the more effective tool in strategy creation and implementation. A must-read'

Hrishi Bhattacharyya, former senior VP, Unilever, and author

'*The Tao of Strategy* infuses Eastern ideas and wisdom into modern management pedagogy—an essential read for entrepreneurs and strategists'

R. Gopalakrishnan, former executive director, Tata Sons Ltd, and author

'Providing a survey of Eastern philosophy to Western readers, *The Tao of Strategy* helps us understand the strategic behavior of Eastern leaders and their companies, teaching Western managers how to apply these concepts to their own thinking and actions. A very useful, interesting and truly original treatment of an important topic'

Phil Rosenzweig, professor, Institute for Management Development, Switzerland, and author

'Successful strategy is an inspired practice, an arena to play out the best of ourselves or the worst of ourselves. *The Tao of Strategy* is the perfect guidebook to become the best of ourselves, both in business and in life'

Maria Rodale, former CEO, Rodale Press

'An inspiring primer on a wide range of Asian philosophies and wisdom with a difference. The difference is in the ample use of real business cases, on the level of strategic decision-making, to provide perspectives and applications of the various philosophies. *The Tao of Strategy* is an enjoyable read for not just business executives but for anyone interested in Asian philosophies and wisdom'

Kingsley Liu, CEO, Casey Companies Ltd, Hong Kong

THE TAO OF STRATEGY

THE TAO OF STRATEGY

How Seven Eastern Philosophies Help Win in Today's World

L. J. BOURGEOIS III, SERGE EYGENSON AND KANOKRAT NAMASONDHI

BLOOMSBURY
NEW DELHI • LONDON • OXFORD • NEW YORK • SYDNEY

BLOOMSBURY INDIA
Bloomsbury Publishing India Pvt. Ltd
Second Floor, LSC Building No. 4, DDA Complex,
Pocket C – 6 & 7, Vasant Kunj,
New Delhi 110070

BLOOMSBURY, BLOOMSBURY INDIA and the Diana logo are
trademarks of Bloomsbury Publishing Plc

First published in the United States of America by University of Virginia Press 2021
First published in India 2025
This edition published 2025

ISBN: PB: 978-93-61313-07-3; ebook: 978-93-61311-17-8
2 4 6 8 10 9 7 5 3 1

MIX
Paper | Supporting
responsible forestry
FSC™ C016779

For sale in the Indian Subcontinent only

Printed and bound in India by Replika Press Pvt. Ltd

To find out more about our authors and books, visit
www.bloomsbury.com and sign up for our newsletters

To Maggie, my lifelong companion, collaborator, intellectual challenger. It has been an exciting run. You always had your bags packed.—Jay

To Irina, Polina, Sergey, and Yakov, the wisest philosophers I've yet to meet.—Serge

To my grandmother, Ponsri; my parents, Suwanna and Kitsana; and my uncle, Boonchai, all of whom brought me up with Buddhist philosophy and Chinese words of wisdom.—Mint

CONTENTS

ACKNOWLEDGMENTS

Although this book has three authors' names on the cover, it is the product of countless others who have taught us and otherwise influenced how we view strategy. Forty years of students at Darden and Stanford have taught the senior author more than he expected. Generous and forthcoming clients have taught us how strategy really works, and produced the seeds of recognition that strategy is much more than an analytical process.

The executives who contributed to this volume allowed us to see the strategy process at work and how contemplative practices such as those covered here are valuable strategic tools when confronting corporate crises. In particular, several senior executives gave us their time and advice as we developed the book, especially Steve Hansel, Maria Rodale, Naresh Kumra, Nok Anulomsombut, and Sumeth Laomoraporn.

We would like to thank Eric Brandt, our editor, who invited us to initiate this venture and coached the writing team along the way. Our two reviewers helped us to mold this work into a final product, and our copyeditor, Lynne Bonenberger, was instrumental in adding professional polish. Finally, we would like to thank our families and friends, who not only put up with our long hours spent poring over source materials and drafting and editing our manuscript, but also served as our sounding boards, coaches, and cheerleaders.

Jay: Thanks to my Darden MBA students—especially coauthors Mint and Serge—who joined me in this exploration by taking the risk of enrolling in the inchoate venture that was the Strategic Intuition and Eastern Philosophy elective. Many of the ideas expressed here were developed with the executives and management teams that allowed me to copilot with them in the intricacies and discoveries of actually getting strategy to happen. I thank my friend William Purvis Bane, who introduced me to the *Tao Te Ching* many years ago; VN Dalmia, who supported my exposure to India and its history; Mary Parrish, my first Vipassana meditation teacher; and Robert Hodge, who welcomed me into his *sangha* and opened my eyes to the vast wisdom of the Buddha.

Serge: Thank you to Jay and Mint, for allowing me to join them on this adventure; to my parents and grandparents, for an upbringing rooted in intellectual curiosity; to Gina, Michael and Dean, for being my rocks and scheming companions; to the wonderful teachers who shared the power of mindfulness and other Eastern practices; and to Allison, for everything.

Mint: I thank my Uncle Boonchai, my tutor in Buddhist philosophy, and Jay, who invited me on this journey. I also appreciate those who referred us to our Thai interviewees: Patcharanan Khomsan, Walee Wangthira-umnuay, Puree Tantivirasut, and Ratanasiri Tilokskulchai.

THE TAO OF STRATEGY

INTRODUCTION

Imagine yourself in any of the following situations:

1. On the heels of a successful turnaround, the chief executive officer (CEO) of a major regional bank receives notice that an aggressive bank consolidator is about to acquire his closest and largest competitor.
2. The CEO of the commodities division of Southeast Asia's largest conglomerate learns that his recent trade in the rice market just lost more than USD200 million due to an unexpected change in Thai government policy.
3. The CEO of a global exporter of residential air conditioners based in Hong Kong finds that a recent change in Amazon's large-item packaging requirements has caused a huge drop in sales, just days before the company is to launch a game-changing fundraise.
4. The chief marketing officer of a high-growth cyberwarfare software provider is disappointed that the company's sophisticated data-driven strategic planning effort produced only incremental changes relative to its current strategy.

In the first three situations, the companies and their CEOs face an existential challenge. In the fourth, management has failed to come up with an innovative strategy to capture additional share in a fast-growing market.

In all of these cases, leaders must make a tough call. Their decisions and actions will dramatically affect the future of their companies and their careers.

Now, consider the following scenarios describing how you might have reacted under the circumstances:

1. Because of the high stakes, you are anxious. You can't sleep at night. Indeed, your self-identity will probably be defined by the outcome. Will you be remembered as a corporate hero or a failure? Although you may not admit it, your ego and identity are inextricably invested in the success or failure of your decision.

2. You sleep well at night. You have little or no anxiety about the outcome—whether successful or not—and you have disengaged your ego from the results. You are calm, emotionally detached, and prepared to either celebrate a positive result or to deal with unpredictable events as they unfold. You find equanimity in the acceptance of how little control anyone actually has over external events.

The second scenario describes our intention for this book. The *Tao of Strategy* is not simply about Taoism and strategy. The word "Tao" in the title has a variety of meanings—the Way, "the nature," the origin of all things—while also connoting Eastern wisdom. The book presents the nature of strategy and the way of strategic thinking through the lenses of seven Eastern philosophies: warfare and the game of Go, Hinduism, Buddhism, mindfulness, Taoism, *chi* (energy), and Confucianism. Our observations of institutions facing strategic challenges, plus recent research positing strategic intuition as the source of novel strategies, led us to explore how Eastern philosophy complements Western strategy-making.

While we believe that sophisticated strategy analytics are essential to informing consequential strategic decisions, we encountered Eastern philosophies as powerful partners to conventional strategy frameworks. As we will see in the stories we chronicle, the calming of the mind can open it to insightful intuition and novel strategies.

Our initial exploration led to the design of an elective, Strategic Intuition and Eastern Philosophy, as a follow-on to our advanced strategy seminar in the University of Virginia's Darden School of Business. The new course's purpose was to introduce the wisdom of the ancients to modern business leaders, and to cultivate presence of mind—what Austrian military strategist Carl von Clausewitz pointed out as the necessary ingredient for a strategist to experience the "aha" of discovery. The course garnered some publicity, leading to the invitation to write this book.

To bring as many of the philosophical principles to life as possible, we populated the book with scores of examples and stories from consulting experiences, case research, and other sources. In order to make the lessons as contemporary as possible, the authors traveled to China, India, and Southeast Asia in July 2018 to interview senior executives who shared three characteristics—an Asian cultural and/or religious upbringing; an MBA or engineering degree earned in a Western institution; and major responsibilities, preferably at the C-Suite level—and who had experienced a recent corporate crisis, challenge, or wicked existential problem that they addressed using both their Eastern heritage and perspective and Western strategic tools.

Our question was simple: How do executives exposed to both traditions reconcile or build on them when making tough choices?

We also included stories from Western companies and executives whose decision processes exemplified our Eastern philosophical concepts. Some of those companies, including Rodale Press and Google, actively embrace practices such as mindfulness and Zen meditation. Other stories illustrate actions and strategies that, through the lens of Eastern philosophy, appear to be solid examples of successes or, in some cases, failures that might have been avoided through the application of these philosophies.

A list of the executives and organizations whose stories we tell is provided in appendix 1.

The actions chronicled in our stories might look familiar to anyone engaged in modern strategic or change-management practices. Our point isn't that the Eastern principles are new. Quite to the contrary; many of our so-called modern management principles can be traced as far back as 500 BCE.

We have written this book in a way that encapsulates key insights from our philosophers and invites you to embark on a lifelong learning journey. Rather than presenting new analytical frameworks, the book is about discovering and practicing a mindset, with the goal of opening your mind to insights you otherwise might not have had when developing strategy. Although we do not give ready-made solutions or guarantee successful outcomes, we invite you to discover your own answers through the lenses of various Eastern philosophies and practices.

The Tao of Strategy is organized according to the unit of analysis being addressed: the external competitive environment (part 1, "Strategy"); the intrapsychic world of the decision maker (part 2, "The Inner Mind"); and lateral relationships with colleagues, organizations, and societies (part 3, "Relationships"). Each chapter introduces practical lessons, and action imperatives are listed at the ends of the chapters. The final section (part 4) draws lessons from across the entire book.

You can read the chapters in the suggested sequence. Or you can selectively read the chapters that attract you in your preferred order. We designed the book with a focus on the flexibility and fluidity emphasized by many of the Eastern traditions. We provide necessary ingredients; you have the choice to codesign your learning journey with us to suit your personality and situation. Even though some Eastern philosophy is about warfare, competitive setting, and organization, this book is ultimately about you. As a decision maker, you can impact yourself, your family, the people around you, your organization, and your community through countless large and small decisions. Our ambition for this book is to offer an additional perspective on how to approach tough issues in your professional and personal lives and to make better strategic decisions.

As you read, we encourage you to reflect on your thinking process and your mind, to experiment with the Eastern practices presented here, and to explore some of the books recommended in the bibliography.

To set the tone, we turn to our first protagonist. Faced with a crisis in Singapore, she travels to her company's headquarters in Europe to visit her boss.

Zurich, Switzerland, 2018

Ravi Menon was despondent. His management team was panicking, and his overseas investors were emailing him incessantly. In a world of solid economic growth, his year-over-year sales had plummeted 38 percent over the past quarter, and he knew that hesitation would attract attacks from nimble European and American competitors. Just as important, he was the public face of Global Horizons, his USD7.8 billion European consumer goods company in Asia. If he failed to take corrective action, his reputation in global business would be destroyed.

Menon entered his boss's office in the company's Zurich headquarters at 8:30 a.m., having stepped off his intercontinental flight less than an hour earlier.

"Henry, I failed," he said. "I am embarrassed. You placed your trust in me—you appointed me one year ago as leader of a $3 billion division covering all of East Asia—and I have let you down.

"I am here to resign."

Calmly, Henry said: "Ravi, you have an obligation to your employees and our retailers. To leave now would not only have you depart in shame, but would leave your executive team and twelve thousand employees adrift. I know it looks and feels like an emergency, but it is your ego that is clouding your mind. Stop, go back to Singapore, and breathe.

"Come back in six months with a new strategy."

Beijing, China, 2017

"What is strategy?" asked Dr. Cheng.

Cheng Gang, professor of philosophy at Tsinghua University, was sitting across from us in the university's faculty lounge. We were calling on him to learn how a Chinese philosopher presents his topic to his Chinese students.

"Before we discuss Eastern philosophy," he said, "perhaps you can help me, Dr. Jay, as I have only a passing understanding of your subject matter."

Somewhat startled at how our visit had started, I answered, "Strategy is an institution's search for and fulfillment of its purpose."

"It is existential, then?"

"Hmm. . . . I never thought of it that way, but yes, I suppose so. In addition, however, it is how the leader of an institution defines its future and the means to achieve it, and marshals the physical, financial, intellectual, and human resources to fulfill that purpose."

"And," continued Professor Cheng, "from where do these strategies come?"

"Many in my profession believe that good data, analytical rigor, and sophisticated models and frameworks can guide one to a sound strategy."

"Forgive me, Professor Jay, for following a philosopher's logic, but it would seem to me that the key, the foundation, to all this is the data. Would that be a valid assumption?"

"It would."

"And that data, whence does it come? Would it be fair to conclude that it can come from only one source, the past?"

"You would be correct," I answered.

"Would that not suggest, then, that all who feed this past data into models and frameworks would arrive at the same strategies?"

"Yes! Unless the strategist can recombine all that data and the stories from which the data derive into a new strategy."

"How does one do that?"

"That is what we are attempting to understand: how a strategist reaches the beginner's mind that the Buddha spoke about. That is the subject of our book."

What Is Strategy?

Professor Cheng had isolated the fundamental question facing Meijin and every other strategist: In order to "win" in a marketplace, an institution must deliver something of value to a client or customer better than anyone else can. In order to secure the financial resources to do so—be it revenues, investments, donations—the organization must be more attractive than rivals and continuously outperform them. In the strategy lexicon, we call this creating a competitive advantage—delivering superior customer value in a way that cannot be copied. But how?

In order to build and sustain a competitive advantage, the strategist must focus limited resources. As Sharon Oster writes, strategy is a choice to pursue one set of actions over another. Leaders choose actions that reconcile their current understanding of the environment with their forecast for the future.[1]

Essentially, the strategist deploys scarce resources in an ambiguous climate to reach an institutional goal or mission.

Doing Strategy

How does one "do" strategy?

The following three scenarios illustrate how strategy typically is made:

1. *The CEO vision.* The chief executive is sitting at her desk, looking out her window and pondering several alternatives handed to her by a planning staff or consultant. After consideration, she announces the company's "strategic intent," a declaration of a future for which current capabilities are potentially inadequate.[2] In articulating this stretch beyond what is visibly possible, she ignites the institution with a newly declared vision—a vision in which every now energized player can see the part that she or he might play. One globally famous statement of strategic intent was articulated by John F. Kennedy when he declared in 1962 that by the end of the decade, the U.S. would land a man on the moon and bring him back safely to earth. This declaration contained the two essential elements of a strategic mission: a destination and a timeline.
2. *The C-Suite definition of a future.* The CEO and top management team[3] are at an off-site meeting where they pore over reams of analytical reports about the economy, competition, internal resources, and projections for the future. Together, they build a shared frame of reference, engage in debate about possible courses of action, and reach a negotiated outcome with targets, timelines, actions, resource requirements, and task assignments. For example, in the late 1990s, the top management team of Bacardi came to an agreement on a strategy of becoming a global company—a dramatic change from the existing five separate companies that arose out of the post-Castro Cuban diaspora in the 1960s.
3. *Strategy happens.* With plan in hand, execution is initiated, and things do not go as anticipated. As described by Clausewitz, we have entered the "fog of war."[4] Or as Dwight D. Eisenhower reputedly told West Point cadets, "Plans are worthless. Planning, however, is priceless." Why is planning so important? Because we need to have processed enough information and logic in order to be able to adapt to circumstances as they present themselves. In this scenario, strategy emerges from action—it is a constantly changing course in which the organization adapts, shifts, dodges, and feints. It is essentially a constructive learning process. If the strategic plan is like a carefully crafted symphony score, the execution is jazz improvisation. As Tom Thorsen, chief financial officer of General Electric, explained

to an MBA strategy class that was studying GE's strategic planning system: "We do strategic planning to discover what our strategies have been. If the strategies ultimately implemented don't look different from the original plan, then our executives have not been sufficiently enterprising. Our planning process begins by looking at the past year and capturing what we learned from the serendipity that occurs during execution."[5]

The visionary CEO in scenario 1 formed his intuition about an optimal future based on what he learned from natural occurrences and discoveries, such as those described in scenario 3. But in order for that intuition to take hold, he needed to have cleared his mind of preconceptions. In scenario 2, all minds present are engaging in building that intuition—some participants from analytical rigor, others from flashes of insight. The result is a blend of these perspectives.

Eastern Philosophy and Strategy

This book, *The Tao of Strategy,* is about making and doing strategy. Specifically, our focus is on how leaders of institutions might achieve the creative insights that provide novel, and potentially winning, courses of action. Our premise is that as important as Western analytical tools are in the process of understanding industries and competitors, true insights and novelty are achieved through what the Buddha called beginner's mind, the state of mind characterized by emotional detachment from outcomes, abandonment of preconceived notions, and openness to learning as conditions unfold. Logic and analyses help, but only as foundations and preparation, not as the source. Hindu, Buddhist, Confucian, and Taoist philosophies and practices provide a path to beginner's mind and offer perspectives on how to achieve this open, unencumbered mindset.

Readers of this book will meet Eastern philosophies and cultures, and hear accounts from executives in Asia, America, and Europe who have applied these philosophies in leading their corporations. The book offers guidance on cultivating presence of mind, interpreting a wide variety of situational dynamics, and deciding on appropriate action or inaction to most effectively identify and reach a strategic goal.

We draw from treatises and practices dealing with warfare, including writings by the ancient Chinese general Sun Tzu, the Indian classic the Bhagavad Gita, and the Chinese board game of Go. We identify a leader's obligations and responsibilities from the Bhagavad Gita, the renowned Chinese philosopher Confucius, and the fourth-century Chinese classic of Taoism, the *Tao Te Ching.* We learn the benefits of releasing the ego and achieving a state of serenity from the Indian sage Gotama Buddha, the Japanese martial art of *Ki-Aikido,* and the Zen practice of mindfulness. We conclude with an invitation to develop and nurture a facility for encountering your own coup d'oeil—the ability to see things simply and comprehensively in order to experience a flash of insight.

This intellectual tour provides a concise package of intuitive concepts and applicable lessons. We hope that, for some, it also generates a thirst for starting their own self-learning journey into Eastern philosophy.

PART I

STRATEGY

We travel from Western approaches to business strategy formulation to the Eastern way of strategy as revealed in ancient warfare treatises and strategic board games.

Overview of Part I

In chapter 1 we encounter traditional treatments of strategy as seen in almost all MBA programs and practiced by most strategic planning professionals. However, we also note how rarely strategy happens as intended. Instead, new strategy often emerges from efforts to implement the intended strategy. We also introduce William Duggan's notion of strategic intuition, where new insights can suddenly emerge when the strategist has beginner's mind, connects two previously unrelated pieces of knowledge, and follows through with resolve.

In chapter 2, we look at how *The Art of War* lays out strategies, tactics, and factors that increase the probability of success on the battlefield. While the 500 BCE general Sun Tzu focused on the army as the unit of analysis, the seventeenth-century samurai swordsman Miyamoto Musashi's *Book of Five Rings* focused on the individual and the development of his or her skills in combat. Musashi introduces the concept of emptiness (similar to Buddhism's beginner's mind). Both authors emphasize the need to remain flexible, adapt to life's circumstances, prepare constantly, and invest in the process of acquiring new knowledge.

In chapter 3, we derive some surprising strategic-thinking benefits from playing the ancient board game Go. Playing Go teaches us the value—indeed, the necessity—of strategic intuition versus attempting to plan everything in advance. Just as important, we study the practice of focusing simultaneously on a number of battles taking place across the board.

1

Strategy, Insight, and Competitive Advantage

Flashes of insight are rarely experienced during the traditional strategic planning process. But strategists must undertake that process to build the foundation necessary for preparing their minds for the unforeseen flashes that will occur along the way—what we will describe as part of a firm's "emergent strategy."

White Sulphur Springs, West Virginia, 2018

"But, we didn't come up with a breakthrough or anything particularly creative."

Clay Cox, the chief marketing officer at Dominion Analytics, was describing his concerns to the senior author, who had led the firm's planning retreat at the Greenbrier resort. "Sure, the strategic initiatives that emerged from our three days of planning are a stretch. But they seem kind of obvious."

"Are you confident in your conclusions and paths forward?" asked the author.

"Yes, but I was expecting us to find a riveting 'aha' moment during the planning process," Clay retorted, somewhat dispiritedly.

Clay's top management colleagues, however, were content. The meeting was over, and the team was now armed with an in-depth industry analysis; a thorough understanding of Dominion's capabilities and competitive advantages; a new mission with a destination and a timeline; and a set of well-thought-out action plans for competing in the defense cyberwarfare industry. Exhausted, they packed their bags and began the journey back to their headquarters in northern Virginia, ready to start executing the new strategic initiatives. Next week, they would start finding the resources to turbocharge their new product development, create a marketing culture, and improve the inner workings of the corporation—three of their new strategic initiatives.

Stockholm, Sweden, 2007

It came in a flash. "Of course! Let's get our cases in front of business executives and MBA students around the world."

The senior author, then associate dean for international affairs at the Darden School of Business at the University of Virginia, was walking past the open door of an executive classroom at Stockholm's Swedish School of Economics. He was on a multischool tour around the world, nourishing existing relationships with other MBA programs and establishing new ones. As he passed the classroom, he noted that the students had on their desks a business case study published by INSEAD, the renowned French business school.

Two years previously, in 2005, the senior author had met with Darden dean Bob Bruner to discuss the school's globalization strategy. The author had asked, "How will the Darden School be different in ten years? What is our strategic vision?"

"We will be recognized as among the best MBA programs in the world," replied Bruner. This was a bold statement, as it was generally acknowledged that Darden was seen as a great regional school that had only recently achieved national ranking in the U.S.

How to do this? Darden had a total of ten thousand alumni at that time, of whom a thousand lived overseas. By contrast, Wharton had eighty-five thousand alumni, of whom thirty-five thousand lived outside the U.S. Certainly, it could not be a numbers-led game of "market share" or on-the-ground critical mass. How could Darden increase its share of mind, if not share of market, in the global arena?

The question vexed the Center for Global Initiatives (CGI), which Bourgeois headed.[1] The center had conducted a typical strategic analysis, taking the following steps:

1. Analyzing trends in the global market for business education—GMAT test-taking, application trends, and the like.
2. Conducting detailed analyses of twenty major global competitors, including Harvard, Wharton, and Chicago in the U.S.; INSEAD, London Business School, and IMD (Switzerland) in Europe; and some Asian business schools such as HKUST in Hong Kong and CEIBS in Shanghai. The analyses were conducted along a variety of dimensions, including the nature of the students, faculty, and alumni, and the extent of the schools' global outreach.
3. Taking inventory of Darden's strengths, such as an outstanding classroom experience, students chosen on the basis of character as well as credentials,

abundance of research resources, and a successful and extremely loyal alumni base.

4. Generating a number of strategic alternatives, including establishing a Darden outpost in Asia, Europe, or South America.

The appeal of an overseas center was strong, because several other globally known players had established them as well. There were two problems. One, how could Darden raise the resources to fund such a center? The strategic plan had estimated a three-year startup period and an operational cost of USD15 million. Could Darden sell this idea to alumni donors? And, two, was this merely a copycat strategy?

The next two years were spent scoping out possible sites and partnerships with schools at each location. Beijing? Hong Kong? Singapore? New Delhi? Bangalore? The dean and associate dean called on several prominent and prosperous alumni, seeking both counsel and support.

But it wasn't until 2007, on the trip to Stockholm, that the senior author had the flash, the "aha" strategic insight. Darden's case-writing skills and its case-publishing arm, Darden Business Publishing, were slowly being honed and positioned to increase the school's outside sales of classroom-ready business cases. But they hadn't been included in the inventory of strengths (step 3 above). Darden students often complained that the case collection was very U.S.-centric and did not promote learning about business around the world.

Seeing the Swedish students using INSEAD cases, it dawned on Bourgeois that one stone—the production of international cases—could kill two birds: globalizing student learning at Darden, and placing the school's brand in front of thousands of executive eyes around the world. The infrastructure was in place, and—most important—CGI had yet to budget for the coming year. Why not offer incentives to Darden faculty to write international cases?

Earlier in the day, Bourgeois had enjoyed a morning jog near his hotel in Stockholm, with the concomitant experience of "thinking about nothing." While he was aware of obstacles on the sidewalk to be avoided and street corners to be turned, his mind was focused solely on the thumping bass line of Paul Simon's "You Can Call Me Al" in his earbuds. In other words, Bourgeois had begun his day clearheaded and undistracted, with what the Buddha called beginner's mind—fertile ground for the kind of insight that occurred to him that afternoon.

The resulting strategy was to set up a program that would subsidize case-writing activities, such that if a case were to address cross-border issues or take place outside the U.S., CGI would provide up to USD8,000 in subsidies to the effort. In addition, CGI would use its network of partner schools, alumni, and corporate contacts to generate new case leads. For example, in

Italy, Bocconi University's business school had offered access to nearby Ferrari.

The first scenario described above (Dominion Analytics) occurs on a regular basis in strategy consulting firms and across corporations all over the world. Solid analytical and economic analyses yield insights into possible futures for the firm and probable competitor and customer reactions, but the results are usually logical and incremental extensions of current strategies. The second scenario, on the other hand, is more descriptive of the strategic insight process that occurs when an executive implements a strategic initiative and takes corrective action when it doesn't go as planned. As Bryan Quinn of Dartmouth said, "To assume your strategy is cast in concrete is to assume that new information has zero value."[2]

Conventional Strategic Planning

Various approaches to strategic analysis are available, and although the details differ they all have fundamental components in common. These approaches typically attempt to find an optimal match between the resources and the capabilities available within the firm (strengths and weaknesses) and the external market conditions and environmental trends (opportunities and threats). This match or coalignment (often called a SWOT analysis) results in a strategy whose efficacy translates into some level of corporate performance. The basic dimensions of this fairly straightforward approach are illustrated in the strategy model shown in figure 1.

A key feature in the basic strategy model is the reciprocal influence of all of the variables. For example, in the late 1980s a partner at Arthur D. Little (ADL), a major science-based consulting firm, was reading a *New York Times* story about how the level of expenditures on health care in the United States was accelerating, a trend likely to continue. He connected this with the recognition that his firm had several professionals on staff who had carried out health-care-related assignments such as designing hospitals and evaluating

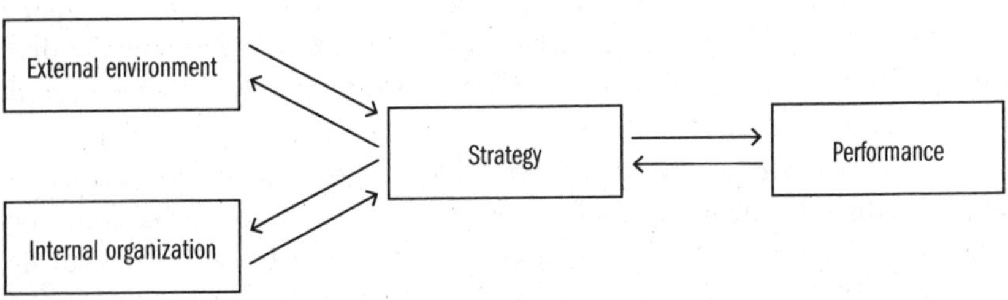

FIGURE 1. The basic strategy model

medical group acquisitions. By responding to the market opportunity and articulating a health-care strategy, ADL would define a new domain (as the arrow drawn from strategy to external environment in fig. 1 illustrates) based on existing internal capabilities (arrow drawn from internal organization to strategy). Having chosen the new domain, the firm would now have to respond to the dictates of the marketplace (arrow from external environment to strategy) by, for example, designing products and services that would be in demand or adapting to whatever governmental regulations might be relevant. To implement the new strategy, ADL might reorganize its staff so that all professionals working on health-care assignments were grouped together (arrow from strategy to internal organization). Over time, this group might increase its proficiency by sharing experience, knowledge, and the like. The degree of success would be manifested in some level of performance (arrow from strategy to performance), and in turn, the performance level would serve as feedback, indicating that further adaptations of strategy might be in order (arrow from performance to strategy).

The model represents a system of interacting parts. But the picture painted thus far is not complete. A "perfect" strategy might be found to violate an organization's noneconomic values.

In our ADL example, there was strong support for the health-care venture among senior management and some of the professional staff. That is, the venture fit the values of top management. However, ADL was originally organized on the model of a research lab, in which professionals were unimpeded by bureaucratic hierarchy and were free to choose their projects. Assignment to projects was by invitation, and assuming the invited persons were billing sufficient time to avoid the pressure to join projects indiscriminately, they could turn projects down. The health-care strategy, in contrast, suggested an organizational unit in which consultants would be expected to dedicate themselves to one major type of activity. This ran smack against the prevailing culture. The strategy was abandoned.

Conversely, management's values may suggest strategies that are not optimal in an economic sense. For example, over the first hundred years of its existence, Aston Martin produced beautiful, expensive, powerful, exotic sports cars. The company was owned by a string of hobbyists and enthusiasts and manufactured the cars at a cost that could not be translated into viable (super-premium) selling prices. Up to around 2000, the company operated with values that were more aesthetic than economic. It wasn't until Aston Martin was owned by Ford Motor Company that the firm focused seriously on profitability.[3]

Therefore, the basic model shown in figure 1, although a "rational" model of strategy, should be amplified to consider the implementability of strategy.

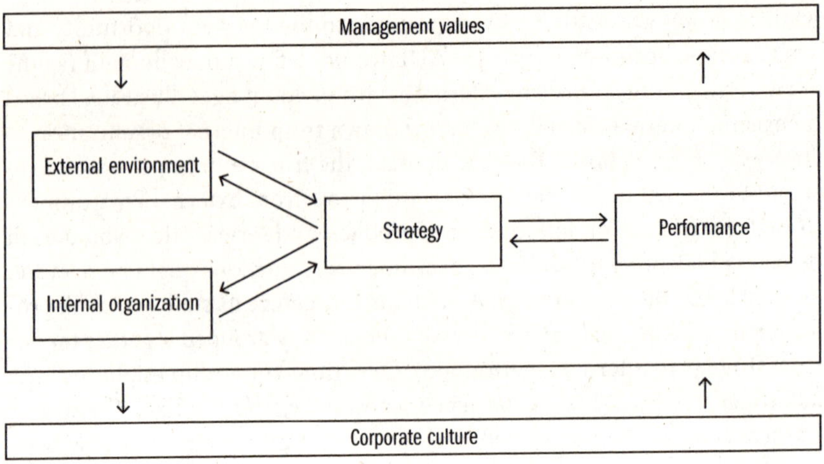

FIGURE 2. The complete strategy model

Management needs to include the "soft" sides of strategy, such as political feasibility and organizational acceptability. Thus, a complete model would include explicit consideration of managerial values and prevailing corporate culture, as shown in figure 2.

The model outlined in figure 2 suggests a sequence of activities in the strategic planning process:

- Environmental trends analysis and scenario building
- Industry and competitive analysis (using, for example, Porter's Five Forces framework)[4]
- Evaluation of current strategy
- Identification of competitive advantages
- Generation of strategic alternatives
- Strategic choice aligned with core values
- Strategic change and action planning

This sequence follows the linear, left-brain analytical approach to strategy proposed in 1838 by Napoleon aide and subsequent military strategist Baron Antoine Jomini.[5] To quote one description of the strategy: "First establish your base of operations, then determine an 'objective point,' and then choose lines of operations from the base to that point to move your army along. That makes three basic steps: first you figure out where you are (Point A), then you decide where you want to be (Point B), and then you make a plan to get from Point A to Point B."[6]

This is the conventional approach. But it is not the full story.

What Is Strategy?

In our reflexive answer to Professor Cheng in the introduction, we defined strategy as an institution's search for and fulfillment of its purpose. That is its overriding role. But there are nuances beyond that.

Ask twenty managers to define strategy and you will hear twenty definitions. Most of these, however, will share some key elements, such as:

- A plan for the future
- A goal, and an outline of the steps to reach it
- A method of facing competition
- A mission
- A path
- A set of integrated decisions
- A battle plan

What these definitions have in common is an orientation toward the future, a sense of deliberate action, and a notion of competitive rivalry. They all conform to the definitions in the introduction, where we saw strategy as a choice to pursue one set of actions over another or the deployment of scarce resources under conditions of ambiguity in order to fulfill a mission. They also correspond fairly well to the dictionary definition, which gives the origin of the word as the Greek *strategos,* or "the art of the general."

These definitions are all appropriate. However, they depict a particular aspect of strategy—that which is thought out in advance, preplanned, or otherwise deliberate or intentional. We might call this "intended strategy." For example, Darden intended to establish an overseas outpost to expand its global footprint and visibility. Between the time when intended strategy is formulated and some point in the future—say two or three years—activities to execute the strategy take place, and the company ends up with what Henry Mintzberg calls realized strategy[7] (see fig. 3).

When asked what percentage of intended strategy is realized, executives will give estimates ranging from 10 to 30 percent. When asked, "Why not 100 percent?" they usually respond with comments like these:

- Conditions changed.
- Customers didn't respond the way we had hoped.

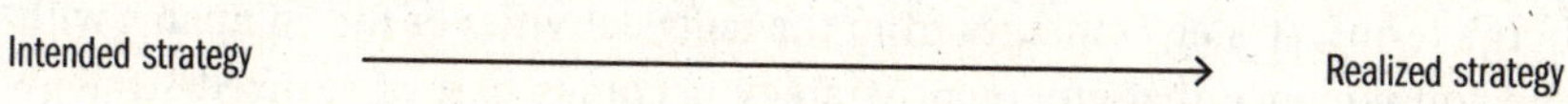

FIGURE 3. Intended and realized strategy

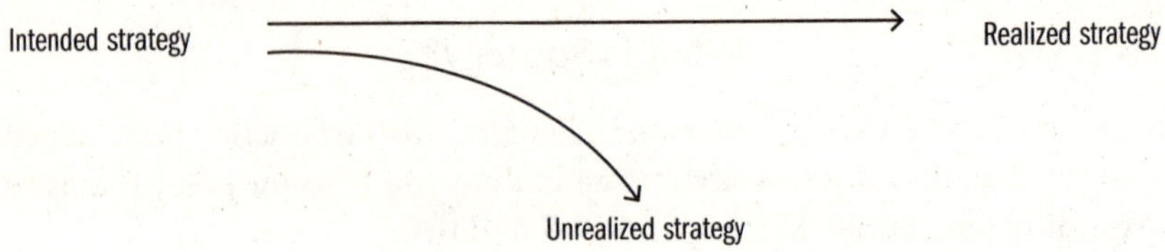

FIGURE 4. Unrealized strategy

- The government changed the rules.
- We didn't have the resources in place in order to execute.
- The organization resisted change.
- The skills needed to execute were not developed in time.
- The plan came from a consultant, and we were not 100 percent committed.
- We didn't think the strategy through clearly enough.

As a consequence, a proportion of intended strategy falls by the wayside and is essentially unrealized (fig. 4).

Additional comments from executives, however, are not stories of failure to implement, but rather stories of seizing opportunities and capitalizing on new strategic insights along the way:

- A competitor dropped out of the market, and we jumped into the void.
- We changed our product specs to respond to a customer request, and a whole new market (not in the original plan) opened up.
- A field salesperson received an inquiry from an unanticipated source, and we shifted our customer base accordingly.
- We made some lucky mistakes.

Or, as one executive put it:

- We discovered new strategies almost by accident. One of us had a flash of insight that was not part of the original plan, but that in hindsight made enormous sense.

Comments like these suggest that much of strategy occurs by trial and error, as well as by accident. In other words, strategy happens. To use Mintzberg's terms, strategy emerges from the daily activities of the company, with the consequence that emergent strategy becomes part of realized strategy (fig. 5).

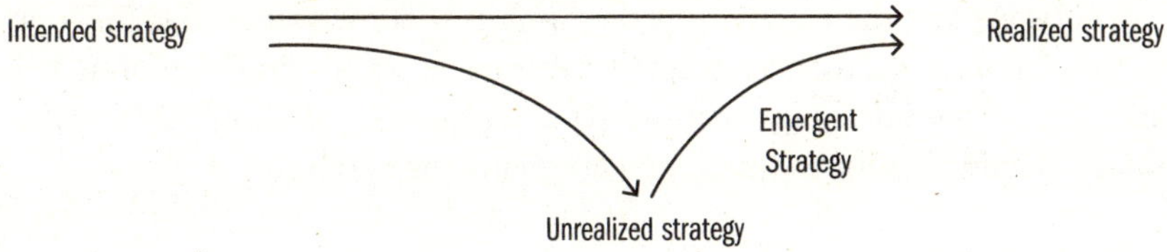

FIGURE 5. Emergent strategy

THE STRATEGY EQUATION

How does one assess the efficacy—the "performance" component—of a realized strategy?

For an organization to serve all of its stakeholders, it must provide quality services or products to its clients at a reasonable cost while paying competitive wages to its employees, serving its community as a responsible environmental steward, and conserving the resources entrusted to it. For a business enterprise, performance includes doing all of the above in a way that contributes a surplus to those who invested their monetary assets with the expectation of a return better than what a savings bank might offer them.

Adding the prospect of growth to an investor gives business enterprises the convenient metric of financial return. This underlying economic premise of business strategy is summarized in the following strategy equation, which holds that a firm's financial performance is a function of two variables: industry attractiveness and competitive advantage or competitive position (same as the two dimensions of the McKinsey matrix, or the two questions underlying Porter's Five Forces framework). The equation reads:

$$\mathbf{FP = f(IA, CA)}$$

where

FP = financial performance
IA = industry attractiveness
CA = competitive advantage

A competitive strategist, however, seeks more than average financial returns. He or she seeks above average or superior returns. In addition, the quest is for the long term, so he or she also seeks sustained superior financial performance. We might rewrite the equation (with new variables bolded) as:

$$\mathbf{SSFP = f\,(IA, CA)}$$

where

SSFP = sustained superior financial performance

Let us expand the equation further. Industry attractiveness is a function of two variables: industry structure (Five Forces) and environmental trends; and competitive advantage is of two types: economic position based and human capability based. So the complete equation would be:

SSFP = f (IA, CA)

↓ ↓

IA = f(**IS, E**) CA = f(**P**, **C**)

where

IS = **i**ndustry **s**tructure (Five Forces) P = **p**osition-based advantages
E = **e**nvironment trends C = **c**apability-based advantages

In summary, sustained economic superiority derives from operating in an attractive industry (IA) and a strategy that creates a competitive advantage (CA) that allows the organization to outperform its industry peers. An attractive industry's health depends on its structure (IS) as well as favorable environmental trends (E); and the strength of its competitive advantage comes from executing a strategy that gives it a favorable position (P), such as market share, as well as unique organizational capabilities (C).

Let us expand on the concept of competitive advantage.

As we saw with Professor Cheng in the introduction, in order to "win" in the marketplace, an institution must deliver something of value to a client or customer better than anyone else can. That is what a competitive advantage gives it—a winning combination of resources and actions. Competitive advantage has traditionally been treated by economists as being based on assets or resources, that is, competitive position. This would include but is not limited to the following:

- Cost leadership (thus able to compete on low prices)
- Differentiation (by, say, unique product characteristics, allowing for higher prices)
- Advantageous location
- Brand equity
- Reputation
- Patents or proprietary technology
- Market share (which usually confers cost advantages)
- Size
- Government protection (such as licenses, patents, etc.)

Note that many if not most of these position-based advantages can be imitated or otherwise circumvented by competitors. By investing in the latest manufacturing technology, one firm can "jump the experience curve" of an entrenched competitor and overcome its cost or location advantage. The Japanese television industry did this to U.S. home entertainment companies such as Sylvania and RCA in the 1980s and 1990s. In the 2000s, Korean and then Chinese firms leapfrogged their predecessors with newer and more efficient flat-screen technologies, each coming in with a lower cost position than the previous low-cost producer. Research by Professor Pankaj Ghemawat at Harvard indicates that most position-based competitive advantages can be copied, imitated, or overcome within seventeen months.

This reality presents the rather stressful specter of always having to scramble to stay one or two steps ahead of one's competitors. In this view, one can never sustain competitive advantage, but must be constantly scurrying to find or create the next, and unfortunately temporary, source of competitive advantage.

Another view, one brought by organizational sociologists such as Professor Jay Barney and strategists such as C. K. Prahalad and Gary Hamel, states that competitive advantage is based not only on economic position, but also on organizational capability. Capability advantages arise from human interactions, energy, coordination, experience, culture, and trust. Examples of capability-based advantages include:

- Technological skills (Amazon)
- Speed (FedEx)
- Creativity (3M)
- Customer responsiveness (Walmart)
- Agility (Nucor)
- Corporate culture (Google)

ORGANIZATIONAL CAPABILITIES AS COMPETITIVE ADVANTAGE

To be a source of sustained competitive advantage, a firm's capabilities must be distinctive.[8] Three conditions must be met:

1. *The capabilities must be valuable.* They must support or lead to a position-based advantage that customers will actually pay for. For example, Apple's culture of innovativeness has led to products that command a significant price premium. In other words, the capabilities must enable the firm to do

things and behave in ways that lead to higher sales, lower costs, or higher margins (price).

2. *They must be rare.* They must have attributes and characteristics that are not commonly found in firms. If everybody's got them, they're not worth much.
3. *They must be inimitable.* Firms without these capabilities must not be able to copy them.[9]

Strategic capabilities can be categorized as follows:

- *Technological capabilities:* The know-how implicit within products, processes, physical plants and facilities, and people's skills and experience.
- *Human capabilities:* The skills, styles, attitudes, and behavior of organizational members. Ultimately, all capabilities are embodied in, or exercised through, human skills.
- *Organizational capabilities:* The structures, systems, and norms that guide and coordinate the behavior of the members of the organization. A useful way of thinking about these capabilities is provided by the concept of organizational culture: the organization's shared and learned beliefs and values, and the behaviors that reflect and reaffirm them.
- *Managerial and leadership capabilities:* The abilities to create, coordinate, and change economic, technological, organizational, and human capabilities. Leadership capabilities determine the ability to translate strategies into action.
- *Strategic insight capabilities:* As in the Arthur D. Little example above, some leaders and their organizations seem uniquely capable of preparing their minds and clearing them sufficiently to discover new strategies from unanticipated sources. (That is what this book is about.)

For example, some intuitive strategists appear to create brilliant and unexpected strategies from thin air, without prior analysis. Steve Jobs, whom we will discuss in further detail in chapter 7, and Apple's development of the iPhone and iPad are often held up as the prototypical examples. But this is naïve. As Jobs described to the senior author in 1981 at a dinner at Stanford, he did voluminous homework to "feed his brain's hard drive" (memory), and he was an avid practitioner of Buddhist meditation practices in order to repeatedly clear his conscious mind. Apple had just gone public, and the author asked Jobs, "Now that you're worth over four hundred million, what now?" Jobs replied:

> I am only twenty-eight. I need to get ready for the next wave. I have read several books on manufacturing and accounting, and am currently in the

> process of building a senior executive team to help me manage this now public corporation. I need them to run the ship while we continue to invent the future.
>
> As an example, we have been recruiting a chief financial officer. We were down to a short list of five individuals. I took each of them to lunch and asked a simple question, "What is the difference between a debit and a credit?" The one who answered in a way that my uneducated mind could grasp quickly got the job. My logic: I want executives who are smarter than I am in their respective professions, and who can teach others what they know without jargon.

Having built his team, Jobs was free to roam Silicon Valley and visit places like Xerox PARC, the corporation's Palo Alto research center, where relatively unsupervised scientists, architects, and tinkerers experimented in an environment of Nerf ping-pong tables, open offices, and whiteboards, and where their next assignment was to "reinvent ourselves" with the aid of mind-clearing meditations.[10] At PARC, Jobs witnessed the use of computer mice and GUIs (graphical user interfaces) in a computing system entirely foreign to either Apple II or MS DOS users. This experience contributed to the creation of Apple's next blockbuster, the Macintosh.

In this example, Jobs was building managerial and leadership capabilities through the process of recruiting a team of senior managers who could also be teachers. Along with regular meditation, that approach freed up space and time for Jobs to exercise his own strategic insight capabilities.

Sustainable competitive advantage is grounded in the systemic nature of capabilities. That is, position-based advantages are by themselves usually not sustainable sources of competitive advantage—they are too easy to mimic. Linked to strategic capabilities, which are much harder to imitate, they become a source of sustainable competitive advantage.

But Again, What *Is* Strategy?

Strategy isn't a thing—it isn't a meeting, a bound document, a PowerPoint presentation, a letter from the CEO in an annual report. Strategy, rather, is an ongoing process. Strategy is a way of thinking about a business and envisioning its possibilities. In other words, strategy isn't something we have, it's something we do and have to keep doing in order to support and grow a successful organization.

Over the past three decades numerous frameworks for how to do strategy have been developed (see table 1), from the famed Five Forces and "blue ocean" strategy to the resource-based view, strategy as options, and the BCG or McKinsey matrices.[11] The question is not which of these frameworks is the most productive or accurate. As Professor Cheng Gang surmised in our introduction, they are all useful for helping us build a thorough, albeit historical, knowledge of our situation. But they alone will not produce or give us our strategy.

This point is exacerbated by the fact that so much of the strategy that comes to fruition is actually emergent. In the end, a firm's strategy is what it does, not necessarily what it had planned to do.

If strategy is a holistic process rather than a set of distinct frameworks, why do we use these frameworks at all? For one, they allow us to codify a process that, for many of the great business leaders, happens intuitively. According to many authors, these people—the Jobses, Buffetts, Gateses, Bezoses, and Musks—seem to wake up every morning with a clear understanding of where the world is going and how to get there sooner and more profitably. For the rest of us, if we were to rely wholly on emergent strategy to drive our organizations' development, we can assume that we would see a great many more business failures. We simply need some way to organize and prioritize the mountains of data that are germane to developing a strategic direction.

We must also remember that the codified frameworks we develop are, at best, proxies for inherent strategic insight, and that our ultimate goal should be to train our insight on ourselves and our institutions through constant practice. As we will see in the next chapter, as well as time and again throughout this book, one of the key lessons from the Eastern teachers is the criticality of practice for building the foundation for subsequent strategic insight.

But what does that mean in terms of actually doing strategy? The tools available to us as strategic thinkers can be brought together to develop as robust a strategic process as possible (see table 1).

WHOLE-ENTERPRISE-DRIVEN STRATEGY

Equally important as the tools used to do strategy is the identification of those who should use those tools. As we saw in the introduction, strategy development is conceived of as the purview of CEOs, planning departments, or external consultants (the "CEO vision" model); little thought is given to the role of the entire enterprise as a source of strategic direction. We believe this framing of the issue is short-sighted at best, and at worst it threatens to leave a firm irrelevant in the face of more nimble competition. The concept of crescive strategic management,[12] taken along with our idea of strategic framework continuums, provides an alternative conception of the strategy creation process.

The crescive model—with its name derived from the Latin *crescere,* "to

TABLE 1. Strategic tools/frameworks

Industry analysis	Typified by Porter's Five Forces, industry analysis asks firms to think thoroughly about the structure and dynamics of their industry and the implications for optimal strategies.
BCG/ McKinsey matrices	Strategic positioning for a multibusiness firm is a matter of plotting the business units relative to each other on a matrix, taking into account industry attractiveness (e.g., growth) and competitive strength (e.g., relative market share). The matrix dimensions are informed by industry analyses and internal resources.
Resource-based view	Resource-based view takes the position that all businesses compete based on distinct resources or capabilities, some of which are stronger, more stable, and more valuable than others.
"Blue ocean" identification	Thinking in terms of "blue oceans" means finding market spaces that avoid the intense competition of established products. This often requires an in-depth understanding of the consumer, leading to the identification of unmet (and often unspoken) needs.
Effectual reasoning*	Akin to resource-based view in its emphasis on an organization's means, effectual reasoning focuses on an organization's current resources and determines how to use those resources in previously unplanned actions, while minimizing the risk involved.
Strategy as options	Options strategy holds that effective planning for an uncertain future requires organizations to place many small bets on different initiatives in order to make themselves viable in a wide range of circumstances.
Strategic intuition	Strategic intuition is a manner of approaching each problem or situation as if it were new and unique, and drawing upon diverse knowledge and sources in order to develop new ways of dealing with problems. Strategic intuition can occur at the top (Jack Welch, GE), during the creation of a firm (Bill Gates, Microsoft), or at lower levels during the course of events (emergent strategy).

* Saras D. Sarasvathy, Effectuation: Elements of Entrepreneurial Expertise, Cheltenham, United Kingdom: Edward Elgar Publishing, 2008. Effectual reasoning is a way of thinking that differs from traditional planning methods, or what Sarasvathy calls causal reasoning, where one marshals available means to accomplish a goal. In comparison, in effectuation one examines the resources at one's disposal and allows these means to show a path and a goal that minimize the possibility and extent of failure. In essence, effectual reasoning takes place "in the moment," where one allows options to present themselves and develop over time.

grow"—most importantly redefines the role of the CEO in strategy development. Rather than crafting and imposing firm strategy from on high (as in the traditional top-down model), the crescive CEO instead takes on the role of strategic mediator, picking from among strategic options presented to him or her and meting out resources accordingly (the "strategy happens" model in the introduction). As a direct result of this change in the CEO's role, the crescive model also redefines the roles of all others within an organization. Put simply, for a CEO to have strategic options from which to choose, he or she must have staff at all levels capable of developing strategic insight and crafting these alternatives.

Of course, it is difficult to picture an organization, no matter how advanced, in which all employees at all levels spend substantial portions of their day planning or developing strategy in the conventional sense. How then can we rectify these two seemingly conflicting ideas? We believe that the analysis/action continuum of strategic tools provides insight. Specifically, we can recast the analysis/action continuum as an executive/front-line continuum (see fig. 6).

Rethinking the continuum in this manner, we are now provided with a guide as to what roles all members of an organization can play in the strategy development process. In essence, this suggests that the closer employees are to the front line, the more their roles allow for in-the-moment strategy development using action-oriented tools like options strategy, effectual thinking, and the like. By contrast, the more people are engaged in management func-

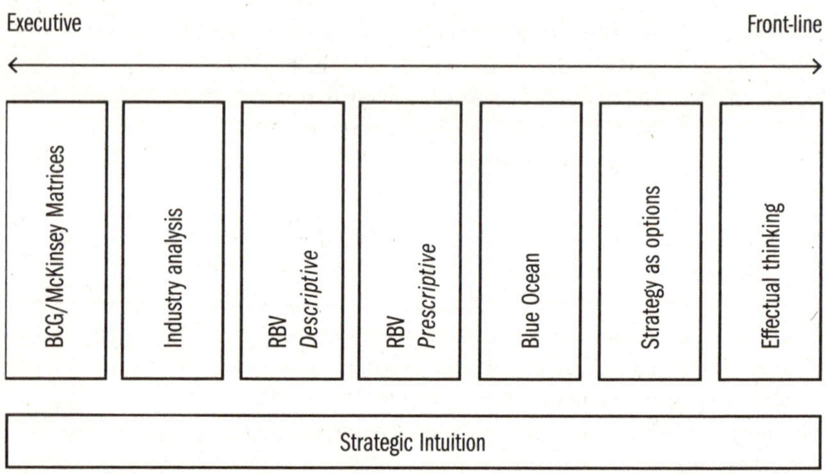

FIGURE 6. Whole-enterprise strategic tools. (Jonathan Pugh and L. J. Bourgeois, "Doing Strategy," *Journal of Strategy and Management*, vol. 4, no. 2 [2011])

tions, the more their roles offer them opportunities to employ comparatively analytical strategic tools.

We will explore an Eastern perspective on whole-enterprise strategy in chapter 10 when we discuss, through the lens of Confucius's teachings on culture, the important role each individual in an organization plays in creating an environment that enables strategic innovation.

STRATEGIC INTUITION

Strategic intuition is an outlier that does not abide by the rules of the executive/front-line framework described above. Rather, based upon the accumulation of experience and insight over time, strategic intuition is a viable method of strategy formulation at all levels of an organization.

Strategic intuition, an idea and term coined by William Duggan, is an attempt to explain and codify the process by which great strategic thinkers arrive at groundbreaking insights and plans. At its essence, this idea, which stands in contrast to both ordinary intuition (gut) and expert intuition (experience), describes the coming together of previous experience and historical knowledge to provide a novel manner of addressing a new problem.

Strategic intuition is the progression through which experience and historical knowledge are stored within our brain and, as a problem is presented to us, are allowed to coalesce and congeal at their own pace to form a wholly new solution. Instead of jumping to a conclusion based on similar problems (as in expert intuition), strategic intuition allows practitioners to draw on disparate experiences to address new challenges. In Duggan's words, strategic intuition occurs when "a flash of insight cuts through the fog of your mind with a clear, shining thought [so that you can] see clearly what to do."[13]

Duggan drew his ideas from a contemporary of Antoine Jomini's, Carl von Clausewitz, who wrote the strategy classic *On War* in 1832. A Prussian military officer, Clausewitz, like Jomini, observed Napoleon's victories, but he came to a different conclusion than Jomini did about his military genius. What Clausewitz observed, he labeled coup d'oeil, a French term meaning a strike of the eye, a flash that produces the recognition of something new and insightful.

Clausewitz's method consisted of four elements:

1. An inventory of stories, histories, and anecdotes that populate the "shelves of one's brain." These examples are stored in the brain's "hard drive," to be accessed when circumstances call for a strategic insight. The examples are complemented by one's own experiences. For example, Steve Jobs read

widely and was constantly seeking new experiences and examples as he toured other Silicon Valley organizations.

2. Presence of mind, "where you expect the unexpected and don't prejudge which examples you will draw on."[14] As in the Jobs example, this is akin to Buddha's beginner's mind, which we cover in chapter 5.
3. The coup d'oeil itself, which combines the appropriate examples from inventory. As Ghyczy points out in *Clausewitz on Strategy,* war is the realm of foggy uncertainty and the province of change. "If the mind is to survive this constant battle with the unexpected, two qualities are indispensable: *first, an intellect that even in this moment of intense darkness retains some trace of the inner light that will lead it to the truth, and second, the courage to go where that faint light leads.* The first is metaphorically described by the French term coup d'oeil, the second is *determination*" (italics in the original).[15] That determination presents the fourth element:
4. Resolution, where one follows through despite the obstacles ahead. This is the execution or implementation of strategy. In the Darden Center for Global Initiatives example, this amounted to earmarking the financial resources and promoting international case opportunities to colleagues.

This book focuses on element number 2: presence of mind. It is this state of clear-mindedness and disassociation from one's ego and preconceptions that can be informed by Eastern philosophies and trained by its practices.

This is not a task or skill limited to the CEO at the top of an organization. As we have argued, in order for a firm to remain agile and competitive, all members of an enterprise must be engaged in the strategy discovery and development process, playing the roles and using the tools most appropriate for their positions. Only with such preparation and engagement can the organization maximize its share of luck.

LAND MINES AND EXIT RAMPS: STRATEGY FOR THE FUTURE

An analogy can help us think though the different ways of doing strategy. Imagine an Aston Martin being driven through a vast open space. Throughout this space, placed irregularly and sometimes at great distances from each other, are land mines and exit ramps that are difficult to see from a distance. As the driver makes his way through the space, he attempts to avoid the mines and find the exit ramps. If the driver is made aware of a possible mine or ramp on the horizon while he is still some distance away, it takes only a small change to his course (i.e., a slight turn of the wheel) to avoid or move toward the object. However, if the driver chooses to ignore the object, preferring to hold his course until he has a better sense of what lies before him, he invites the chance that he will need to make larger corrections as he gets closer. Taken to the extreme, if the driver waits until he is right on top of the mine or ramp, he will have to jerk the steering wheel violently in order to avoid the mine or make the ramp, possibly causing great damage to himself or the car.

This is our job as strategists, both as managers and as front-line intuitors. While it is imperative that we keep one eye on the road in front of us, above all else we need to maintain a clear view of the horizon, watching for any mines that might be in our way or ramps that might allow us access to more appealing markets. If we glimpse them early, we can make small adjustments to move us in the right direction. If, however, we wait until the future is absolutely certain, we run the risk of complete ruin.

Strategy is, at its core, nothing more than making the most of our current situation and planning so that we are even better positioned in the future. By taking full advantage of all the strategic tools available to us and being aware of what lies ahead, we can ensure that we are as prepared as possible to sustain our superior performance for periods to come.

Strategy is about learning, discovering, and inventing. Strategy analysis tools aid our learning about the industry, our realized strategies, our capabilities and economics. The tools are also tools of discovery: What options appear as we analyze the data? Both learning and discovery should reveal the low-hanging fruit that will help us bring about incremental improvements to our current position. It is only after much homework and intellectual sweat that the inventions and potential "blue oceans" sparked by strategic insight come to the fore.

Arlington, Virginia, 2018

When Clay Cox, the Dominion Analytics executive introduced at the beginning of this chapter, stepped outside his house to retrieve his morning newspaper, he encountered a man walking five dogs of varying breeds on leashes. The golden retriever was pulling toward the street, while the spaniel had stopped to sniff a tree. The dogs were pulling their human walker in opposite directions while he tried valiantly to control all five.

Clay had spent the earlier part of the morning listening to a favorite album, Artur Rubinstein's *The Chopin I Love,* and had come out to get the paper in a serene state, unaffected by the coming day's busy agenda. As he watched the dog walker, he was amused.

Then, bang! It dawned on him that Dominion's new product development strategy was an attempt to solve a problem not all that different from the dilemma facing the dog walker. Supercomputers had long ago solved the problem of parallel processing, by which multiple strands of analyses run simultaneously. What Dominion needed was simply to write the software that would harness the simultaneous but disparately focused energies of its research scientists and software engineers. Some of them worked quickly. Some worked on large projects. Some worked at night, and some worked sporadically. This is how Dominion would harness its already existing resources to implement the new product development strategy it had declared four weeks earlier at its Greenbrier meeting.

Forgetting the newspaper, Clay ran back into the house, anxious to get to the office with his newfound strategic insight.

Strategy Lesson from Chapter 1

1. Build and reinforce a culture and system where new strategies emerge naturally from all parts of the organization.

2

Warfare in Eastern Philosophy

Geneva, Switzerland, March 2009

Ulrich Bez, CEO of Aston Martin Lagonda, was poised to introduce the world's first luxury crossover vehicle. Until now, no other carmaker in the ultra-luxury segment had produced an SUV. Mass-luxury brands such as Mercedes, BMW, Lexus, Porsche, and Audi had successfully introduced SUVs, but neither Ferrari, Bentley, Lamborghini, McLaren, nor Rolls-Royce had done so. (Each of the ultra-luxury "Group of Six" sold between twenty-five hundred and eighty-four hundred cars per year, whereas Porsche alone sold eighty-four thousand.) Bez had spent months forecasting the short-term investments and long-term gains from a line of crossovers, and the design department had produced a prototype. Considering that Aston would be the first of this competitor group to enter the EUR150,000[1] price segment, it had the opportunity to establish itself as the uncontested pioneer. It would take Aston Martin's Group of Six competitors at least four years to catch up, if they decided to enter.

Prior to its reveal at the Geneva Motor Show, Bez was highly optimistic about the crossover. In fact, he projected its "strong presence in 100 territories, vastly increasing the global brand reach"[2] to Russia, the Middle East, South America, India, and China, while also catering to customers in Europe and North America. The financials assumed an 11 percent adoption rate by the high-net-worth market segment, and the analysis presented a break-even in five years and a net present value of GBP230 million in year nine.[3]

The automotive press, however, mocked both the concept and the look of the vehicle, calling it "ugly."

The stakes for this decision were particularly high. Not only were the automotive press and Aston Martin's competitors eagerly awaiting the company's next move, but Bez would also have to convince the company's investors that the crossover was worth the investment of GBP339 million.

With the unexpected criticism from the press indicating that consumer demand for the car might be dramatically low, Bez had to decide whether to forge ahead with his vision for the vehicle. After all, Aston Martin would be implementing Sun Tzu's famous dictum of "go where the enemy is not."

Warfare in Eastern Philosophy

War is man's default condition: Of the 3,400 years of recorded human history, peace has prevailed in only 268 of them. As Chris Hedges points out in *War Is a Force That Gives Us Meaning,* "civil war, brutality . . . and murderous repression are part of the human condition . . . almost the daily fare for many but a privileged minority."[4]

Storytellers, children at play, historians, and rulers are fascinated by war and its inherent violence. As depicted in classic literature from *The Iliad* to the Bhagavad Gita to the Bible and the Torah of Abrahamic scriptures, waging war is at once man's destiny, his duty, his curse, and his downfall.

Why the fascination? War is brutal, gory, homicidal, cruel. War can also be noble, seductive, thrilling, and mythically glorious. Indeed, throughout history we have celebrated warriors as one of the exalted classes in most societies around the globe. Sparta's military citizens, Plato's auxiliaries, feudal Europe's knights, Japan's samurai, India's Kshatriyas, and China's shi all occupied a top slot in their cultures' major class structures.

Given the ubiquity of warfare and the exaltation of warriors, it is no surprise that war has been a favorite topic of authors and thinkers. However, in spite of thousands of titles on military strategy in circulation and many more published over the millennia,[5] only a handful are the perceived classics: Carl von Clausewitz's *On War,* the U.S Marines manual *Warfighting,* Sun Tzu's *The Art of War,* and Miyamoto Musashi's *The Book of Five Rings,* among others.

Few business leaders will be surprised by our view that these classic military texts hold valuable lessons for decision makers looking to develop organizational strategy. The use of war as a metaphor for the competitive business landscape of today's global economy is commonplace to the point of cliché.

As an introduction to Eastern philosophy, it is fitting to start with what are perhaps the most familiar Chinese and Japanese contributions. *The Art of War* is one of the most studied and cited strategy books in both the East and the West. While historically less well-known, *The Book of Five Rings* has become an increasingly influential text in both the military and strategy spheres. Sun Tzu focuses on the army as the unit of analysis, while *Five Rings* focuses on the individual and the development of his or her skills in battle. *Art of War* emphasizes information, knowledge, and deception as key ingredients for a winning strategy. It also instructs the strategist to avoid direct conflict; in perhaps Sun Tzu's most well-known contribution to the strategic canon, *Art of War* argues that the best way to win a battle is by avoiding physical engagement entirely. *Five Rings* focuses on knowledge of weaponry and the harmony between an individual's intellectual, physical, and psychological traits. It also introduces the concept of emptiness, or unencumbered mental state. Both authors emphasize the need for flexibility and the power of remaining adaptable, as well as the value of constantly preparing and investing in the process of acquiring knowledge.

This chapter will review the contents of both books, outline their common themes and lessons for modern leaders and strategists, and apply the relevant lessons to Ulrich Bez and Aston Martin.

Sun Tzu's *The Art of War*

Sun Tzu is the most famous military strategist in China's history. Composed in the Spring and Autumn period of the Zhou Dynasty, which lasted from approximately 771 to 476 BCE, his writings on the philosophical underpinnings of success on the battlefield may well be history's most famous treatise on the subject.

Unsurprisingly, many of Sun Tzu's dictums on warfare (such as "know your enemy and know yourself" and "every battle is won before it is fought") have become so well known in his native land that they have entered the common lexicon of Chinese students, scholars, and strategists. His thinking also enjoys almost unparalleled popularity in the region. Many Japanese companies make *The Art of War* required reading for executives.

The Art of War will also look familiar to Westerners.[6] Without diminishing the power of Sun Tzu's wisdom, one could argue that the popularity of *Art of War* among business readers for decades can be attributed to the powerful alignment between the book's principles and the core frameworks found in any business strategist's toolkit. For example, one of Sun Tzu's most quoted passages in the annals of both strategy and war mirrors the ubiquitous SWOT analysis (internal strengths and weaknesses, external opportunities and threats) of most strategic planning designs:

> If you know the enemy and know yourself, you will need not fear the result of a hundred battles. If you know yourself but not the enemy, for every victory gained you will also suffer a defeat. If you know neither the enemy nor yourself, you will succumb in every battle.[7]

Art of War's core message can be organized into four broad lessons:

- Avoid direct confrontation with your opponent
- Build your strategy on a foundation of information advantage

- Stay adaptable and flexible, especially in the face of new information
- Practice deception

The following sections will elaborate on each of these lessons. Also, because *Art of War* contains so many treasures of foundational material, we have chosen a few quotes from each of its thirteen chapters and presented them in appendix 2, "The Contents of *The Art of War.*"

1. AVOID DIRECT CONFRONTATION: "THE SHEATHED SWORD"

Sun Tzu's wisdom rests at the intersection of two seemingly contradictory dictums. While *Art of War* from its opening lines assumes warfare to be an inevitable and even necessary part of the affairs of state, Sun Tzu advises that "to fight and conquer in all your battles is not supreme excellence; supreme excellence consists in breaking the enemy's resistance without fighting." For example, in 2004, ICI Australia, a major chemicals manufacturer, was able to dissuade a foreign competitor from building a new chemical plant in Cairns by announcing its own expansion nearby and getting local government support to do so.

Sun Tzu gives this most famous advice—to win a war before it is fought, avoid battle if possible—not because he believes it is possible to govern without encountering military conflict, but because he believes conflict to be inevitable. If conflict is an inevitable byproduct of competitive geopolitical dynamics, Sun Tzu argues, successful leaders have no choice but to acknowledge the practical realities of forgoing the potential glory of heroic but costly victory in pitched battle in favor of employing limited resources efficiently to overcome the enemy. While *Art of War* offers numerous strategic and tactical recommendations for how to get there—including advice on careful planning, finding opponents' weaknesses, and decision-making that anticipates their next move—it is Sun Tzu's emphasis on achieving military victory in the least expensive and least violent way possible that serves as the undergirding paradigm of *Art of War.*

Sun Tzu argues that "the skillful leader subdues the enemy's troops without any fighting; he captures their cities without laying siege to them; he overthrows their kingdom without lengthy operations in the field. With his forces intact, he disputes the mastery of the empire, and thus, without losing a man, his triumph is complete. This is the method . . . of using the sheathed sword."[8] (We will see the power of this lesson in chapter 3 on how one wins at the competitive game of Go.)

In preparation for its move to block its competitor's new plant, ICI Australia had done considerable industry and market analysis, and, in the secrecy of an offshore meeting, had conducted a simulated war game to be able to anticipate its competitor's probable countermoves. Sun Tzu's sheathed sword highlights the importance of developing a thorough understanding of the market and the competitors in the industry; understanding how available resources stack up against those of competitors; and attacking the market where competitors do not anticipate, the market is underserved, and one can exploit one's own relative strengths. Similarly, Aston Martin was poised to enter a market that was not served by any of the Group of Six.

In sum, great generals, and strategists, are not defined by victories in direct confrontation, but by the ability to overcome opponents while avoiding costly battles altogether.

2. BUILD STRATEGY ON INFORMATION ASYMMETRY: "OUR EYES ONLY"

Sun Tzu's writing is remarkably tactical, and *Art of War,* interpreted literally, is very much an instruction manual for success on the field of battle. Like a chef transcribing a recipe, Sun Tzu shares a series of repeatable steps for achieving positive results in military entanglements in the long term. Chief among his ingredients is developing, maintaining, and maximizing information superiority. Sun Tzu's information-driven strategies center on developing a deep knowledge regarding one's own resources, gathering the best available information about one's opponents, and ensuring that peers, competitors, and even allies are privy only to limited or downright false data about you. With the appropriate knowledge, you are able to identify the best uses of your limited resources, know the best time to engage your enemy, and reduce the risk of a devastating failure.

While few modern strategists would disagree with the importance of developing high-quality competitive intelligence, even a twenty-first-century reader of *Art of War* may be surprised by the primacy that Sun Tzu places on the process. To him, information superiority is important not just as a foundation for successful decision-making, it *is* the strategy. For example, ICI Australia, by virtue of its longstanding relationships with regional and local regulators, had a thorough understanding of the predilections and priorities of the local government. It was able to use that knowledge to help craft a strategy that counteracted foreign competitors' attempts to invade ICI's market.

"The general is skillful in attack whose opponent does not know what to defend; and he is skillful in defense whose opponent does not know what to attack."[9] Whether for an entrepreneur building a startup that competes against established Goliaths or a corporate executive defending a company's leadership position against would-be disrupters, Sun Tzu's advice would be the same: Before taking any other action, invest in creating information superiority.

3. CULTIVATE ADAPTABILITY AND FLEXIBILITY: "MAKING MUSIC FROM ONLY FIVE NOTES"

While Mike Tyson is not often mentioned among the ranks of great philosophers or strategists, his dictum that "everyone has a plan until they get punched in the mouth"[10] is an apt metaphor for the importance of emergent strategy—a bedrock principle of Sun Tzu's approach to warfare that modern-day strategists would do well to take to heart. As indicated in the introduction, crafting intended strategy is useful for choosing a course of action, but it is the quality of emergent strategy that most often separates the victors from the also-rans in the boxing ring, the field of battle, and the corporate market.

Cleverness alone is not enough. Leaders need to be adaptable, nimble, and receptive to change, continuously on the move with flexibility, unpredictable moves, originality, and creativity. Edwin Land exhibited this when he founded and ran Polaroid. Land was always introducing new models and features, usually on an unannounced schedule. He was known for his antics at annual meetings, where he might have clowns juggling, and for spouting statements such as "if anything is worth doing, it is worth doing to excess." When Kodak entered the instant camera market in 1982, it was Land's unpredictability, creativity, and nimbleness that kept his competitor constantly on guard.[11] Due to Polaroid's aggressive responses, Kodak exited the instant camera field just four years later.

Sun Tzu notes that "there are not more than five musical notes, yet the combinations of these five give rise to more melodies than can ever be heard. . . . There are not more than five cardinal tastes—sour, acrid, salt, sweet, bitter—yet combinations of them yield more flavors than can ever be tasted."[12] He urges his readers to follow these examples from the natural world to develop the flexibility and adaptability necessary to create unlimited possibilities out of limited resources and information. When he furthers the nature metaphor by noting that "military tactics are like unto water; for water in its natural course runs away from high places and hastens downwards," he is urging his readers to cultivate not just mastery in each of the individual tactics he advises, but also the ability to adroitly switch tactics in response to whatever unexpected events might impact their competitive engagement.

Aspiring emergent strategists would do well to heed Sun Tzu's advice. Emergent strategy is always the product of unexpected conditions that are by definition impossible to predict. Therefore, as we saw in chapter 1, strategists must cultivate a capacity to be prepared to execute their organization's intended strategy and, simultaneously, to interpret and respond appropriately to evolving market conditions, competitive dynamics, and internal developments.

The nuance of Sun Tzu's advice regarding adaptability becomes particularly apparent when considered in conjunction with his simultaneous focus on intelligence-gathering before entering the field of battle, as described above. On the one hand, successful leaders must prepare diligently before engaging a foe; on the other, they must be willing to let go of their intended plans if the conditions they encounter require a different set of actions. While the juxtaposition of diligent preparation and fluid adaptability makes intuitive sense, business and military history is littered with the cautionary tales of leaders and organizations who, due to an excess of hubris or a lack of situational awareness, never reached their full potential as a result of failing to maintain this equilibrium.

Sun Tzu makes clear that "the general who wins a battle makes many calculations in his temple before the battle is fought,"[13] yet "he who can modify his tactics in relation to his opponent and thereby succeed in winning, may be called a heaven-born captain."[14]

4. PRACTICE DECEPTION: "CONSTRUCTING A TROJAN HORSE"

From optimal formations, to pace of attack, to communicating with subordinates, Sun Tzu's recommendations cover a panoply of scenarios, stakeholders, and subject matter. Yet the purpose of his wide-ranging advice can be boiled down to a single motivation—creating strategic advantage. If leaders' level of strategic ability is defined by the effectiveness with which they can marshal the resources available to them, then strategic advantage can be measured by the difference between two competitors' respective abilities to do so. Hence, to maximize strategic advantage, strategists must attempt to broaden this gap by both cultivating their own abilities and attempting to hinder their opponents' effectiveness. While the three principles identified above—avoiding direct confrontation in favor of more subtle engagement, gathering superior information, and remaining fluidly adaptable to changes in the prevailing environment—are primarily strategies for strengthening one's own abilities, Sun Tzu also offers a powerful tool for tilting the balance by limiting one's opponents:

> All warfare is based on deception. Hence, when able to attack, we must seem unable; when using our forces, we must seem inactive; when we are near, we must make the enemy believe we are far away; when far away, we

> must make him believe we are near. Hold out baits to entice the enemy. Feign disorder, and crush him.[15]

A leader must not only create processes to gather comprehensive, accurate, and timely data, but also leverage deceptive tactics to ensure the inaccuracy of the information his or her opponents will use to deploy resources. To Sun Tzu, deceptive tactics fall into two categories: broadcasting inaccurate information in ways that one's opponent will find credible and are likely to cause the desired reaction; and ensuring that the opponent does not access any material information on oneself. Combined with Sun Tzu's other guidance, deception empowers a leader to prey on opponents' weakness and neutralize their strengths:

> If [your opponent] is secure at all points, be prepared for him. If he is in superior strength, evade him. If your opponent is of choleric temper, seek to irritate him. Pretend to be weak, that he may grow arrogant. If he is taking his ease, give him no rest. If his forces are united, separate them. Attack him where he is unprepared, appear where you are not expected. Practice dissimulation and you will succeed. . . . Let your plans be dark and impenetrable as night, and when you move, fall like a thunderbolt.[16]

> O divine art of subtlety and secrecy! Through you we learn to be invisible, through you inaudible, and hence we can hold the enemy's fate in our hands.[17]

Much of the timelessness of the lessons to be found in *The Art of War* comes from their potential to offer effective guidance in a near limitless variety of scenarios, whether in a business or a military context. The beauty of the author's prose, humanity's millennia-long fascination with warfare, and the applicability across generations have helped *Art of War* achieve its enshrined status along with history's other great literary works.

Musashi's *The Book of Five Rings*

Like *The Art of War,* Miyamoto Musashi's *Book of Five Rings* is a tactical manual for victory in combat. Written in mid-seventeenth-century Japan, *Five Rings* is distinct from its better-known predecessor not only in historical context and geographical origin, but also in some of the lessons modern strategists can draw from its pages. A famed samurai, Musashi wrote *Five Rings* after a victorious career in which he won sixty duels and founded an influential school of samurai swordsmanship. Completed shortly before his death, *Five Rings* serves as an anthology of the philosophies and methods Musashi taught his students. He outlines how to achieve victory in hand-to-hand combat, giving the lion's share of the book to the techniques, tactics, and philosophy that should govern one's physical, mental, and emotional behavior,[18] which results in an entirely different paradigm from Sun Tzu's.

Musashi's focus on the psychology and philosophy of warfare holds powerful lessons. These lessons can be uncovered in the book's five sections, each representing one of the rings of the title. These rings echo the Buddhist belief in the five core elements of earth, water, fire, wind, and emptiness.[19]

- Earth (or "ground," in some translations) represents solidity and hardness. Musashi views earth as symbolic of the practical knowledge, skills, and tools that a warrior must possess and master. Devoting the first section of the book to these principles, Musashi describes the earth chapter as "an outline of the 'Way of the Martial Arts' and the view of my own style. Strategy is the craft of the warrior [gentleman]."[20] To succeed at this craft, Musashi urges his students to draw lessons from the other professions that dominated seventeenth-century Japanese society, or the three other "Ways"—farmer, artisan, and merchant. "Liken a soldier to a carpenter," he explains. "The latter sharpens his tools, . . . prepares the various instruments of his trade . . . and performs his duties well, down to the smallest detail."
- Water, representing fluidity and purity, is Musashi's metaphor for the flexibility that a warrior must exhibit to adjust appropriately when unexpected circumstances interfere with his planned technique. He explains that a warrior "makes the mind like water. Water follows the form . . . of [its] container."
- Fire represents energy, heat, unpredictable and rapid change, and the intensity of battle.
- Wind (the kanji character is the same as for the word "style") represents the diverse range of martial arts and approaches to combat a warrior might encounter across a lifetime of engaging opponents. Musashi urges his students to learn a number of styles so as to minimize the potential for defeat at the hands of a competitor employing an unfamiliar technique.
- Drawing on Taoist concepts of the Tao, or Way (see chapter 8), the book's final section centers on emptiness (or "void"), described by Musashi as "the place from which all other activities come." After explaining numerous techniques in great detail, Musashi concludes his manual with the wisdom that "having attained these principles, you leave them." True mastery does not rely on a set of prescriptive techniques. Rather, students should internalize the techniques and strive to achieve a level of comfort that

allows them to release their grip on formal training. "In the Way of the Martial Arts there is a natural freedom: you naturally gain an extraordinary strength, you know the rhythm of the moment, you strike naturally, and you hit naturally."

Each of the five sections builds on and is intrinsically linked to the other parts of the book, creating an interconnected web from which strategists can draw two lessons:

1. CONSTANTLY LEARN AND DEVELOP A VARIETY OF SKILLS: "THE SWORD AND THE PEN"

"It is said the warrior's is the twofold Way of pen and sword, and he should have a taste for both Ways." In these opening lines of the Earth book, Musashi refers to the need for aspiring samurai to focus not only on the study of battlefield tactics ("sword"), but also of poetry and calligraphy ("pen"), in order to achieve mastery.

Musashi spent the majority of his life traveling across Japan on a constant search for new opponents. More than simply besting his competitors or enjoying the glory of victory, Musashi's ceaseless quest was motivated by a desire to learn from his opponents and, from this, to strengthen his own skills.

In addition to martial arts and military practices, Musashi studied a wide variety of fields, from calligraphy to sculpture, building a broad base of knowledge that he maintained was essential to his improvement as a samurai.

To Musashi, constantly expanding his capabilities provided two vital advantages on the battlefield: access to the benefits of a wide-ranging skill set and knowledge base, and the opportunity to avoid the pitfalls of over-reliance on a single tactic, tool, or weapon.

In *Five Rings*, Musashi repeatedly discusses "the Way"—an all-encompassing term referring to the training, responsibilities, social standing, lifestyle, and cosmic path inherent to various occupations—which he put in the context of other "Ways" familiar to the denizens of seventeenth-century Japan: "Buddhism is a Way of salvation, Confucianism venerates a Way of culture, and medicine is a Way of curing various diseases. Moreover, poets teach the Way of Japanese verse; and then there are tea masters, archers and others who teach the various arts."[21] These comparisons are used to define the path a samurai must take to master his craft by drawing distinctions with the training involved to achieve mastery in other disciplines. Such comparisons underscore the value of exploring a broad array of disciplines to better understand one's own core competency.

Musashi was an accomplished calligrapher, artist, and poet, and lived a life devoted to this principle of variety. He believed that cultivating a range of knowledge and interests allows for moments of creativity that are impossible to access otherwise. This insight is related to the core principle of strategic intuition: Cultivating knowledge of varying disciplines enables the mind, through a flash of insight, to leverage different points of view to arrive at unexpected solutions to challenging problems.

The benefits of a continually expanding base of knowledge do not end there, but extend to the pitfalls the samurai will avoid. Musashi advises that "you should not have a favorite weapon. To become over-familiar with one weapon is as much a fault as not knowing it sufficiently well. . . . It is bad for commanders and troopers to have likes and dislikes."[22] An over-reliance on any given competitive approach, Musashi intimates, opens one up to attack by combatants who can effectively exploit the shortcomings specific to that strategy, tactic, or weapon.

Twenty-first-century leaders face the challenging balancing act of remaining connected to the values, culture, and strategy at the heart of their organizations' success while simultaneously developing and maintaining the organizations' capacity to remain nimble and unpredictable. While Musashi does not provide a silver bullet to solve this intractable challenge, he does offer a philosophical point of view, centered on the importance of continually expanding one's skills and knowledge, to undergird any potential strategic solution. Musashi urges his readers to "study the Ways of different arts one by one. When you cannot be deceived by men you will have realized the wisdom of strategy."[23]

2. FOCUSED, CONTINUOUS PRACTICE MAKES PERFECT: "SAMURAI TRAINING"

"A sword feels heavy and difficult to wield for anyone at first and a bow is difficult to draw. But you get used to any weapon: for the bow, you gain strength, and if you practice with the sword you will gain strength in its Way and come to handle it well."[24]

Like scores of philosophers, teachers, and sages before and after him, Musashi emphasized the irreplaceable value of sustained, directed effort in order to achieve mastery over the foundational skills at the heart of his school of swordsmanship.

Yet Musashi goes a step farther. When discussing the benefits of diligent practice, he repeatedly underscores and describes in detail the specific, limited set of skills, psychological attitudes, and habits a student must focus on in his training. For Musashi, a jack of all trades who dabbles in a variety of fields but masters no single discipline is destined for failure. The lack of deep understanding and mastery in any given area will doom its practitioners to defeat at the hands of a master who has fully grasped one particularly effective approach. As Musashi describes it: "The Way of the warrior does not include other Ways, such as Confucianism, Buddhism, certain traditions, artistic accomplishments and dancing. . . . Men must polish their particular Way."[25]

This emphasis on the need for absolute concentration on mastering a limited set of skills may appear to contradict Musashi's writing on the benefits of exploring a wide range of disciplines and creative pursuits. In fact, these two strains of advice are synergistic building blocks that bolster each other.

Consider these two principles in the context of a twenty-first-century business environment. To succeed in attracting and maintaining customers, a business must have a competitive advantage that separates the value its products and services offer to a specific set of clients from that of the competition. Simultaneously, that same organization will benefit and thrive further if its strategy is informed by concepts drawn not only from a deep understanding of competitor strategies and market dynamics, but also from insights inspired by unrelated fields and industries. The classic example of this was mentioned in Steve Jobs's 2005 commencement address at Stanford, where he described how his "for fun" college course on calligraphy informed the variety of iconic word processing fonts embedded in the original Lisa computer (precursor to the Macintosh).

Common Themes between Sun Tzu and Musashi

When comparing Sun Tzu's and Musashi's writings, one encounters the common emphasis on the importance of cultivating the right virtues, the determination to train diligently, the discipline to study one's opponent and the situation, the flexibility to adapt to the circumstances, the craftiness to deceive one's opponent, the mindfulness to see the opportunity, and the resolve to act quickly and decisively.

The recipe is quite simple. Victory is attained by those who train, study, observe, adapt, and act. Simple to understand, of course, is rarely synonymous with easy to implement.

Having read and analyzed these works, an astute student might ask, "How will this advice help me win the competitive battle at hand if the enemy also reads *The Art of War* and *The Book of Five Rings?*" How can organizations win when others use the same frameworks and have access to similar sets of data? In attempting to answer this question, one gains renewed appreciation for Musashi and Sun Tzu's wisdom. While Sun Tzu underscores the vital importance of achieving information asymmetry and Musashi devotes great effort to explaining the superiority of his technique relative to alternative styles of swordsmanship, it is when these foundational points of potential advantage are neutralized by a worthy competitor that the full genius of the strategic insights of *The Art of War* and *The Book of Five Rings* is fully revealed.

A decision maker well-versed in a broad range of tactics and strategies, but unattached to employing any particular combination of these tools, and prepared to identify emerging opportunities and respond at a moment's notice can overcome an opponent who may be equally or better resourced, informed, or prepared at the beginning of the battle. Simultaneously, like the infinite number of tunes one can create with just five notes, generals must select and combine existing frameworks, data, and insights with no fear of trying the new and experimental. This will give strategists unpredictable patterns, inexhaustible creativity, and original strategies. Strategists, as also suggested by Duggan in *Strategic Intuition*, should look for existing practices outside their position, functional area, business, industry, and geography, and apply them to their current business. This capacity to generate novel solutions is the key that opens the lock of flexibility and novelty.

Gaydon, England, June 2009

Back at Aston Martin headquarters, Ulrich Bez presented his SUV project to his two investor groups, highlighting that there was no other SUV in the ultra-luxury segment. By moving now with a projected 2013 launch, Aston Martin would avoid direct conflict with Bentley, Ferrari, Lamborghini, McLaren, and Rolls-Royce. The only existing SUVs even near the segment were the mass-luxury brands of Porsche, Audi, Mercedes, Lexus, and Infinity.

But in the shadow of the recent global financial crisis, Bez could not convince his Kuwaiti and Italian investors to spend an additional GBP339 million after having already spent USD848 million to buy the company from Ford in 2007. After all, Aston Martin had generated profits in only one year of its ninety-six years of existence. As far as the investors were concerned, Aston Martin was still in crisis. They vetoed the project.

By 2015, however, the global economy and the appetite for luxury crossovers had changed. In 2016 Bentley introduced its Bentayga, which became its best-selling model. Lamborghini launched its Urus in 2017, Rolls-Royce its Cullinan in May 2018, and a few months later Ferrari announced its Purosangue. In addition, among the mass-luxury brands, Jaguar introduced the F-Pace in 2015 and Maserati its Levante in 2016, both at price points below Porsche's Cayenne.

Andy Palmer was appointed CEO of Aston Martin in October 2014, after twenty years with Nissan in Japan. At the Geneva Motor Show in March 2015,

Palmer announced his new crossover concept, the DBX, and the company went on to build a facility in Wales to produce it. The DBX was due in dealerships by the end of 2019, three years after the first of Palmer's competitors had entered the former SUV white space. And now they were all there, ready to take on Aston Martin. Sun Tzu would have instructed those hesitant Italian and Kuwaiti investors to fill the void in 2013 and secure the high ground long before any of the others could venture in.

By not "going where the enemy is not," as Bentley did, Aston Martin missed the window in 2009. The DBX finally launched in May 2020, just as the coronavirus epidemic was ravaging the global economy and creating particular volatility in the Chinese market, where Aston Martin had planned to sell the majority of its SUVs.

Strategy Lessons from Chapter 2

1. Avoid direct confrontation with the enemy.
2. Build strategy on information asymmetry.
3. Cultivate adaptability and flexibility.
4. Practice deception.
5. Constantly learn and develop a variety of skills.
6. Practice, practice, practice.
7. To generate novel solutions, look for existing practices outside your rank, functional area, business, industry, and geography.
8. Select and combine existing frameworks, data, and insights; try the new and experimental fearlessly.

3

Competitive Dynamics and the Chinese Game of Go

Chengdu, China, December 1949

The Communist troops were pouring over the horizon as General Chiang Kai-shek watched Mao's army breach the perimeter of Chengdu, the last stronghold of Chiang's Kuomintang (KMT) party. Months before, Mao Zedong had surrounded Nanking, the Nationalist capital in the east; then he surrounded Canton in the south, followed by Chonqing in the West and, now, Chiang's last central China strongholds in Sichang and then Chengdu. Although far better resourced at the outset of the conflict, Chiang's troops were exhausted, his resources drained, and all avenues of escape closed off. On December 10, 1949, Chiang retreated from China and crossed the Formosa Strait to the island of Taiwan, essentially capitulating after the long civil war. With most of China's territory now held by the People's Liberation Army (PLA), Mao declared victory and established in Beijing the government of the newly formed People's Republic of China.

The decisive victory of the PLA derived from a number of factors, including global geopolitical forces in the post–World War II era, widespread corruption within the KMT's leadership, and broad social unrest caused by China's economic stagnation throughout the mid- 1940s. Military historians also underscore how Mao's strategic decision-making, and the effective execution of that strategy by the highly unified and well-organized PLA, played a decisive role in defeating the uncoordinated efforts of the independent armies that made up Chiang's KMT.

In the decades that followed, students of Mao's strategy drew parallels between his methods and Go (or *Wei-ch'i*, as it is known in China), a centuries-old board game popular across the Asian continent. Mao's military success mirrored the game's complex methods, in which a player encircles, isolates, and captures enemy pieces and geography. Often referred to in the West as the game of Chinese encirclement, Go originated as the preferred pastime of Chinese generals and intellectuals about four thousand years ago,[1] predating the emergence of chess by more than thirty-three hundred years.[2] *Wei-ch'i* is also played in Japan (where it is called *Igo*) and Korea (*Baduk*). Go is the game's English name.[3]

While the link between Go and martial combat far predates Mao—Japanese samurai were known to travel with both swords and Go boards—Mao appears to have eagerly embraced the tradition. He insisted that his generals study the game, and the tactics the PLA employed to wage a protracted guerilla war against Chiang Kai-shek's Nationalist forces in the 1930s, combat Japanese invaders in World War II, and ultimately expel the KMT in 1949 all carry the hallmark of Go principles. Even today, senior officers of the Chinese military must know the game well in order to progress through the ranks.[4]

New York City, May 1997

Headlines across the world reverberated with the news that Gary Kasparov, perhaps the greatest chess player of all time, had been defeated by Deep Blue, an IBM supercomputer. Global media breathlessly reported on the contest as a sign that artificial intelligence was catching up to the limits of human intellect. "The Brain's Last Stand!" proclaimed the cover of *Newsweek*. For technology pessimists, this foretold a fast-approaching future where humans would be overtaken by an army of hyperintelligent machines. For optimists, Deep Blue's victory signaled the growing potential of computer technology to improve outcomes in fields of human endeavor ranging from medicine and the sciences to business and the arts.

The media scrutiny and public attention were as much about conflicting opinions regarding the impact of technological progress as they were about perceptions of the game of chess. Sometimes referred to as "the game of kings," chess is perceived in the West as the ultimate test of individual mastery over logic, analytical capacity, and pattern recognition. Deep Blue's 1997 defeat of Kasparov signaled the victory of machine over man in a contest of the purest distillation of human reasoning.

As the hoopla calmed after Deep Blue's achievement, a growing chorus of voices pointed to Go, another immensely popular strategic board game where even an amateur player could defeat the most advanced computing technology of the time.

Contrasting Chess and Go

Go and chess are both games of strategy.[5] But unlike chess, where one wins by capturing the opponent's king, Go is won by slowly extending control over territory. Chess is a game of direct confrontation with force and power. Go, on the other hand, embodies Sun Tzu's principles of avoidance, deception,

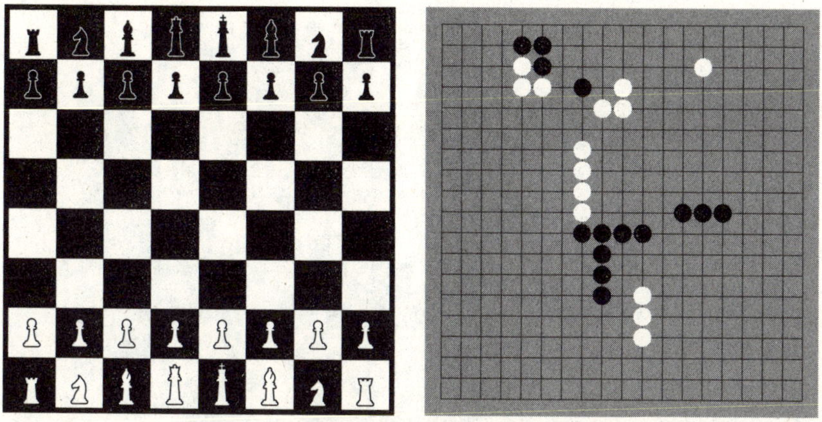

FIGURE 7. Chess and Go boards. (Michael Maggs and Donar Reiskoffer, Wikimedia CC BY-SA 3.0)

and guerilla-like moves of warfare.[6] Quoting Mao: "In guerilla warfare, select the tactic of seeming to come from the east and attacking from the west; avoid the solid, attack the hollow; attack; withdraw; deliver a lightning blow, seek a lightning decision."[7]

In chess, the pieces are placed on assigned squares. Go begins with a 19 by 19 grid (see figure 7) on which players place alternating black and white stones. The stones all have equal power. (There is no queen and no pawn.) Chess pieces are moved throughout the game, while in Go, stones stay in place unless they are surrounded and removed by the opposing player. In chess, pieces are removed one by one during play, reducing the number of variables as the game progresses. Go becomes more complex as stones are added to the board. A game of Go typically concludes when all available positions on the board are either occupied or fully encircled by a group of stones. The player whose stones occupy the larger share of territory is declared the winner (see figure 8, where black wins).

While chess and Go both require players to think strategically, differences in rules and gameplay translate to contrasts in the strategic principles that govern each. Paramount among these are the ways in which chess and Go treat the role of the individual pieces and the differences in how victory is defined.

The path to victory in chess is basically a series of conquests by an individual piece over another, where a player uses chessmen to capture opposing pieces one by one. In Go, stones are captured only when a player completely encircles an opponent's position. Go stones have uniform capabilities, but their power grows as a result of their relationship to the position of other

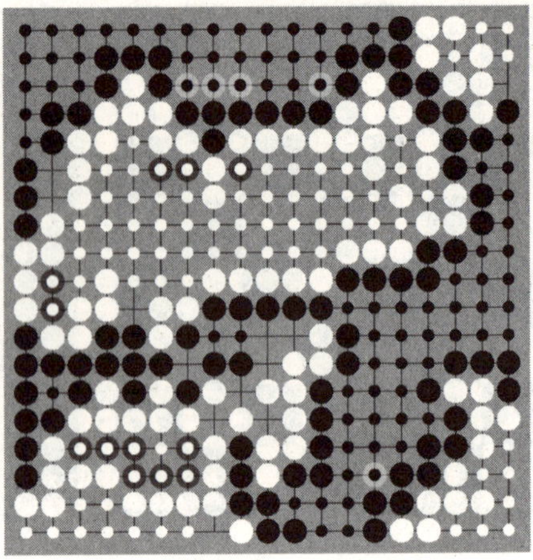

FIGURE 8. Go game result. (Hautala, Wikimedia CC BY-SA 2.0)

stones. In chess, pieces can move multiple times. In Go, a placed stone must remain in position unless it is captured. Accordingly, stones placed next to each other lose their individual identities, and their relevance is determined by their contribution to the broader patterns already on the board.

This power distinction between the pieces in chess versus Go is also observed in the differences in the end objective of each game. The ultimate goal of chess is to capture a specific piece—the opponent's king. All of the other minor victories and captures along the way are valuable only insofar as they increase the player's ability to capture the king. In Go, a player achieves victory by securing and controlling the most territory. In chess, victory or defeat is absolute, determined by the capture of the king. Conquest of this sort is rare in Go. The outcome between skilled Go players is often a narrow margin of victory determined only by a slight difference in territorial totals.

As in games, so in cultures. Chess is about individual roles and power. Go is about the strength of the group and the individual relationships within it. These differences between the games have led experts in various fields to highlight cultural differences in the competitive approaches taken by Westerners and Easterners in fields ranging from business and technology to geopolitics.[8]

Armonk, New York, 1997

In preparation for the match with Gary Kasparov, engineers at IBM headquarters consulted top-tier chess players to develop an arsenal of effective strategies.[9] They then trained Deep Blue over thousands of simulated games to establish correlations between individual scenarios and the effectiveness of specific moves. Armed with unprecedented raw computing power, Deep Blue would mine this library of data when facing Kasparov to make the optimal move at each stage of a match.

Even as IBM basked in the publicity surrounding Deep Blue's success, the company admitted that the engineering approach and computing power enabling victory over Kasparov would not translate to Go. IBM's engineers had trained a machine to access a vast library of predetermined strategic responses in service of a singular, specific, unchanging goal—checkmating the opposing king.

Victory in Go is a much more fluid concept. What it means to capture more territory than one's opponent changes from game to game and move to move. The importance of any given stone can shift dramatically based on where the next stone is placed on the board. The constantly shifting power dynamics and relational nature of Go simply did not lend themselves to Deep Blue's capabilities.

In fact, it would be nearly two decades before AlphaGo, a program developed by DeepMind, a Google subsidiary specializing in artificial intelligence, would defeat Lee Sedol, one of the world's best Go players. In developing AlphaGo, DeepMind did not discard the fundamental principles employed by Deep Blue. AlphaGo was trained over millions of simulated Go games. But unlike Deep Blue, this training was not used to equip AlphaGo with a deep but finite set of strategic responses. Rather, the engineers leveraged deep learning, neural networks, and other recent advances in data science to give AlphaGo the ability to make decisions specifically suited to each game's shifting dynamics.

Lessons for Strategy

A strategist can develop a number of skills by playing Go, such as building comprehensive awareness of the competitive landscape; learning how to isolate enablers of victory and avoid distracting skirmishes; understanding the importance of relational dynamics; probing to gather key information; dividing and ruling; and pursuing victory instead of just defeating a foe.

1. CULTIVATE COMPREHENSIVE BOARD AWARENESS

> You should observe reflectively, with overall awareness of the large picture as well as precise attention to small details.
>
> —Miyamoto Musashi, *The Book of Five Rings*

In the mid-1980s, the dominance of U.S. steel production was an unquestioned fact of global trade. In those years, this book's senior author visited China Steel in Taiwan, where he happened to meet a senior engineer from U.S. Steel who had been engaged in a manufacturing process consultation. At lunch at the company mess hall, the author asked the engineer, "Who are your major competitors?" The American engineer's response—"Bethlehem Steel, Allegheny, Republic, Jones & Laughlin, and Lackawanna"—was a catalog of the leading U.S. firms then dominating global markets. Later, in strategy meetings with China Steel executives, the author posed the same question. The answer from the Chinese executives was "Korea, Japan, Malaysia, and soon, Thailand."

In the ensuing years, the U.S. steel industry's major incumbents were blindsided by the onslaught of cheap, high-quality steel imports from Asia flooding global markets. By 2000, only U.S. Steel and Bethlehem maintained a significant manufacturing presence. By 2017, China, India, and Japan ranked ahead of the U.S. in steel production, with South Korea following close behind.

As the China Steel executives did in identifying their major competitors, Go players learn to make decisions with a broad-minded perspective, continuously surveilling and maintaining a keen awareness of the entire playing surface. The board's grid of nineteen perpendicular lines gives players 361 intersections on which to place their first stone. Certain areas of the board, such as the four corners, offer some inherent advantages.[10] Yet, with each game starting with an empty board, the relative importance of the various geographies varies dramatically from game to game. Throughout the course of a match, multiple battles are likely to break out in different regions. A Go player must remain aware of the dynamics of each conflict while also recognizing how these conflicts combine to propagate a boardwide dynamic.

Decisions focused on dominating one's portion of the playing surface, as U.S. Steel attempted to do in its home market, can lead to a player's ruin if not considered in terms of their implications for the dynamics of the entire match. As we saw with the steel industry, peripheral vision is often constrained by success on one's home turf.

In 2012, for example, the management team and board of directors of Seaver Solutions, a multinational conglomerate specializing in enterprise technology, was besieged by JLT, an aggressive activist investor that had taken a minority position in the company. JLT stated publicly that Seaver management's struggles to identify new revenue sources and minimize overhead costs had resulted in a prolonged period of slowing margin growth and declining investor returns. JLT wanted to replace several board members and significantly alter Seaver's strategy.

In response, Seaver's CEO and senior management pursued an aggressive public relations campaign. They vigorously engaged employees, clients, other large shareholders, and the media to argue publicly that JLT was interested not in Seaver's long-term success, but only in boosting short-term shareholder returns and jeopardizing the company's future through a series of divestitures and dramatic cost-cutting initiatives. The PR campaign painted JLT's proposals as "solutions in search of a problem" and unnecessarily belligerent.

Seaver's ploy worked. A shareholder proxy vote rebuffed the activist's proposed changes to the board, and company management celebrated what they viewed as a significant victory.

Seaver's senior leaders were likely right that JLT, regarded widely in the industry as a corporate raider, did not have the company's best interests at heart, and management may have been wise to invest significant resources in defeating the takeover attempt. However, Seaver's aggressive communication strategy had unintended consequences. Not only did its single-minded focus on defeating JLT take its attention away from long-term strategy and day-to-day operations, its actions were interpreted by many other major institutional investors as unwillingness to adapt in response to constructive shareholder criticism.

Focusing for the better part of a year on defeating JLT at any cost resulted in Seaver's eventual downfall. Within nine months, the company's market value declined significantly. The investing public had grown increasingly skeptical of Seaver's "steady as she goes" market strategy, and several key rivals announced major new product lines. The public perception at fiscal year-end was that management had been caught flat-footed. With shareholder pressure mounting, more than half of the senior management team lost their jobs in the ensuing fallout. With the stock in free fall, JLT expanded its holdings in Seaver and eventually became its single largest investor.

This lack of "full board awareness" by management had dramatic strategic implications. By seeking only to defeat JLT rather than considering how the specific conflict might be resolved in a way that served the firm's broader strategy, Seaver's senior leaders positioned their company for failure. Whether because of a reflexive competitive streak or a defense mechanism activated by fear over job security, management zeroed in on eliminating the threat posed by JLT as their top priority.

Perhaps if these leaders had focused on better understanding and addressing the issues underlying the investor's sentiment—such as slow profitability growth, trailing innovation, and underwhelming performance—they would have found an alternative path to defending against the challenge or taken a different course of action with higher probability of positive long-term outcomes.

As a contrast, Seth Winogrond, CEO of Aggregate Materials Industries (AMI), illustrates the success that can be unlocked through full board awareness. AMI, a supplier of aggregates and other heavy materials, blasted, harvested, and crushed rock and gravel for use in the construction of buildings, roads, and shorelines.

Given the expense, logistics, and effort required to transport large quantities of aggregates, a key driver of success in the industry was a producer's ability to locate its facilities near customer projects. Furthermore, road construction projects represented a significant share of total demand for aggregates. At Winogrond's direction, AMI's strategy team cataloged the locations of every large road construction project in North America over several years. The mapping exercise revealed that many of the projects were located in close proximity to interstate highways. Connecting this insight to a business strategy, Winogrond identified developing a robust system of quarries near interstate highways as the path to AMI's long-term strategic growth.

With his priority defined, Winogrond focused on his objective with full board awareness.

Winogrond's office in Albany, Georgia, was dominated by a large map of the United States. Plotted on the map were the interstate highway system, the locations of every major competitor's properties, AMI's own locations, and the locations of yet-to-be-bought private aggregate companies. Each morning Winogrond studied the map, his eyes scanning it in concentric circles, focusing on areas where AMI had no operations, properties that were under consideration by competitors, and small players opportune for acquisition. Through the exercise, Winogrond maintained a keen awareness of the nationwide industry landscape and could filter every individual decision through this holistic understanding.

Winogrond's broad-view perspective pervaded every facet of the company strategy. Executives across the country were empowered to and rewarded for identifying and forming relationships with the owners of quarries in highway-adjacent geographies that AMI had yet to penetrate, as well as those whose ownership would enhance the value of AMI's existing properties. In addition, the executives' compensation included bonuses for identifying and bringing to the attention of senior management properties that were eventually pursued, acquired, and brought into the AMI fold.

As a result, even as competitors pursued their own aggressive acquisition strategies, AMI began to establish a dominant market position in highway-adjacent quarries. AMI was soon able to consistently undercut competitor prices to win lucrative road construction contracts across the country, thanks to its lower transportation costs. After only a few years of Winogrond's leadership, AMI became the leading aggregate, cement, and concrete provider in North America, with the highest market share and profits.

2. PRIORITIZE THAT WHICH IS MOST CLOSELY LINKED TO STRATEGIC VICTORY

> One who knows when he can fight, and when he cannot fight, will be victorious.
>
> The victorious army first realizes the conditions for victory, and then seeks to engage in battle. The vanquished army fights first, and then seeks victory.
>
> —Sun Tzu, *The Art of War*

While full board awareness is a prerequisite for identifying the range of potential threats and opportunities, Go players must also effectively prioritize the many battles in which they might further engage before making a move.

In deciding where to place the next stone, players must understand the short- and long-term implications of each of the available positions and select the option that is most powerfully linked with developing ultimate strategic advantage. Even when multiple relatively attractive opportunities are available, a player now has the criteria for which battles to pursue.

For example, Spirit Airlines experienced explosive growth after it switched to an ultra-low-cost business model in 2007. The Florida-based airline, famous for being the first U.S. carrier to charge passengers a separate fee for carry-on bags in 2010, was absolutely clear on its value proposition (exceptionally cheap airfare) and its operational priority (extreme efficiency and intense cost management). By focusing ruthlessly on these objectives and deemphasizing other important elements of the client experience (such as in-flight comfort and customer service) and operations (such as timeliness), Spirit empowered the entire organization, from upper management to front-line personnel, to make decisions with a clear understanding of which values should be prioritized. While Spirit ranked near the bottom of all U.S. airlines in terms of on-time performance and customer service experience, the company's growth outpaced nearly all competitors. By resisting the pressure to pursue other attractive strategies, Spirit grew to become America's seventh-largest airline.

Spirit's early growth, moreover, enabled it to invest subsequently in what were once subordinate priorities. For example, after years of ranking as the worst American airline in on-time performance, Spirit focused on timeliness and by late 2018 was consistently finishing near the top of the on-time rank-ings. Although customer service performance ratings continued to lag, Spirit accepted this as it continued to pursue lowest cost and timeliness. It recognized that other strategic, secondary priorities could remain just that—secondary.

3. EXPLOIT THE IMPORTANCE OF THE RELATIONAL

> Unite with your allies on focal terrain. Do not remain on isolated terrains.
>
> —Sun Tzu, *The Art of War*

The full board awareness that Go players must cultivate is insufficient if it is just awareness of the board's present dynamics. Full board awareness must also include a capacity to identify future opportunities in relation to the resources that a player can bring to bear.

For example, several small, isolated groups of stones in disparate parts of a Go board do not in themselves represent a competitive advantage. In fact, these isolated groups may be vulnerable. Because each group is separated from the player's other stones (in, for example, opposite corners of the board), an opponent could more easily encircle any of these stand-alone clusters than if the stones were clumped together in a single, larger mass.

Despite this perceived vulnerability, expert players often seek to establish this dynamic. While several groups of stones in distant parts of the board might appear vulnerable, they also present potential for advantage. A skilled player will add stones in subsequent turns to form connections between separate groups. When connected, the disparate groups transform into a powerful bloc spanning large portions of the board, creating the potential for encircling larger adjacent territories.

Fashion pioneer Karl Lagerfeld's revitalization of the high-fashion label Chanel in the early 1980s exemplifies the power that new resources brought to bear strategically can have on the fortunes of an organization. When Lagerfeld became creative director at Chanel in 1983, the brand was considered by industry experts to be in a prolonged decline since the death of founder Gabrielle "Coco" Chanel in 1971. In the rapidly evolving high-fashion landscape, Chanel had continued to focus on styles and designs that reflected the brand's classic lineage. Critics and consumers alike increasingly perceived Chanel as dated, fussy, and out of touch, more in tune with the brand's heyday of the 1920s through the 1940s.

Lagerfeld took this perceived weakness—the association of the brand with iconic but dated designs—and turned it into the foundation for Chanel's reemergence. In his initial collections, Lagerfeld combined Chanel's most classic themes—such as the "double C" logo, instantly recognizable to any aficionado—with highly irreverent and boundary-pushing symbolism. In a particularly famous example, Lagerfeld posed a group of supermodels as a motorcycle gang dressed in Chanel's bouclé women's suits, a favorite of Jacqueline Kennedy's that had skyrocketed to popularity in the 1950s as a symbol of classically feminine style. Lagerfeld's decision to pose the models in the suits while standing next to motorcycles and wearing leather accessories created a powerful contrast between the suits' femininity and the gruff masculinity associated with biker culture.

The combination of controversial imagery with Chanel's classic heritage shook the fashion world and translated to growing interest from both the mainstream press and high-end retail buyers. By the early 1990s, not only was Chanel seen as being on the cutting edge of haute couture, but the sales generated by its retail ready-to-wear offerings led all high-end brands.

Lagerfeld was hardly the first fashion designer to employ controversy and shock to draw attentions to his designs. But the juxtaposition of his tactics with Chanel's classic lineage—widely considered too old-fashioned to inspire excitement among 1980s consumers—catalyzed the brand's return to prominence. Like a Go player connecting two weak-seeming groupings to form a powerful position, Lagerfeld ably transformed a weakness of the brand's image into a cornerstone for Chanel's successes from the 1980s through the 2020s.

Whether considering Go, fashion, or other industries, this principle reveals the power of relational thinking. As strategists consider the environment in which their firm must operate, and the resources available to them to deploy in that environment, their decision-making may be improved if a fundamental lesson of Go is considered. The stones on a Go board are all identical. Their relative impact and power are derived solely from their position and relationship to other stones on the board. Similarly, to fully understand the potential inherent in an organization's available resources, decision makers must place importance on how these resources relate to each other and the competitive landscapes.

4. USE PROBES TO GLEAN COMPETITOR INFORMATION

> The means by which enlightened rulers and sagacious generals moved and conquered others, that their achievements surpassed the masses, was advance knowledge.
>
> Advance knowledge cannot be gained from ghosts and spirits, inferred from phenomena, or projected from the measures of Heaven, but must be gained from men for it is the knowledge of the enemy's true situation.
>
> —Sun Tzu, *The Art of War*

Eastern and Western philosophers, military leaders, and business executives all realize the value of competitive intelligence to understanding an opponent's strategic thinking and intentions. This is often accomplished through intensive research and counter-intelligence. A second way to probe for competitor information is through bluffing—attempting to mislead the opponent by communicating a falsified version of one's own plans, and thereby tricking the opponent into revealing his own strategy.

Go reveals a third approach. A skilled player will test his opponent's intention through a series of probing maneuvers. Probes ("asking moves" in Go parlance) are made to test an adversary's reactions. An effective probe will force the opponent into one of a limited number of responses that, if interpreted correctly, can offer guidance for future strategies. For example, if an opponent responds to a probe that appears to threaten one of her strongholds by fortifying her defenses, the player might consider pursuing a strategy focused on other portions of the board, having interpreted the opponent's behavior as indicative of a significant focus on existing positions. Alternatively, if she had responded by pursuing a strategy elsewhere on the board, the player might consider a more aggressive attack on the stronghold, since the opponent may be viewing that particular position as a secondary priority.

Skilled probing can help a company draw broader insights about opponents' plans and priorities. During the memory chip wars that dominated Silicon Valley in the 1980s, Texas Instruments (TI) announced plans to build a 52,000-square-foot facility to manufacture memory chips that would be priced at sixty-nine cents per hundred. Shortly after, Intel announced a 68,000-square-foot plant for chips priced at sixty-two cents per hundred. Three weeks later, Motorola announced a 102,000-square-foot plant for chips priced at forty-nine cents per hundred. TI responded to this news by announcing that there would be no new facility after all, and that it would outsource chip manufacture to a Japanese facility going forward. In effect, TI had uncovered information on, or even provoked, Intel's and Motorola's strategies. Empowered with this new information, TI could then make its strategic decision with a much clearer view of the competitive landscape.

5. DIVIDE AND RULE

> Display profits to entice them. Create disorder in their forces and take them. If they are substantial, prepare for them; if they are strong, avoid them. If they are angry, perturb them; be deferential to foster their arrogance. If they are rested, force them to exert themselves. . . . If they are united, cause them to be separated. Go forth where they will not expect it. These are the ways military strategies are victorious.
>
> —Sun Tzu, *The Art of War*

As mentioned earlier, a Go player who is able to connect groups of stones from disparate parts of the board can dramatically increase the probability of victory. Just as important is the ability to prevent an opponent from generating the same kind of synergies with his own troops. Instead of attacking enemy positions directly, a skilled player can take an alternative path to limiting an opponent's capacity to acquire territory. Sometimes referred to in Go as "cutting," the player places stones in positions that limit the opponent's ability to connect separate groups into a single unit. This strategy has two benefits. First, the opponent's ability to attack is limited because the maneuver has prevented the realization of synergies between his groups. Second, keeping opposing stones disconnected forces the opponent to defend a larger number of individual groups, increases his defensive challenges, and limits the bandwidth available for offensive maneuvers.

In 1991, Steve Hansel took over as president of Louisiana's Hibernia Bank, a large regional bank on the verge of bankruptcy. After two years of targeted acquisitions and a focused recapitalization strategy, Hansel restored Hibernia to profitability. Meanwhile, a wave of geography-expanding consolidations was sweeping through commercial and retail banking. California's Bank of America had acquired a number of banks in the western United States; North Carolina's NationsBank had consolidated the largest independent banks in the East; and Banc One of Columbus, Ohio, was buying and absorbing banks in the center of the country. Declaring Louisiana and Texas as its next targets for geographic expansion, in mid-1997 Banc One announced plans to acquire First Commerce, Hibernia's largest local competitor. If Banc One succeeded, it would immediately inherit an established network of locations around the state. The acquisition would leave Banc One well positioned to leverage its scale and the "power of the relational" to put pressure on Hibernia.

Over the coming months, Hansel engaged his executives in a series of intensive war games centered on answering two questions: How could they fend off the threat of a now much-larger competitor, and how could Hibernia take advantage of the inevitable disruption that the post-merger integration process would create within First Commerce? The team zeroed in on the next twelve months as their window of opportunity: Banc One was unlikely to pursue aggressive expansion in the coming six-to-nine-month regulatory approval period, or in the ensuing three-to-six-month integration process when they would merge information systems, procedures, and customer records.

To take advantage of these twelve months, Hibernia executives created the "Home Team" strategy. First, Hibernia launched an intensive advertising campaign touting itself as "Louisiana's Bank" and encouraging First Commerce clients who preferred a bank with local ownership to switch to Hibernia. Building on the campaign, Hansel and other senior executives visited CEOs of large private businesses that banked with First Commerce. Hansel often would guide the meeting through a series of questions meant to create discomfort with First Commerce's new arrangement. He would note: "We were founded in 1870. We know you, and you know us. Banc One is inevitably going to change things. Are you comfortable trusting your business to bankers who will now report to an out-of-state conglomerate?"[11] According to Hansel, "We pushed hardest when turmoil was greatest—right after the closing. We would end our meetings with a handshake and, 'If this [merger] doesn't work for you, let us know.'"

Hibernia's strategy deftly employed the cutting principle. To facilitate a speedy and untroubled acquisition, First Commerce would have to dedicate its resources to the intensive regulatory approval and post-merger integration processes. But to remain an attractive investment for Banc One, First Commerce also could not allow Hibernia to lure away large portions of its customer base, a major reason for the acquirer's interest in the purchase. In the coming months, First Commerce was forced on the defensive, attempting to balance the demands of the merger with the need to fend off Hibernia's pursuit of its customers. As a result, First Commerce spread its resources thinly. Not only did the competing priorities slow the acquisition process, but many customers, upset by the rocky integration, left First Commerce, taking Hansel and his team up on their offer. In the coming months, Hibernia was able to gain significant market share in the New Orleans business community and the rest of Louisiana.

Like skilled Go players isolating their opponents' positions, Hansel and his team had managed to leverage cutting to improve their position, even in the midst of Banc One's attempt to bring its scale to bear in the market.

6. PURSUE YOUR OWN SUCCESS RATHER THAN YOUR OPPONENT'S DEFEAT

> Those that excelled in warfare first made themselves unconquerable in order to await the moment when the enemy could be conquered. Being unconquerable lies with yourself; being conquerable lies with enemy.
>
> —Sun Tzu, *The Art of War*

When two fairly evenly matched Go players compete, outright victory through capturing all the opponent's territory is extremely rare. Much more likely, the winner will claim victory by capturing just slightly more territory than the opponent.

In business, leaders should decouple achieving effective growth in their organization from a psychological or emotional need to defeat competitors by, for example, challenging their core competencies. Not only would this require extensive resources to overcome a competitor's strength in the target segment, but the rival's perception of this segment as a core strength could trigger a disproportionate—and hard to counter—response.

In these situations, traditional Go strategy would advise against challenging in the sections of the board where the opponent is strongest, unless absolutely necessary. The resources that this type of contest would require would be better utilized for other purposes. For example, stones could be more usefully deployed in developing a foothold in a part of the board where the competitor hasn't established a commanding presence. Given the lower cost of achieving a competitive advantage in empty spaces, the impact of the deployed resources is likely to be more powerful.

Furthermore, instead of trying to attack an opponent's core strengths, resources may also be better invested in strengthening the defenses around one's own most important assets, whether they be territories on a Go board or product and service lines of a business. By developing strong defenses that give the appearance of invincibility and communicating a willingness to attack with overwhelming force in response to any encroachment, a player dramatically reduces the probability of being on the receiving end of an attack.

For instance, in the decade following the 2008 global financial crisis, emerging new technologies, tighter regulatory standards, and changing customer preferences led to a dramatic decline in securities trading for all major financial institutions. Large U.S. commercial and investment banks reacted in a number of ways. Some doubled down on the trading business, engaging with each other in bloody price competition. Other banks, accustomed to working with investors and corporate executives, focused on offering a broader range of financial products, such as helping high-net-worth individuals manage their personal assets. Given the small universe of potential clients, this led to fierce competition for the ultra-high-net-worth segment.

Goldman Sachs, long viewed as an elite institution whose private banking services were available only to the wealthiest clients, was hit hard by the competition for a shrinking market. Like its peers, Goldman pursued several strategies to grow revenues and cut costs in both the trading and the private wealth divisions. Yet, as Goldman's leadership surveyed the post-crisis landscape, they identified an opportunity in a market underserved by its direct competitors. In 2016, after a series of investments, acquisitions, and strategic hires, Goldman launched Marcus, a lending and savings account platform targeted at the mass market of low-dollar borrowers and savers. Marcus offered individual loans that waived the plethora of fees other banks typically charged small borrowers, provided savings accounts with no minimum deposit, and paid savings account interest rates that far exceeded those of the competition. Undergirded by Goldman's strong technological infrastructure, the Marcus platform offered clients a top-notch user interface and gave Goldman an effective platform to evaluate consumer preferences.

By mid-2020, Goldman was still in the midst of a full-scale deployment of the Marcus platform. Prior to the impact of the coronavirus, the initiative had proven to be a major success. It had attracted millions of new customers, provided a platform to develop other profitable new consumer banking services, and was projected to add more than a billion dollars to Goldman's profitability in the coming years. As might be expected, Goldman's competitors had announced plans to establish similar units, but they would be playing catch-up while Goldman enjoyed a substantial first-mover advantage. By focusing on creating a path to its own success, rather than simply defeating opponents on the existing field of competition, Goldman effectively created a new avenue for additional profitability.

Peoria, Illinois, 1981

Almost anyone with a Caterpillar Tractor Company (CAT) franchise became a millionaire in the years after World War II, when the baby boom in the U.S. triggered residential and suburban construction, the Marshall Plan launched the rebuilding of Europe, and President Dwight Eisenhower initiated the interstate highway system.[12] All these developments fueled the need for the light and heavy earth-moving equipment (EME) in which CAT specialized, and the company and its 87 U.S. and 129 overseas dealers prospered. With average sales per dealer at USD13 million[13] and gross margins of 25 percent, the average net worth of a CAT dealer reached USD13 million by 1981.

At that time, CAT viewed its world in three parts: North and South America; Europe, the Middle East, and Africa (EMEA); and the "Far East" of Australia, India, and a Mitsubishi partnership in Japan. Despite CAT's global presence, nearly all its worldwide marketing and sales efforts were managed by executives based at its headquarters in Peoria. This Midwestern-centric mindset was reflected and reinforced in CAT's culture. For instance, more than two-thirds of the firm's executives had been born in Illinois. When assigned overseas, they lived in company compounds and traveled to work together in company buses.

In 1981, CAT was winning the global EME game. Or so it thought.

Osaka, Japan, 1985

In January 1985, Komatsu Ltd. was closing in on CAT's global domination.[14] Komatsu chairman Ryoichi Kawai was surprised to see the size of CAT's 1984 loss of USD428 million, following two unprofitable years. CAT's global market share had dropped from 51 percent in 1971 to 43 percent in 1984. Over the same period, Komatsu's share had grown from 10 percent to 25 percent, making it the world's second-largest EME player. With the U.S. recession in full swing, International Harvester had divested its EME business, Germany's IBH was going bankrupt, and other competitors were selling off excess capacity. Komatsu continued to remain consistently profitable.

CAT did not see Komatsu's incursion coming. A mere shadow of CAT in the 1960s, Komatsu dominated the Japanese market but had no overseas presence. When CAT entered Japan, Komatsu prevailed with the Japanese Ministry of Economy, Trade, and Industry to declare EME a critical Japanese industry and block competition from non-Japanese firms. Consequently, CAT was limited to entering via a mildly effective joint venture with Mitsubishi.

While CAT was held at bay, Komatsu operated in the background. Before expanding outside Japan, it shored up its product lines through investments in new technology and quality assurance. It next tackled margins, pursuing a series of intensive cost-cutting initiatives. By the time Komatsu started competing outside of Japan, it had an advantage in both quality and cost over most other EME manufacturers.

Komatsu's progression overseas included entry in the 1960s into China, the Soviet Union, and the Eastern Bloc countries in Europe, secondary markets below the radar of CAT executives. In the mid-1970s it established operations in Southeast Asia and Africa. By 1983, Komatsu had outlets in Warsaw, Moscow, Havana, and Beijing, as well as Brazil and Mexico. By the time the firm had established itself in other parts of the globe, its scale and cost structure allowed it to underprice CAT by 30 to 40 percent.

How would one describe Komatsu's extraordinary—and profitable—capture of so much market share in a world dominated by Caterpillar and other U.S. EME manufacturers? According to Kawai, the answer lay in its in-house slogan, "*Maru-C*," which translates roughly into "encircle Caterpillar."

Strategy Lessons from Chapter 3

1. Cultivate global awareness and peripheral vision.
2. Prioritize that which is most closely linked to strategic victory.
3. Exploit the relationships among the individual parts of your organization for competitive advantage.
4. Use probes to glean competitor information.
5. Divide and rule.
6. Pursue your own success rather than your opponent's defeat.
7. Win by encircling your opponent rather than by direct confrontation.

PART II

THE INNER MIND

Strategic choices—no matter their frequency or scale—are bound to create mental and emotional challenges for decision makers.

Overview of Part II

Having studied strategy, war, and war games against external adversaries, we now turn to the inner mind of the strategist. In chapters 4 through 7 we explore how strategists can develop the contemplative abilities that will open them to beginner's mind and new strategic insights.

With the Bhagavad Gita in chapter 4, we explore the role of duty—our dharma—even when our hearts and minds are crying out for us to run the other way. We acknowledge that humans are imperfect beings, with a shortcoming inherent in every leader: Our focus on present desires and objects produces an awareness distorted by our egos.

In chapter 5, we encounter the Buddha's life and learn that strategists need to return to themselves, alone in seclusion, to quietly reflect on what they have absorbed from research and information gathering. We see that it is far more important for strategists to be practical and deal with the situation at hand than to overanalyze.

As Nobel laureate Herb Simon noted, we are efficiency-seeking creatures of habit who make decisions based on old frames, memories, and associations—especially when faced with ambiguity.[1] As we'll see in chapter 6, the practice of mindfulness allows us to see how our mind reacts to thoughts, sensations, and information and to discern the habitual patterns that guide our choices. This awareness enables us to open the space for beginner's mind and allows us to explore new alternatives, new definitions of reality, and new strategic opportunities.

Zen Buddhism's lessons for today's strategists lie in promoting self-awareness and clear-mindedness. Described as "the art of seeing into the nature of one's being,"[2] Zen focuses on the essence of Buddhism and "strips all outer castings" by, among other things, concentrating on simplicity and detachment from conventional thinking. As described in chapter 7, the principles of Zen encourage strategists to constantly evolve, acquiring new knowledge to "fill the shelves of their brains" (Duggan's metaphor in *Strategic Intuition*) without developing attachment to any particular framework.

4

Dharma and the Bhagavad Gita

> My will is paralyzed, and I am utterly confused. Tell me which is the better path for me.
>
> —Prince Arjuna, in the Bhagavad Gita

The senior author's sister was in the powder room, door open, washing her hands. John, his six-year-old son, came in from outdoors, walked past his aunt, lifted the toilet seat, and peed. After flushing he walked out, saying, "A man's gotta do what a man's gotta do."

It might be unusual for a boy of six to be self-aware enough to be commenting on duty, but he got the lingo right. "Duty" implies adherence to a code defined by principles beyond an individual's self-interest. Honor and duty are familiar words to trained warriors. Although this book's chapters on strategy (part 1) were focused on achieving victory and gaining a competitive edge, winning is not necessarily the ultimate objective in warfare. As the battle rages and chaos reigns, we must release ourselves from a myopic obsession with victory. Our focus, as in any situation, should remain on how best to achieve the optimal outcome. A clear, unquestionable defeat of the opponent may sometimes lead us there, but not necessarily.

Duty is one of the Western interpretations of dharma, the Hindu concept of a moral order that upholds the universe and society. Dharma in this context refers to duty that goes beyond self, the forfeiting of one's personal desires to the obligations of one's destined role or purpose. (Note that when we come to chapter 5 on the Buddha, we'll see an additional meaning for dharma. There, dharma refers to the Buddha's teachings, truth, or remedies for suffering.)

Strategy: Consequential, Irreversible, and Often Painful Decisions

The Bhagavad Gita, or Gita, as it is often referred to, is one of the great texts of Eastern philosophy and a foundational part of Hindu scripture. Written sometime between the fifth and second centuries BCE, the Gita takes us into the mind of a legendary leader on the precipice of making a particularly wrenching decision.

The story's hero, Prince Arjuna, must decide whether to lead his army into battle against enemy forces composed of rogue members of his own family. He is anguished. Should he fulfill his moral duty to combat injustice and wage war on his own kin, or abide by his instinct for family preservation and be complicit in their immorality?

In the millennia since the Gita was written, dilemma and inner turmoil of all sorts have kept generations of leaders from a good night's sleep. To some degree this tension is inevitable—the higher one's position, the higher the stakes and the tougher the choices. As any executive stymied at the crossroads of a major decision will testify, the battle is experienced not only in the context of a struggle between ourselves and external opponents. Frequently, the most intense conflicts take place within.

The Art of War and *The Book of Five Rings*, as examined in chapter 2, armed us with tools, tactics, and philosophies for how to overcome our opponents on the battlefield, in the boardroom, in geopolitics, and beyond. However, even supplied with comprehensive frameworks, well-considered methodology, and insights gleaned from Sun Tzu and Musashi, decision makers will inevitably be challenged by thorny dilemmas—tough choices with no certainty about which path might lead to success.

Should I fight or retreat? Should I pursue an attractive opportunity or avoid the hazards of a risky investment? What is the best solution in this situation? Am I making the right decision? Will it turn out as well as I expect? Even the best strategists encounter these questions as they approach the precipice of consequential organizational decisions.

In late 2018, hedge fund manager Edward Lampert was brutalized by the business press as he considered Sears, Roebuck's existential dilemma. Lampert had invested heavily in Sears and had, through his ESL Investments fund, loaned the struggling retail icon in excess of USD200 million. Now he would have to decide whether to encourage Sears to shutter its remaining stores or try to keep the retailer's rapidly declining operations afloat. Even as public criticism mounted, Lampert appeared determined to uphold his wunderkind billionaire reputation, keeping Sears open in an attempt to turn the business around.[1]

Was this folly, or his dharma? More important, how was he to decide not only which alternative to choose, but the process he should use to reach his decision? Should he risk injecting an additional USD300 million in bankruptcy financing? Should he attempt to preserve his own reputation and pursue a high-risk strategy to protect the capital of his hedge fund investors?

Should he cut his losses and risk creating new unemployment for the already troubled economy of Chicago, Sears's hometown? Who would benefit from each move? Who would get hurt? What was his dharma dictating?

While the specific contextual details may vary, the essence of this inner turmoil is captured with remarkable nuance in the Gita. From its opening scene, where Arjuna struggles with profound personal and strategic decisions, the Gita serves as a meditation on the intense angst that accompanies making difficult choices and a guide for leaders working through such turmoil.

Notably distinct from the religious texts of the Abrahamic religions familiar to Westerners, the Gita is structured as a prolonged dialogue between Arjuna and Krishna, Arjuna's charioteer and advisor. Having arrived on a battlefield on the brink of war, Arjuna and Krishna discuss whether Arjuna should engage in the conflict despite his many misgivings. The Gita leverages this narrative device, a battlefield debate, to shed light on virtue, duty, and decision-making in the most challenging of circumstances.[2] Krishna's most vital argument to Arjuna is that there are specific ways of acting that, if followed, can ensure that one's actions will avoid generating bad karma—that is, one's store of good and bad actions, accumulated over lifetimes, that determines one's present circumstances and condition. Thus, one reaps what one sows, both in this life and in future ones.

The Gita is also a narrative guide for rediscovering our essence by removing the egocentric habits that obscure our natural goodness and compassion.[3] The Gita inspired American transcendentalists Ralph Waldo Emerson and Henry David Thoreau as they developed their ideas about the self. Notably, Thoreau carried the Gita with him to Walden Pond in 1845, finding virtue in Krishna's preference for action over inaction.[4]

Content and Key Themes of the Bhagavad Gita

The Bhagavad Gita, meaning "the song of Lord," is set on a battlefield in the moments before the onset of a brutal war. Yet this seven-hundred-verse, eighteen-chapter treatise is only superficially about conflicts with external opponents. The Gita's true focus is on resolving the conflicts within one's self.[5]

In the early pages, the reader encounters Arjuna as he prepares for battle against his power-hungry cousins, ready to engage in whatever violence will be necessary to reclaim the throne to which his brother is the rightful heir. Yet, as Arjuna and his loyal charioteer Krishna (whom Arjuna does not recognize as Krishna's true self, an incarnation of the god Vishnu) ride onto the field of battle, Arjuna realizes that the conflict will be unlike any he has fought before. Observing his army, as well as the opposing forces, he recognizes "fathers and grandfathers, teachers, uncles, brothers, sons and grandsons, in-laws and friends" in both the armies.[6] Evil, greedy, and selfish though his adversaries may be, Arjuna sees among the opposing forces family members and companions with whom he has associated all his life.

Arjuna believes himself incapable of attacking his family and is tormented by the question of whether the pursuit of justice can justify slaying them. "What can we hope from this killing of kinsmen?" he asks. "If we kill them our sin is greater. How could we dare spill the blood that unites us?"[7] In fact, Arjuna proclaims himself willing to be killed unarmed rather than fight the battle.

This is the intense, visceral dilemma Arjuna encounters: Should he wage war to support a cause he knows to be noble and righteous, or steer clear of the conflict and avoid having to square off with family members, mentors, and friends in a fight to the death? Arjuna's quest to resolve this quandary is the basis for his dialogue with Krishna. That conversation, in turn, serves as Arjuna's—and the reader's—gateway into a journey of spiritual discovery.

In helping resolve Arjuna's dilemma, the dialogue between Arjuna and Krishna lays out not only spiritual guidelines for how to live a virtuous life, but also the considerations we must weigh in order to make effective decisions.

Lessons for Strategists and Leaders

1. KNOW YOUR DHARMA AND PERFORM YOUR DUTY

As Arjuna expresses worry and confusion about the dilemma in front of him, Krishna admonishes him that "this despair and weakness in a time of crisis are . . . unworthy of you."[8] Krishna advises Arjuna to "fight in good cause" and to fight for his values, not for himself:

> They are forever free [those] who renounce all selfish desires and break away from the ego-cage of "I," "me," and "mine."[9] . . . The ignorant work for their own profit, Arjuna; the wise work for welfare of the world, without thought for themselves.[10]

In the midst of confusion and uncertainty, Krishna encourages Arjuna to return his focus to his motivations.

Even when making decisions far more mundane than those involving war against our families, we may experience the stress of having to make choices without clarity about potential outcomes. The Gita argues that by understanding and continually clarifying our motivations, we can simplify the daunting task of selecting from a range of seemingly attractive alternatives.

The Gita underscores the importance of establishing a clear intention. Furthermore, the text sets out a hierarchy for prioritizing our motives. Krishna suggests to Arjuna that a decision-making compass oriented toward benefiting others, broader communities, and a higher power will yield more powerful results than one oriented toward individual gain. "Act selflessly, without any thought of personal profit," he implores.[11]

This advice may seem trite to twenty-first-century readers. Stressing the importance of making decisions based on what will most benefit your fellow human is far from groundbreaking. However, understanding the "why" behind Krishna's advice reveals nuanced insights for organizational strategy.

L. J. B., the former CEO of Esso Brasil, describes a sense of never being satisfied, "a restless heart," as a foundation for his success. But simple dissatisfaction with the organizational status quo can keep the heart restless only for so long, he argues. After our objectives are achieved, the temptation to rest on our laurels may prove powerful.

The energy of a powerful selflessness, however, can prove to be a more enduring stimulus. Instead of drawing its energy from organizational shortcomings, a restless heart might focus on a desire for more justice, well-being, and peace in the world. When our decisions are driven by the desire to right these deficiencies, we are unlikely to come up short of examples to spark our motivation.

Such energy can serve as powerful fuel for strategists pursuing an ambitious organizational agenda. Yet, as L. J. B.'s example would suggest, that energy is likely to be sustained only if it arises from a place deeper than simple dissatisfaction with the present moment.

Following Krishna's advice, Arjuna decides to fight the war, believing it to be his duty. Strategists, too, can learn to navigate through tough decisions and uncertain circumstances by connecting to a powerful dharma, whether it be the betterment of employees, customers, and other stakeholders or other causes larger than themselves.

Mahatma Gandhi faced extraordinary challenges and choices during his life. As both a lawyer and a practicing Hindu, Gandhi deeply understood the law, but believed himself to be governed by more fundamental values: truth, nonviolence, and service to others. In pursuing these principles, he positioned responsibilities—duty—rather than individual rights at the center of his moral and governing philosophies.[12] Summarizing lessons to be drawn from Gandhi's teachings, Keshavan Nair points out the contrast between responsibility- and rights-oriented social constructs: "A society driven by responsibilities is oriented toward service . . . and progress—whereas a society driven by rights is oriented toward [personal] acquisition [and] confrontation."[13]

2. TAKE SELFLESS ACTIONS AND RELINQUISH EGO ATTACHMENT TO RESULTS

Now with a selfless end in mind, Krishna guided Arjuna to perform his duty with similarly selfless actions. The notion of selfless ends, along the same lines as concern for stakeholders, may feel familiar, at least as a concept. But what are the implications for strategy?

As Krishna explained: "You have the right to work, but never to the fruit of work. You should never engage in action for the sake of reward, nor should you long for inaction. Perform work in this world, Arjuna, as a man established within himself—without selfish attachments, and alike in success and defeat."[14]

Mahatma Gandhi built on the Gita's message, stating: "You must not worry whether the desired result follows from your action or not, so long as your motive is pure, your means correct. . . . But renunciation of fruit in no way means indifference to the result."[15] Ralph Waldo Emerson was also influenced by the Gita's emphasis on selfless action, drawing from it a belief that, as Barbara Stoler Miller described it, "works must be done without thought of reward and a person may have a tranquil mind even in activity."[16] Or, as Emerson himself wrote, "The reward of a thing well done, is to have done it."[17]

Detachment does not imply inaction in the face of difficulty. Certainly, when the path deviates from the goal, we must pursue corrective action, increase our efforts, and inspire our followers. But we must also accept a rising improbability of success with equanimity. Eknath Easwaran, a noted translator of the Gita, argued in his commentary: "This attitude frees us completely. Whatever comes—success or failure, praise or blame, victory or defeat—we can give our best with a clear, unruffled mind."[18]

Paradoxically, the Gita suggests that by freeing the mind from the constraints of a sole focus on outcomes, we are better prepared to identify the right course of action:

> The wise . . . have abandoned all external supports. Their security is unaffected by the results of their action; even while acting, they really do nothing at all.[19]

How can we rise above senses and emotions? The Gita emphasizes having the equanimity to allow undistorted reality to reveal itself to us.

Practicing selfless actions with emotional indifference to success and pain, praise and condemnation, strategists will hold clearer views toward the world. They must cultivate the capability to remain unreactive, even while becoming completely present to the unfolding circumstances. This notion of balancing a deep understanding of the present moment with a total lack of desire to change the experience in any way serves as a guide for strategy-making. Strategists must be aware of the present moment to recognize subtly arising opportunities that other players in the market may not see. At the same time, they must also remain equanimous enough to avoid chasing trends and overreacting to market dynamics.

Having accepted the value of presence combined with nonreactivity, Arjuna asked Krishna for guidance on how to practice equanimity. Krishna replied:

> It is true that the mind is restless and difficult to control. But it can be conquered, Arjuna, through regular practice and detachment. Those who lack self-control will find it difficult to progress in meditation; but those who are self-controlled, striving earnestly through the right means, will attain the goal.[20]

This is encouraging news. The Gita does not suggest that the ability to balance awareness and equanimity is an innate trait or the product of karma from past lives. Rather, Krishna describes it as a developed skill built through determined practice. No strategist, therefore, should be disappointed when equanimity, awareness, or both seem out of reach in a challenging moment. Rather, our ability to hold the balance is developed over time through disciplined practice repeated across many decisions. Perhaps the intensity of the moment will overtake us the first, second, and even tenth time we are grappling with tough predicaments. But if we consistently strive to cultivate a nonreactive, aware presence, we too can develop this capability over time.

3. STRATEGIC INSIGHT IS AVAILABLE TO ALL OF US

This emphasis on developed skill is at the heart of the Gita's wisdom. Some are born with a talent for the strategic, but that does not mean that those who are not naturally gifted cannot become successful strategists, nor that the amply gifted will always be successful. Right thoughts and actions rather than destiny determine successful strategists.

Challenges are bound to arise, and perseverance in the face of obstacles is the key ingredient in the Gita's recipe for success. Right thoughts and right mindsets alone are not enough; right action is required for us to accomplish our objectives. Persons who conduct themselves dutifully, selflessly, and with integrity—who, in the Hindu lexicon, do "right deeds"—will have better lives than those who do not. They can create new foundations in life today for a better tomorrow and break through their inherited or self-created negative karma cycle.

In the Gita, right actions are a practice, not a onetime event. As we saw in chapter 1, Clausewitz's fourth step in strategic insight is resolution, or the resolve to carry out the strategy that one's coup d'oeil has revealed. Krishna's advice extends beyond intention, underscoring the importance of diligent execution.

As an example of the need for diligent execution, and of a "get things done" culture, consider the path taken by Microsoft since the early 2000s. When Steve Ballmer succeeded Bill Gates as CEO in 2000, his personal management style was often marked by bluster and histrionics. In terms of strategy, Ballmer's forays into markets already dominated by others, such as cell phones, were seen as leading Microsoft into obsolescence. It appeared that Microsoft was unable to make headway into "almost every significant computing trend of the 2000s—mobile phones, search engines, social networking—while letting its main source of revenue, Windows . . . stagnate."[21]

To his credit, Ballmer identified and developed Satya Nadella as his successor. Nadella was the opposite of Ballmer—a mild-mannered, no-nonsense engineer with a librarian's temperament who grew up in Hyderabad, India. He is now credited with Microsoft's reemergence as a tech power, for instilling corporate mindsets of "empathy" and "growth,"[22] and for positioning Microsoft as a key player in cloud computing and artificial intelligence.

What was it about Nadella that caught Ballmer's eye? Nadella is seen as a self-effacing, bland, unruffled, "no swagger" person with little ego. But that is not all. In Ballmer's words, he "doesn't piss off other people" and, more important, "gets shit done."[23]

4. ANOTHER PERSON IS NEEDED UNLESS STRATEGISTS CAN CREATE AN ALTER EGO

For strategists to be successful, they need right thoughts and clear mindsets to formulate strategies and navigate their execution. But humans are imperfect beings. Our awareness of the present moment and of other people and objects—including our family, our friends, and our belongings—is distorted by our egos. Therefore, a strategist may benefit from another person—a colleague, a partner, a wise and skeptical friend—serving as a sounding board and foil.

Krishna's guidance is crucial for helping Arjuna navigate the hardest dilemma of his life to the right decision. The interplay between the two of them serves as the backbone of the text's narrative structure. In a very different vein, European kings had their court jesters to prevent them from becoming overly self-obsessed. Walt Disney had his grounded brother, Roy, as a counterbalance,[24] and wild-eyed Soichiro Honda had Takeo Fujisawa to keep their business on a solid path.[25]

To be successful, strategists should find their own people who counterbalance to show them light when in darkness, and to wake them up when they're basking in praise and success.

In 1981 billionaire N. R. Narayana Murthy cofounded Infosys, a USD13 billion IT consulting firm in Bangalore, India. During an interview in 2017, Murthy was asked to elaborate on why his vision for Infosys was "to earn respect from all stakeholders" and "to be India's most respected company."[26]

Murthy, who had trained at the Indian Institute of Technology Kanpur and earned his MBA at the Indian Institute of Management Ahmedabad, said in the interview that "even though good governance is to maximize shareholder value, society is the most important player because it contributes to employees, customers, investors, and vendors. Therefore, if we could earn respect from society, our company could go far." He emphasized that "in every decision that any corporation takes . . . they all should ask this simple question: Will this decision of mine enhance respect for my company from this society? And will this decision of mine enhance respect for me from my colleagues?"

When asked to share his vision for the next five to ten years, Murthy said: "Automation is coming. This is a huge opportunity for big corporations, but executives have to spend time and effort to re-deploy and re-train their employees so that the livelihood of their families would not be affected." As new ideas, new technology, and new innovation are entering our lives, he urged corporations to ensure that society would not suffer from the trend.

When asked how he defined success, Murthy referred to Thomas Jefferson's words: "It is not the conditions that you have been put in because of chance that matter. It is your occupation; it is your conscience; it is what you do to contribute that matter." Murthy also said: "Success to me is the ability to bring smiles to the faces of people when I enter the room. . . . They know that I care for them as they are my family members." He referred to a Sanskrit saying: "The whole world is one family."

Hong Kong, 2017

"There was nothing we could do wrong," said Naresh Kumra, CEO of Jmatek, a global leader in evaporative air coolers and portable air conditioners. Describing the early days of Jmatek, Kumra noted:

> I had bought into the partnership with a management buy-in in April 2012, and with existing management in place, we grew sales and increased gross margins, and went from loss-making in 2013 to industry-leading profitability by 2016. We had big growth all over the world, with offices in Buenos Aires, Mexico City, two offices in Europe, a few in Asia, and in New Jersey. We were the leaders in e-commerce in our segment, with a good position on Amazon, and retail in Lowe's, Best Buy, and other, smaller, shops, and had global exclusive rights to represent Honeywell.[27]

By January 2017, Jmatek's sales in the United States had risen significantly, and Amazon had become its biggest channel. "The time was ripe for an infusion of new capital, so we prepared for the next consequential round of cash from outside investors," Kumra said. The stakes were significant. Kumra had invested his own capital in the management buy-in, and managers and employees themselves were shareholders.

During the cold months of December 2016 to April 2017, Jmatek's sales through Amazon slowed as expected. Come May, the month when Jmatek typically saw the start of a summer-long surge in sales, management noticed that the company's sales on Amazon were running significantly behind 2016. Scrambling to understand the cause of the decline, management learned that Jmatek's products, which had previously occupied prime positions for their categories on the first page of Amazon's search results, had dropped as far as the fifth and sixth pages.

"We were new to this e-commerce thing, and didn't understand what was happening to our business," Kumra said. "My fellow shareholder partners were really nervous; we were in the middle of a fundraiser, we were going back and forth, and my partners are saying, 'We need to cut the cost, we need to do this.' Just a lot of stuff going on—I'm right in the middle of it, and I don't know what to do."

Kumra's Cultural Upbringing in Rajpura

In the midst of British India's 1947 partition into two independent states, India and Pakistan, Naresh Kumra's parents made the forced migration from Pakistan to Rajpura, a small town in northern India.

Most people in Rajpura never ventured more than twenty to thirty miles from home. Though ambitious, Kumra did not have a clear view of how to pursue a different path. His answer came in the form of the National Talent Search, an examination to identify India's highest-potential tenth-graders. To his surprise, Kumra's outstanding test results earned him one of two thousand scholarships awarded annually across all of India, a country of more than one billion people. His strong performance gave him the confidence to move to a city twenty-five miles away for his last two years of high school. There, he was encouraged to apply—successfully—to the elite Indian Institute of Technology Delhi, "an entire 150 miles away!"

While at the university, Kumra heard a classmate describing the value of an MBA from a top American university. He had never heard of the degree nor seriously considered an education abroad. But he was intrigued by his friend's description. After completing his undergraduate studies, Kumra spent several years working for a global oil field services provider across France, Scotland, and India before enrolling at the University of Virginia's Darden School of Business.

Having excelled at Darden, Kumra followed the path of many top MBA graduates and joined McKinsey & Company as a consultant. His entry into the elite ranks of Western business came as a jolt. He recalled:

> I was raised to be kind, giving, supporting—no limelight. This was a barrier in the capitalist corporate world—I was seen as always giving up. I was told I needed to be more assertive, more forceful.
>
> First at Darden, then at McKinsey, I learned that you can give negative feedback without offending to help the person improve and find the fitting role or job. I came to the realization that if I give negative feedback with love, it is because I care for you; if I don't give you the negative feedback, it's actually not good for you because you're not advancing in your career. Sooner or later, you'll be bitter and not be happy. I had to find a way to flourish in the capitalist world without compromising the values I had inherited. (There was no way I could fire anybody, but I had to teach myself that, too.)
>
> So, how do you get yourself to the middle way? First you cut the umbilical cord—then you are unconstrained to pursue the desired change. I experimented with going to an extreme: Every day, for several weeks, I would order a steak for lunch. [Like many Hindus, Kumra was raised not eating beef.] Every day. I could not even chew it. I did not know what it meant. Well cooked. Rare. Or medium. . . . I experimented with it all. So, by going to the other extreme, I was able to end up in the middle—my new normal.
>
> The idea was, I wanted to get past my mental barrier. . . . I realized that if I really want to include an objective Western view, I needed to detach myself from the past. And the best way to do that is force yourself to live at the opposite end of the spectrum, so that it forces you to detach from the past. That's something I've used again and again in my career, in my life.
>
> This experience led me to my leadership style, which I would character-

ize as running a business as a "caring meritocracy." I recognized the need to take people's insecurity and fear out of their business lives, while still inspiring them to stretch beyond their current capacities. How can you get that stretch without fear of failing? With love.[28]

Back to Hong Kong and the Amazon Dilemma

Kumra described the anxiety he felt in 2017 as Jmatek's sales continued to plummet:

> It's August . . . but our sales are very down from 2016. Summer is ending, and we have no idea what's happening. We were in the middle of our first institutional fundraise . . . and now our business is just falling off the cliff.
>
> So we initially pursued what seemed like the rational, analytical approach. But what complicated this was . . . we had people whose bonuses, whose salaries were tied to the company performance. . . . So we're talking about five hundred people that are going to be affected by this. My own family's investment was at stake.
>
> So we have all of this complexity, and a duty to protect all of them and their expectations and financial well-being. And yet, you are in a situation where you don't quite know exactly what is happening.
>
> I went through the gamut of emotions: depression, turmoil, fear, feeling responsible, a sense of injustice (I had done everything right, hadn't I?), and worst, doubting myself, doubting my confidence as a leader.
>
> My priority was solving the problems with an analytical way. But the emotions happen regardless. There's the typical Western side of me: The first thought was okay, let's set the emotions aside. I need to focus on the analytical problem.
>
> So the very first thing that I did was realize emotionally what was happening. How do I rein in the stallion? Get some space? Make the right decision and do the right thing?
>
> The hardest thing was to calm down. I told myself, don't get stressed. That's just how life is going, and I think it's a reminder that whatever goes up must come down, whatever goes down must come up, so having that optimism about the future that whatever you are seeing is only transient, it's temporary, it calms you down.
>
> The second thing was to detach from the past as well as the near-term future. I could not live on our previous successes or the slowdowns of 2017. I had to take a fresh look at what was going on, maybe a transformation that was needed, and for that I needed to learn and experiment. But first I had to acknowledge that 2017 was different, and I didn't want a private

fund breathing down my neck putting additional pressure. How do we just take a break for a while so we figure this out? . . .

So we decided to put the fundraise on hold.

That was a tough decision, but was really important because without the pause I couldn't have focused all my energies on solving the problem, instead of managing the stakeholders. That was the next thing in terms of detaching and acknowledging the worst-case scenario and moving on.

Third, I realized that solving the problem for the short term, like cutting costs and dressing it up, was not going to do it. We really had to solve it for the long term. And that was going to take some time and some experimentation.

The fourth thing was to manage my stress. And one of the best practices is to start with the acknowledgement that okay, here's the worst-case scenario. Let's say it happens. And then you start your thinking from there. You don't get stressed, because after that, everything seems like an upside.

I acknowledged that okay, it's a bad year. It's not going to be as good. Maybe it'll take us a few years to come out of it. And I went and had a conversation with our team and with our fellow shareholders and the board, saying, "Here's the situation. Let's acknowledge it. Let's see how we build from it." It was tough, because I was admitting, in a way, failure. But from there on, what it allowed us to do was to focus only on the problem at hand and not on all the noises and the competing inputs that were coming. And I think that was paramount, because it's a whole new digital world that we would need to learn about, and we were quite clueless.

Fifth, if you want your team to go with you in a war, you want them to feel comfortable that if they die in the war . . . you will do whatever you can to take care of their family. That's the confidence with which a soldier goes to war. When you're fighting a business battle like that, it's no different, especially in the entrepreneurial journey. You have to make sure that you tell your team that come what may, whether we succeed or we fail, I am with you every step of the way. And I will make sure that you, your personal life, and your family are not affected. . . .

It's magical. It's magical when you give people that kind of safety net. And from there on, it all becomes about pursuing all the rational ideas that we considered. But people are now pursuing all those rational ideas with the idea of making it better. They're not personally fearful. Their emotions are not coming in the way. Their insecurities are not coming in the way.

So we did some experiments around the platform, to learn exactly what happened: Okay, how do we take a step back and reassess the strategy? How big of an experiment could we run? We don't really know what's going on, but we're willing to try a few things to test some hypotheses.

> The first hypothesis we had was that something in the Amazon universe changed, because it was too short of a time period for the buyers to have changed. We tried several cheap experiments of, what happens when we do this for a day or a week? How about other brands? Are we the only ones suffering this problem? Other brands were now showing up on page one, and they were having a feast day.
>
> We ultimately found that, because for four, five cold months we were not selling at all, our sales velocity was zero when we got back online. And so our products, which used to show up at the top of page one, were now showing up on page four, page five, page six.
>
> Perhaps the most important thing was telling everybody on our team that let's all get smarter on digital and e-commerce. Don't worry about the short term. We are not playing this game for the short term. We're not playing it for this quarter, we're not playing it for this year, we are trying to figure out the best we can be ten years out.
>
> We decided we wanted to get really good at [e-commerce], reading articles, going to training programs, sharing knowledge within the firm. We just became a learning organization overnight, trying to solve our business model for the long term.
>
> Today [October 2018], our sales are higher than they were in 2016 and so is our market share. And we are continuing to explore new ideas, including offering our knowledge of e-commerce as a service to other companies to help them sell online.

Pursuing a Gita-inspired approach, Kumra was able not only to manage his emotions and help his team navigate the crisis, but to find solutions that positioned Jmatek for long-term growth. As we will see in the next three chapters, the equanimity and calm Kumra displayed in his decision-making also align to many of the ideas at the core of the Buddha's teachings.

Strategy Lessons from Chapter 4

1. Know your dharma and perform your duty.
2. Take selfless actions and relinquish ego attachment to results.
3. Open yourself to strategic insight by conducting yourself dutifully, selflessly, and with integrity.
4. Build a diligent execution culture that perseveres in the face of obstacles.
5. Find a wise and skeptical colleague to serve as a sounding board and devil's advocate.

5

The Buddha and His Teaching

Question: "How much is enough?"

Answer: "More."

Ephesus, Turkey, July 2017

A stream with curative powers runs next to the Virgin Mary's last home. Downhill from the house, along a brick wall, are three faucets from which a visitor may drink or otherwise refresh him or herself with the holy water. Each faucet provides a divine gift: health, wealth, or love. The catch is, the visitor may tap only two of the three faucets.

Which two gifts would you choose? Which one would you leave behind? During the senior author's visit, the young guide suggested that health and wealth would attract the third, love. The author's smiling response to her was yes, perhaps, but possibly the wrong kind.

These three choices are a reflection of Western culture. A manifestation of our evolutionary survival instincts, they reflect the need to procreate (attractiveness), provide shelter (security), and fend off danger (power). As a consequence, we tend to value physical beauty and health, material wealth, and the power that comes with social prestige. Still, we struggle to limit our desires or to identify how much is enough to satisfy our needs. Indeed, as private companies considering going public know well, financial markets themselves will impose the relentless demand for more, more, more. The Buddha's teaching is one path to finding a balance beyond the drive to relentless acquisition and accumulation.

As seen in our previous chapter, the Gita advises us to value duty for purposes larger than ourselves with selfless ends and selfless actions. Buddhism is different. It does not provide the answer for optimal outcomes in difficult circumstances. But it does prepare us to assume a state of mind—beginner's mind—that allows a breakthrough solution to reveal itself. Buddhist philosophy helps eliminate barriers to beginner's mind and guides us on how to prolong that state while we are in the midst of endless external noise.

This chapter and the next two are about the Buddha and Buddhist practices. In this chapter, we provide a brief biography, describe Buddha's basic philosophy, and take you through the first five steps of his practical Eightfold Path. We will see how basic human desires lead to unfulfillable expectations and disappointments—what Buddha defines as suffering—and how we can begin to free ourselves from such dissatisfaction and assaults on clear-headed thinking. The last part of the Eightfold Path, including steps 6, 7, and 8, is given its own chapter because of its powerful application to developing the state of beginner's mind critical to strategic insight. A third chapter explores the lessons strategists can glean from Zen, a strain of Buddhism adapted by and for Chinese and Japanese cultures.

Nakhon Ratchasima, Thailand, July 2018

Charoen Pokphand Group (CP) is Thailand's largest private company and one of the world's largest conglomerates. CP's businesses include agribusiness, retail, and telecommunications, operating in more than thirty countries with three hundred thousand employees. CP is one of the largest foreign investors in mainland China, where it controls two hundred businesses and subsidiaries.

Sumeth Laomoraporn was CEO of several divisions of CP, including CP Leadership Institute (CPLI) and CP Intertrade (CPI). CPLI is at the heart of CP's renowned leadership culture, while CPI serves as the commodity trading arm of CP. Under Sumeth's leadership, CPI had grown rapidly, building a 1.5 million-metric-ton production facility and reaching USD1 billion in revenue.

Sitting with Sumeth in the extravagantly decorated reception area of the Leadership Institute, Mint and Jay asked him to recount experiences where his Buddhist philosophy and practices guided his decision-making and yielded strategic insights. After a few minutes of reflection, Sumeth pointed to a decade-old crisis that had nearly destroyed CP's rice business.

The global rice business is not only cyclical, but is subject to large swings due to unpredictable weather patterns, macroeconomics, and politics and public policy. The year 2008 was the pinnacle of CPI's corporate success. The firm's record profits followed a commodity boom that saw an appreciation of global rice prices and, subsequently, the company's inventory value. In 2011, attempting to emulate the success of three years earlier, CPI took a large long position in the rice market. A rice-buying program recently announced by the government of Thailand was expected to drive a significant rise in prices. CPI procured enormous stockpiles of rice at great costs in anticipation of a price hike.

As CPI had anticipated, the Thai government program did indeed generate significant new demand in the rice market. Yet, shortly after the program's launch, other rice-exporting nations such as India and Vietnam dramatically increased their own rice production in an attempt to avoid losing market share to Thailand. The resulting jump in rice supply far outweighed any increase in demand driven by the Thai program. Rice prices plummeted, and Sumeth realized that he was on the wrong side of the trade.

It was not long before the board of directors got wind of CPI's vulnerability, and members began urging Sumeth and his management team to fix the problem as soon as possible. However, no matter how much the team devoted their brainpower, time, and energy to the issue, nothing improved their position as rice prices continued to decline. Morale also suffered; dejected, depleted, and compromised psychologically, the team was in a state of despair. Sumeth contemplated stepping down from his position as a gesture of accepting responsibility.

Readers may notice similarities between Sumeth's story and that of Ravi Menon in the introduction to this book. Both faced the difficult decision of whether to leave their firm in a moment of crisis. But they approached the situation differently. Ravi boarded a plane to Zurich and submitted his resignation. By contrast, as was his wont when dealing with such questions, Sumeth retreated into himself, spending hours in quiet contemplation of a solution. "All answers are in you, but your mind is too clouded to let you see them," he said during our interview.

After pondering the question of resignation for many days, Sumeth came to a conclusion: "To leave or to stay is not the problem. It is about the 'can-do' mindset and not treating this outcome as a failure but as a learning process through the deeds of our entire course of action, effort, and character. Resignation—running away and abandoning the team members—would be a black scar. It is a sign of a loser. I do not want to run away like a loser."

Sumeth's most profound realization was that his ego and CPI's recent string of successes had clouded his judgment. He described it as a misled belief that "we can limitlessly surpass the beacon of our triumph and all the worldly conquests that man can accomplish—thinking we are more than who we really are."

Sumeth asked the board for twelve months to solve the problem. If the situation did not recover, he would resign. Next, a clear-minded and calm Sumeth addressed his distraught executive team: "We should resign when we are champions, not losers. If we do it right, the outcome will be right."

Having restored the morale of his team, Sumeth returned to solitude that evening to ponder the facts of the situation. He considered the root causes of the team's failure and potential solutions. Leaning on his Buddhist practice, Sumeth focused on avoiding attachment to the outcome. He said:

> When your business encounters financial challenge, you will react with bias and prejudice. You need to step out from the financial figures. The right mindset is very important. Success and failure are not different but are merely two sides of the same coin. Despite their seemingly opposite and total contrast, both and each are paradoxically one of the same thing. Without success there would be no failure. And conversely, without failure one would not see nor comprehend the embodiment of success. Detachment from the numbers gives you courage to confront a problem. Sometimes we are worried too much about the outcome. We need to focus on causes. If we create good causes, the desired outcomes will come after.

Sumeth realized that his feeling of crisis was self-inflicted, with the downward spiral of stress, pressure, and anxiety also infecting his team. This insight came to him after he had eaten dinner, taken a bath, watched a sports movie, meditated, and prepared for bed. This was typical—he often experienced flashes of insight regarding key business decisions after meditation, when his mind was at its most peaceful.

Calmed and centered, Sumeth devised a multipronged strategy to dispose of the excess rice inventory while minimizing losses. Now at peace with the situation, he was able to impart both his strategic plan and his sense of equanimity to his team. Taking an even-keeled approach focused on process over outcomes, the team put the strategy into action over several months. While fluctuations in the rice market continued to create hurdles for CPI, Sumeth watched with admiration as his subordinates resolved the issues without unnecessary panic or anxiety. He allowed himself a moment of satisfaction when CP's directors declared the crisis resolved several months ahead of the deadline.

After witnessing firsthand the personal and professional benefits of Buddhist practices at work, Sumeth began subtly integrating Buddhist principles into CP's corporate culture. Some initiatives were explicitly Buddhist. For example, CP portfolio companies engaged a Thai monk to teach at their offices every month. Others were more subtle. Sumeth embedded Buddhist teaching and practices into CPI's executive education curriculum; now, before beginning the first session each day at CP Leadership Institute, participants are encouraged to reflect in silence for ten to fifteen minutes on the previous day's lessons.

Reflecting on the challenges of 2011 nearly a decade later, Sumeth recounted how the crisis and his Buddhist principles have informed his views on business performance and organizational leadership: "The state of uncertainty is the ultimate certainty. Blinded by the truth, it is us who instead choose not to appreciate this natural unity of success and failure—thus we are the architect of our own demise. Above all, the culprit is perhaps our own reprehensibly inflated ego, when in fact we are insignificantly small and diminutively irrelevant compared to the vastness of our oceans."

Bangkok, Thailand, 2018

Sea Ltd. is a leading integrated internet company in Southeast Asia consisting of an online gaming business (Garena), an e-commerce platform (Shopee), and a digital financial services offering (AirPay). Founded in 2009, this Singapore startup expanded its gaming business to Thailand, which quickly became Sea's largest market.

While enjoying the view of Bangkok from the large window in Sea's waiting area, two of this book's authors were welcomed by the soft voice of CEO Maneerut (Nok) Anulomsombut. She led us to her warmly decorated office, where two couches were filled with pillows depicting Sea's mascots, a series of cartoon characters. After our opening conversation, we posed the same question we had asked Sumeth: "How does your MBA and your Buddhism inform your strategic insights? Can you tell us about a tough, wicked decision that you confronted?"

Glancing away for a while, Nok recalled a challenging period in 2014, shortly after she had joined Sea Thailand as COO. Unfounded rumors about technical shortcomings in a soon-to-launch Garena software package were quickly spreading among Thailand's cybercafes, an important group of business partners who served as local distributors of Sea's online PC games. The rumors fomented doubt in the Garena brand, putting at risk a major source of revenue for the entire Sea group. Nok was particularly caught off guard when local media began publishing erroneous reports about Garena and the new software.

Nok's stress grew after a close friend called to ask if the accusation was true. "I was very upset and frustrated," Nok confessed. "The company had good intentions, but they were misinterpreted. Now, it was not just our partners. My friend questioned my ethics. I was disappointed." Nok felt pressure mounting from inside and outside the company, with executives, staff, partners, and media pressing her for answers and decisions.

At the peak of the crisis, Nok had eaten little and not slept for three days. Sleeplessness and lack of appetite are not uncommon for leaders and decision makers in moments of extreme stress. For many executives, the default response is to push through fatigue to continue pursuing the traditional tools of strategy-making: gather more information, analyze the data again in hopes of gleaning new insights, and continue analyzing the pros and cons of various options. But Nok—a Stanford MBA, ex-investment banker, and ex-BCG management consultant—took a different path grounded in Buddhist principles and practices to discover answers from within.

Nok elaborated that when we are in doubt, we need a break. "You can only make the right decision when your mind is at peace. I cleared my mind—similar to setting my mind to zero—then allowed logical thinking to come in." To prepare for a peaceful decision-making process, Nok shut herself off from the chaos for one hour, alone and in seclusion, and meditated. Relaxed, she then watched a funny TV show. Having returned her mind to a peaceful state appropriate for contemplating the challenge at hand, Nok committed herself to an attitude of "no attachment" and began looking inward for a solution.

Describing how she applied this mindset, Nok formed a ball with her cupped hands in front of her chest: "I visualize a problem as a rock or an object lying separately from myself in front of me." She pushed her hands, still cupped, away from her: "Then, I would look at that 'rock' and think how I would tackle it." The visualization helped Nok detach her ego and weigh her options without excessive emotional turbulence.

Having found seclusion, calmed her mind, and allowed for emotional detachment, Nok was prepared to contemplate a solution to the crisis. She began by inventorying her understanding of the situation and the resources available to her, and became comfortable with the harsh reality of what she described as "the real world." As is often the case, the solution came to her suddenly, an unexpected flash of insight later that night. "The whole process actually went very fast," she said.

> I was quite frustrated and upset about what happened, so I stayed later than usual in the office. I left the office around 9 p.m. and realized when I reached home that I had missed sending my son to bed. I remember sitting by myself and thinking about all that had happened. I came to the point where I realized that I had gotten my emotions involved too deeply to the point where I wasn't myself. I let the problem in and let it control my thoughts, causing me to forget that I have more important things to think about. So I tried to forget about what happened and meditated. I then took a shower, watched my favorite TV series, and just relaxed a bit. I think it was about one hour, then I went to bed.
>
> I came up with the solution while I was doing my routine prayer before going to bed. There were two groups of people causing this rumor: (1) a small group of owners of big chains of one hundred to two hundred cafes—there were not too many of them, but since they owned big chains they could make a louder noise, and (2) our competitors, who probably pushed negative info to the media and tried to spread the word.

First of all, I decided not to respond to any media since whatever statement we put out, our competitors or those who didn't mean us well would find a loophole and attack us again. I then talked to the team to understand what the real concern was from those big chains. Eventually, we learned they were afraid they would lose the benefit we provided before. So we assured them (one by one my team went to talk to each of them) that they wouldn't lose any benefit we provided and that we looked at them as our long-term partners. With face-to-face conversation, those owners felt better and they stopped talking about this. On the very same day, we made the official announcement about our Cafe Thai program and [the new software], with details about the package we offered and the services the cafe owners who signed up for it would get, clarifying that it was not mandatory to install the program but the benefit and add-on services would be different depending on the package (like a premium package). We posted this on our Facebook page as well as our official communication channel that we had with all cafe owners, so literally it only took a day for them to see our official announcement.

The solution may sound quite simple and direct. I should have thought about this quite fast, but I couldn't do so before simply because I didn't have a clear mind. I was frustrated with the issues, letting me be a part of the problem. If only I knew how to separate myself from the problem, I would not have to suffer or think too much about all those negative comments from external parties. I felt that I became stronger and learned to understand the phrase "this too shall pass" a lot better.

Here are some of the Buddhist lessons Nok recounted as her foundation:

Be mindful. Things happen . . . They happen for a reason.
Be present and do your best.
Do not be too sad if things turn out bad. Do not be too happy if things turn out good. It does not matter which direction, it will be good in the end.
Do not think too hard. It will be okay. Emotions will pass anyway. So, just acknowledge them, but do not let them affect you and hurt your mind. Then ask yourself, "Now what?"

Nok was promoted to CEO of Sea Thailand in 2016. In October 2017, Sea went public on the New York Stock Exchange, raising net proceeds of USD936 million. By 2018, Garena had become the No. 1 gaming company in Thailand, fielding esports tournaments of 240,000 spectators in Bangkok and 10 million online viewers. In March 2019, *Forbes* reported that the share price of Sea had increased by 45 percent and that Sea's sales and founder Forrest Li's net worth had both passed the USD1 billion mark.[1]

Nok Anulomsombut and Sumeth Laomoraporn not only had learned Western analytical skills and practiced Buddhist philosophy, they had merged the two in how they approached solving major organizational challenges.

When we asked them how they could master the philosophy and fluently apply it in the real world, they each humbly indicated that they were not experts and needed continuous study and practice of the teachings of the Buddha. In their respective situations, they both experienced stress, anxiety, and extreme tension. What their problem-solving and decision-making processes had in common were seclusion, silence, relaxation, acceptance, and finally, coup d'oeil. How did they find mental calm in the midst of crisis? What allowed them to pause at the right time? Why did their positive mindset kick in when they needed it most? Can we learn to do the same?

Who Was the Buddha?

Siddhattha Gotama—the Buddha, as he was referred to after his enlightenment—never presented himself as a deity.[2] When asked for explanations of cosmic phenomenon or the sacred order, he would demur, usually stating that what he had to offer was not a theory but a method, an actionable set of steps that leads to enlightenment and clear-mindedness. He also did not set out to enroll all of his adherents as wandering monks dedicated solely to his teachings. His target audience included regular householders, merchants, and government officers. In other words, he appealed to those without whom society could not function and prosper.

His mission was simple: to guide humans to liberate themselves from the desires and thirsts that he diagnosed as the root causes of all suffering. By letting go of these attachments, the Buddha taught, one can enter a space of calmness, presence, and peace—a state of enlightenment and liberation he described as *nibbana*. With this core insight as the foundation, the Buddha developed a system to enable others to embark on their journeys toward *nibbana*. This methodology, a how-to guide of step-by-step instructions anyone could follow, includes a range of tools, including lessons from the Buddha's life story and insights regarding the nature of the physical world and the human condition.

In the approximately twenty-five hundred years since the life of the Buddha, his principles have been enhanced by interpretation, study, and practice by an extraordinary range of scholars, monks, and everyday devotees. Although there are many sophisticated interpretations of the Buddha's teachings, we will limit ourselves here to the core concepts that undergird most Buddhist traditions.[3]

Schools of Buddhism

A range of interpretations of Buddhism materialized after the Buddha's death in 483 BCE. Two of the leading traditions present today are Theravada and Mahayana. The Theravada tradition, most commonly encountered in Sri Lanka, Cambodia, Laos, Burma, and Thailand, is generally considered the more traditional of the two schools. Theravada teachings include an emphasis on practices such as yoga that have strong ties to Hinduism and predate the rise of Buddhism. The Mahayana tradition prevails in Tibet, Nepal, China, Korea, and Japan, and is perceived to have a more action-oriented approach, prioritizing individual practice over ritual.

One example that illustrates the distinctions between the two schools can be found in the individuals each chooses to honor. The Theravada tradition venerates accomplished monks who achieved extraordinary levels of individual enlightenment. Mahayana, on the other hand, focuses on celebrating *Bodhisattas*, individuals who may have had the potential to themselves reach Buddha-hood, but who instead focused their energy on teaching the principles of Buddhism to the masses.[4]

This chapter relies primarily on Theravada writings as our source on the Buddha's life and original teachings. In chapter 7, we will offer readers insight into the Mahayana tradition.

The Buddha in Historical Context: The Axial Age

The Buddha's life coincided with a global inflection point in human history. Plato in Greece, Elijah in Israel, Confucius and Lao Tzu in China, and Buddha in India were virtual contemporaries in what is considered the "beginning of humanity" as we know it, between the eighth and third centuries BCE. This period, dubbed the Axial Age by German philosopher Karl Jaspers, has been characterized as a pivotal time in which dramatic shifts in human thought took place across four geographically distinct regions of the world. (See table 2 for dates and locations of the emergence of these major philosophers.)

The Axial Age marks the time during which influential thinkers began the search for the "why" of human existence. It saw the emergence of Taoism and Confucianism in China, Jainism and Buddhism in India, monotheism in Persia and Israel, and Greek rationalism in Europe.[5] In India, the formation of an urban marketplace and the development of a new class—merchants—

TABLE 2. The Axial Age, 850–350 BCE

Date	Philosopher/prophet	Locale	Tradition
849	Elijah	Israel	Abrahamic
712	Kojiki	Japan	Shinto
621–551	Zoroaster	Persia	Zoroastrian (monotheistic)
599–527	Mahalia	India	Jain
563–483	Buddha	India	Buddhism
?–531	Lao Tzu	China	Taoism
551–479	Confucius	China	Confucianism
470–399	Socrates	Greece	Rationalism
427–347	Plato	Greece	Rationalism

challenged the old caste system. New ways of living catalyzed the wellspring of new ideas, including religious ideologies.

A Brief Biography of the Buddha

Unlike the founding documents of Abrahamic religions, such as the Jewish Torah, Christian Bible, and Islamic Quran, early Buddhist scriptures reveal little about the founder's birth and first years of life. Compared to Abraham, Jesus, or Muhammed, Siddhattha himself seems to play a minor role in many of the foundational documents of the tradition rooted in his teachings.

Modern scholars suggest that this lack of biographical detail was intentional. The Buddha's earliest followers appear to have focused on living in accordance with the dharma, a term used to describe the Buddha's teachings, rather than on venerating the Buddha himself. Fortunately, many of the early Buddhist teachers shared at least some details regarding the Buddha's life in order to provide context for his core insights, as well as an example of dharma behavior in action.

As we saw in the previous chapter, dharma in the Hindu context refers to one's duty. Here, dharma means truth, or the teachings of the Buddha. The word dharma, which has its origins in Sanskrit, is equivalent to *dhamma* in Pali, the language of the common people of the Indian subcontinent in the time of the Buddha. *Dhamma* literally means the natural order of the world; physical and mental qualities and behaviors that allow individuals to live in accordance with that order; and teachings that allow individuals to cultivate these qualities and behaviors. To that end, the Buddha's teachings collectively are often referred to as the *dhamma.*

GOTAMA'S EARLY LIFE

Gotama was born in 563 in India, near the foot of the Himalayan Mountains, to the ruling family of the local kingdom of Sakka.[6] His father, King Suddhodana, invited some Brahmins of the priestly caste to foretell Siddhattha's future. They prophesied that Siddhattha would take one of two paths: He would become the "Universal Monarch" to succeed Suddhodana, or he would become a Buddha—an enlightened one. Determined that his son would wield power as a ruler, Suddhodana sequestered him in the royal castle, shielding him from life's unpleasantries. Siddhattha's early years were marked by extraordinary luxury, his every need attended to by servants and his days filled with lessons taught by the wisest scholars, melodies played by court musicians, and meals prepared from the kingdom's best ingredients. Siddhattha proved himself to be an exemplary prince, excelling at languages, mathematics, martial arts, and the other disciplines pursued by the elite of the time. He became a popular future monarch admired by his father's subjects. By age twenty-nine, his life was unfolding smoothly according to his father's plans.

But then Siddhattha's world changed.

Bored with the routine of his luxurious life, Siddhattha convinced his servant Channa to accompany him on a clandestine sojourn beyond the palace walls. That afternoon, as he explored a public garden, Siddhattha saw for the first time a feeble old man, whose appearance startled him.

"What happened to this man?" Siddhattha asked.

"He is simply old. Aging happens to all beings. You, your beautiful wife, and your adorable son will become old as well," replied Channa.

A shaken Siddhattha would go on to encounter a sick person suffering from disease, a dead body, and a monk clad in traditional yellow robes. By the day's end, he had been transformed by the realization that all beings were destined to experience suffering. He felt a special resonance with the monk they had encountered.

After dinner a few evenings later, the nightly music and dances ended as usual. Siddhattha—overwhelmed by the suffering he now saw just below the surface of the pleasures that had until then defined his life—noticed the intoxicated, incoherent muttering of the revelers and the grotesquely collapsed forms of the drunken young women who had entertained the royal family with beautiful dances.

At that moment, Siddhattha renounced his household life. He summoned Channa, took a final look at his sleeping wife and son, and left the palace with his servant for what would be the last time. He made his way to a riverbank on the outskirts of town, shaved his head, donned the yellow robe of a monk, and instructed the alarmed Channa to return to the palace. With that, Siddhattha began his quest to bring about the cessation of all suffering.

GOTAMA'S SEARCH AND DISCOVERY

Siddhattha set out to find a teacher who could guide him on the path to enlightenment and the cessation of sufferings. On his journey, he studied intensively under teachers of various yogic practices, meditation, and extreme asceticism. He reached the highest level in each of the practices, but despite his success he felt no closer to *nibbana*—the lasting, peaceful state of mind that frees one from suffering.

Gotama was an empiricist. As he approached mastery in the traditions, he assessed their efficacy. He regularly tested whether the teachings of each tradition were effective in eradicating the sensations of desire and craving that caused suffering. While each experience brought him a new level of understanding of the human condition, he was able to separate these benefits from actual progress toward achievement of his ultimate goal.

After his experience with asceticism, in which he focused on almost total self-denial of food, water, shelter, sleep, hygiene, and sometimes even oxygen, Gotama experienced his initial flash of insight: The path to enlightenment was to be found through neither severe austerity nor the extravagant self-indulgence of his upbringing. It was in this moment that Gotama experienced his first coup d'oeil—a moment of connecting existing dots in a previously unexplored way. Having resolved to work with human nature rather than fight it, he recognized that *nibbana* was to be achieved through a "Middle Way" that resided halfway between the extremes of his prior experiences.

His newfound insight in hand, Siddhattha assumed a seat under a bodhi tree and vowed to remain there until he achieved enlightenment, proclaiming: "Let my skin and sinews and bones dry up, together with all the flesh and blood of my body! I will welcome it! . . . But I will not move from this spot until I have attained the supreme and final wisdom."[7]

And so he began purifying his mind through the practices he had mastered in his studies, seeking victory over the various sources of suffering—delusion, passion, and desire. He remained in his seat, unmoving, for forty-nine days until he suddenly found himself not only permanently free of suffering, but also having realized the truth of life and nature—*dhamma*. There, under the bodhi tree, Siddhattha Gotama became the Buddha at the age of thirty-five.

The Buddha's Teachings

For the remaining forty-five years of his life the Buddha devoted his waking hours to teaching others that they too could follow the path to *nibbana*. While the Buddha was purported to have discussed some eighty-four thousand topics, in public discourses and private coaching he focused on a single goal—the cessation of suffering. Despite his availability to anyone who approached him, he famously refused to answer any questions that, no matter how intellectually stimulating, were not directly related to that topic. He eloquently described this dynamic in the parable of the arrow: When struck with a poisoned arrow, one is poorly served by devoting one's energy to investigating the direction from which the arrow came. Far more fruitful is to remove the arrow and heal the wound.[8] Ever the empiricist, when asked "Is this *the* way?" he would answer, "All I can say to you is to try it. See if it works for you."

At the heart of Buddhist wisdom are three conceptual frameworks: the Three Marks, or facts of life; the Four Noble Truths, or the Buddha's diagnosis of what prevents us from achieving equanimity and reaching *nibbana* or, in context of strategy, a clear mind; and the Eightfold Path, the Buddha's prescription for how we can reach enlightenment and peace.

THE THREE MARKS (*TILAKKHANA*)

It is not hard to imagine the Buddha observing the modern-day popularity of mindfulness and meditation with jovial skepticism. These practices in and of themselves can certainly be helpful in calming the mind. However, from a Buddhist perspective, without an understanding of the foundational principles that undergird human reality, meditation will do little to help a seeker progress on the path to *nibbana*, clear-mindedness, and even strategic insights.

The Buddha identified three philosophical cornerstones as the foundation of the human experience. He defined these Three Marks as impermanence (*anicca*), suffering (*dukkha*), and nonself (*anatta*).

Impermanence (*Anicca*)

The first of the Three Marks is the notion that it is the nature of all to change. The Buddha emphasized that every aspect of worldly existence—people, places, objects, thoughts, ideas, emotions, experiences—is subject to a continuous process of birth, extinction, and evolution.

While the process is predictable, its timing is not. Often, we have little insight into when our world will shift around us. In our personal and professional lives, we can observe the inevitability and unpredictability of change. No matter how well-planned their projections, businesses are subject to unpredictable forces of disruption, technological obsolescence, and competitive pressure. Still, many organizations continue to insist on casting ten-year plans and base forecasts on what has just transpired in the current business cycle. On a personal level, our great joys and sufferings are just as likely to disappear, transform, or emerge at any moment. These are the facts of life.

Our instinct, often, is to cling to that which we desire and run from that which we want to avoid. Yet, everything around us remains impermanent, destined to change sooner or later. Denial of this truth—along with our natural desire to want to hold on to our relationships, family members, prestige, and the status quo—causes us to form attachments to these impermanent objects. Suffering is the unavoidable outcome of such attachments.

Suffering (*Dukkha*)

The Buddha's insight was that because all is impermanent, attachments to anyone or anything invariably result in disappointment. Furthermore, the stronger our attachment, the more intense the sense of suffering when the object of the attachment disappears, having fallen prey to the universe's inevitable cycle of impermanence. Opening our eyes to the poisonous consequences of attachment delivers the possibility that we might learn how to weaken the cycle of craving and aversion and its inevitable connection to suffering.

Nonself (*Anatta*)

In nonself we have perhaps the least intuitive of the Three Marks. As a way into the concept, consider a brief math mind game. Answer the question "What is zero?"

Most of us have no difficulty with the number zero—adding it, multiplying it, dividing by it. Even children are comfortable with it as a placeholder, as in 0, 1, 2, 3, 4, 5, 6, 7, 8, 9. But what is it? Nothing? Blank? It is one of the most abstract of our mathematical symbols. (Infinity is another.) Indeed, the Greeks—originators of formal geometry and logic—could not conceive of or accept zero as a rational possibility. Logically, it does not exist, literally. It was Hindu mathematicians who, by inventing zero more than twenty-one hundred years ago, provided the avenue to higher mathematics, fractions, negative numbers, infinity, and irrational numbers.[9]

Zero, for Hindus, was not a difficult concept to bring to mathematics. After all, the concept of nonbeing was already embedded in ancient Eastern philosophy, and it persisted for millennia after this, as we saw in Musashi's treatment of emptiness two thousand years later. And Hindus have no problem entertaining the yin and yang opposites of being and nonbeing (see chapter 8 on the Tao). Culturally and philosophically, they were ripe for the introduction of zero. Not only that, but by having no intellectual tradition of formal logic, they were free from the linear either/or orientation of Greek rationalism.

The Buddha was a Hindu. As such, he was likely to have little trouble conceptualizing the third mark of *anatta*—nonself.

With this mark the Buddha aimed to dispel the notion of a permanent, unchanging self in the cognitive, psychological, emotional, or metaphysical state. This concept can cause distress in those readers who object to the conception of their core identity—whether it be their belief system, physical body, or psychological makeup—as not existing. Still, it is undeniable that the ego separates oneself from others with "I," "me," "my," and "mine." As we saw in chapter 4 on the Bhagavad Gita, attachment to the ego can cloud one's objective and intuitive mind.

One manifestation of the nonself reveals itself in the Easterner's experience of existence as defined by being part of a collective, a community. In the West, it is much more common to individuate. Descartes's classic *cogito ergo sum*—"I think, therefore I am"—requires no other human being to be present. To many Eastern cultures, this is a truly foreign idea. "I am" makes sense only in the context of family, clan, or community.

Why is this third mark important to strategists? Consider the concept through the prism of the Buddha's ruthless sense of practicality. Whatever notions we use to define ourselves—physical, mental, emotional, or otherwise—are subject to unpredictable changes. Moments of unexpected illness, racing thoughts, or roller coaster emotions are examples of when we might experience such oscillations. If we also accept the notion that attachment to any impermanent entity is a cause of suffering, it appears logical to categorize a fixed self-identity as just such an attachment.

The Buddha's focus was on how to best rid our lives of suffering. In this context, taking on the assumption that no permanent self exists (regardless of whether that is really the case) appears to provide an elegant solution. Since it is impossible to form an attachment to that which does not exist, assuming no permanent self eliminates one possibility of a strong potential cause for suffering. This foundational principle is what allowed Sumeth Laomoraporn of CP Group to proceed without concern for ego reward and to live with such exquisite humility.

THE FOUR NOBLE TRUTHS

The Three Marks are prerequisite to preparing the mind for detachment. They serve as the cardinal directions for those navigating the path toward *nibbana.* But additional information is still necessary.

The Four Noble Truths can be thought of as complementary elements of an analytical framework. Like any framework, the truths are designed to offer a step-by-step process for resolving a strategic quandary such as the cessation of suffering. Similar to many modern problem-solving frameworks, the Noble Truths start by defining the problem (suffering), exploring the problem's root causes (desire or aversion), offering a conceptual solution to the problem (cessation of suffering), and recommending a set of actionable steps to implement the solution (the Eightfold Path). Like any framework worth its salt, each of the truths offers rigorous yet elegantly straightforward analysis and practical action steps.

First Noble Truth: Suffering

The First Noble Truth is a remarkably intuitive statement: Life contains inevitable, unavoidable suffering.

In the Buddha's own words: "And, what is the Noble Truth of Suffering? Birth is suffering, aging is suffering, death is suffering, sorrow, lamentation, pain, sadness and distress are suffering. Being attached to the unloved is suffering, being separated from the loved is suffering, not getting what one wants is suffering."[10]

The Buddha's definition includes both external phenomena over which we have little to no control (birth, death, aging) and internal emotional experiences (sorrow, lamentation, pain, sadness, distress). Therefore, suffering encompasses both the unfortunate events an individual is destined to encounter and the painful emotional and mental reactions these events elicit.

The 38 percent sales plummet Ravi Menon experienced (described in the introduction), Sumeth's massive loss in his rice business, and the rumors threatening the very survival of Nok Anulomsombut's company were for them forms of suffering. Likewise, the overwhelming anxiety, stress, and uncertainty these leaders faced in response to these external stimuli were also forms of suffering.

The Buddha teaches that painful experiences are an inevitable part of human existence. Problems are real, and they are going to arise when we least expect them. In the business world, if we expand the Buddha's definition of suffering to include disappointments, setbacks, and even catastrophes, we might appreciate that many of our modern management tools are sophisticated attempts to control outcomes and avoid these painful experiences. Balanced scorecards, incentives and rewards, management control systems, vertical integration, contingency planning, and currency hedging are such mechanisms. They are useful tools and appropriate means of strategy implementation.

The first of the Three Marks—impermanence—awakens us to the reality that while Western tools and techniques give the illusion of control, they do not address unpredictable outcomes or failures.

As we highlighted in chapter 1, no matter how well thought out and rigorously analyzed, strategies are destined for at least some deflection. After all, as the Buddha teaches, all is subject to the law of impermanence, including even our most thoroughly tested strategic assumptions. As we craft strategy that aims to avoid falling prey to such problematic circumstances, we can increase the probability of success by accounting for the inevitability of hard-to-predict pitfalls. The goal, then, becomes not to live lives and lead organizations that avoid challenging circumstances. Rather, the focus shifts to developing outlooks that are resilient in the face of these challenges. While we cannot control events, we can, as we will see in the Buddha's Eightfold Path, learn to control our reactions to those events.

Among the most fundamental strategic insights from Eastern philosophy, this—becoming adept at remaining equanimous in the face of uncontrollable events—would be near the top of the list.

Second Noble Truth: Cause of Suffering

If the First Noble Truth serves to deliver the bad news (we are destined to suffer), the Second Noble Truth brings us a step closer to a more optimistic perspective (there is a way out of suffering) by pinpointing the root cause of our distresses.

The Buddha's diagnosis? Clinging and aversion. Our mind's natural tendency is to generate expectations about ourselves, our enterprises, and the world around us. We form strong beliefs about the way things ought to be and, just as importantly, ought not to be. Yet the objects of these expectations and beliefs are almost always stimuli that are beyond our immediate control: other people's behavior, macroeconomic trends, the weather, aging and disease, our own emotional states. The list is infinite.

Furthermore, all of these people, objects, and phenomena are subject to *anicca* (impermanence) and therefore are constantly evolving and changing. Sooner or later, unpredictable, ever-changing reality is bound to deviate from our expectations. Things we wish to happen do not take place, and things we wish not to happen do. It is this moment of tension between the world as it is and how we wish it to be that gives birth to the experience of suffering.

In the Buddha's own words: "And what is the Noble Truth of the Origin of Suffering? It is that craving which gives rise to rebirth, bound up with pleasure and lust, finding fresh delight now here, now there: that is to say sensual craving, craving for existence, and craving for nonexistence."[11]

The Buddha identified three types of craving as the root of all suffering:

Sensual craving results from the interaction between our senses and pleasurable things, such as the taste of chocolate cake on day three of a diet, the sensation of our pillow after we complete a late-night work project, and the comforts experienced from luxury, music, or sex, or even the enjoyment of stress-free transport on the company jet.

Craving for the existence of that which we desire could involve a professional recognition or award, a particular behavior by our family members or coworkers, or sunny weather on our wedding day. Many of us have experienced the pleasant jolt that comes from a promotion, an invitation to an exclusive club, or small victories over those whose successes or personal attributes—looks, wealth, athletic ability—usually leave us feeling inferior by comparison.

Craving for nonexistence is akin to the desire to avoid that which we find disagreeable, a sensation familiar to anyone who has received a substandard performance report, faced a breakup with a significant other, or had a flat tire on the way to an important meeting. A demotion at work, an unexpected physical ailment, or a 38 percent drop in sales all qualify.

When we actually encounter the experience of suffering, we rarely feel the discomfort of any of these sensations in isolation. Rather, the various cravings usually collaborate with remarkably unpleasant synergy in our most painful moments.

Consider Ravi Menon's situation. While he deeply wished that the decline in sales had never occurred (*craving for nonexistence*), his desire to see a recovery in his company's performance was just as intense (*craving for existence*). Amid the ceaseless questions of his panicked management team and overseas investors, it is fair to assume Ravi would have strongly preferred to hear some encouraging words of support (*sensual craving*).

Perhaps most devastatingly, the initial craving-induced suffering can create new emotions, thoughts, and actions that become the source of further craving and suffering. Noticing our reactions to that which we know we are better off disregarding, we now feel an additional wave of frustration. Our craving initiates a perpetual cycle that ensures its continued presence in our lives.

Third Noble Truth: Cessation of Suffering

With the problem concretely defined (the presence of suffering) and a root cause (craving) identified, the Buddha's Third Noble Truth offers a solution as elegant as it is intuitive: To end suffering, one must end the cycle of craving. The logical steps of the prior Noble Truths have led us here. As the Buddha said: "And what is the Noble Truth of the Cessation of Suffering? It is the complete fading-away and extinction of this craving, its forsaking and abandonment, liberation from it, detachment from it."[12]

For our modern-day readers, our natural instincts are reinforced and amplified by prevailing cultural values—including competition, achievement, and consumption—that prioritize a desire to have, do, be, and achieve more as pathways to happiness.

In fact, we are designed to crave. Over millions of years of human evolution, our brains and bodies evolved to prioritize those traits most highly correlated with a single goal: the propagation of our genes to future generations. Natural selection favored mental traits that were most likely to ensure not happiness but survival as a species. The experience of dissatisfaction, whether it be with our physical attributes, material possessions, or social standing, was a highly effective tool to spur our ancestors into action.

As a result, modern humans are hardwired to respond in ways that, while effective for ensuring intergenerational survival, also create, as a noxious byproduct, the continuous cycle of emotional turbulence that the Buddha identified as suffering.

Given this context, the radical nature of the Buddha's prescription—to undo millions of years of psychological evolutionary programming—becomes clear. The Buddha distinguished himself as one of history's great sages not only by offering this powerful proposition, but by also providing a set of instructions for how any individual could pursue a goal so extraordinary. That set of instructions, the Eightfold Path, is at the center of the Buddha's Fourth, and final, Noble Truth.

Fourth Noble Truth: Way out of Suffering, or the Eightfold Path

With the Fourth Noble Truth, the Buddha offered a set of eight turn-by-turn directions for navigating from the origin (a life of inevitable suffering) to the destination (*nibbana*).

THE EIGHTFOLD PATH

The Path's eight elements are usually grouped into three stages of training—wisdom (seeing life as it is and disengaging from the ego), morality (ethical behavior), and mental discipline (focus and concentration):

Wisdom
1. Right understanding
2. Right purpose, or intent

Morality
3. Right speech
4. Right conduct
5. Right occupation

Mental discipline
6. Right effort
7. Right mindfulness, or attention
8. Right concentration

The eight practices and the three stages are interdependent. The Buddha taught that practicing any two of the three but ignoring the third will make attaining *nibbana* impossible.

Wisdom helps us develop an understanding of our eventual destination and find logical solutions to the obstacles encountered on the way. Still, without mental discipline's clarity and morality's impactful action, wisdom is academic.

Morality, by helping us to avoid regrettable actions, can guard our minds from fear, worry, and guilt, thereby building a firm ground for mental discipline. Mental discipline can help cultivate calm and still the mind. But without the benefit of wisdom and morality, it is impossible to effectively leverage that clarity.

The Buddha's elegant combination of clear vision (wisdom), appropriate action (morality), and unrelenting focus (mental discipline) is a powerful triad at the heart of effective strategic planning and execution. For example, an entrepreneur looking to disrupt an industry must lean on a clear understanding of his advantage relative to established players (wisdom), pursue a set of right actions that allow him to overcome a resource deficit (morality), and relentlessly focus on ensuring that what limited resources are available are devoted to capitalizing on that advantage (mental discipline).

Before we proceed, a word about the meaning of "right" in the context of the Eightfold Path. Rather than signifying "correct" or "not wrong," the Buddha's "right" has the connotation of being complete, in tune, fitting, centering, or the righting of an imbalance.

Although the Eightfold Path in tabular form appears to imply a sequential set of steps, the Buddha perceived of the Path as a continuous, circular process.

The Buddha's approach mirrors Tony Athos and Richard Pascale's Seven-S model of the 1980s, where strategy and execution were seen not as separate entities but as an interconnected bundle of strategy, structure, systems, staff, skills, style (culture), and shared values.[13] Not one of the S's dominates. The model was usually diagrammed as seven circles arranged in a larger circular form, with lines connecting each circle with the other six. The purpose was to dislodge strategists' tendency to see managerial levers in linear terms. Similarly, imagine the Eightfold Path as a circle of interconnected circles, with each circle representing one of the eight steps.

1. Right Understanding

Buddhist scripture tells us that "while some preliminary wisdom is needed to start on the Path, the final flowering of the higher wisdom follows after development of morality and concentration."[14] The Path begins with wisdom and ends with higher wisdom. The first step on the Path toward achieving that wisdom, and eventual enlightenment, is right understanding—"seeing life as it is."[15] In the Buddhist context, the Three Marks and the Four Noble Truths serve as the entry point for cultivating that understanding of life's fundamental realities.

2. Right Purpose

Given a firm grasp of right understanding, one can begin to cultivate right purpose, or intent or motivation. That is to say, one develops a worldview that aligns with right understanding, a "willing, desiring, and thinking that is in line with life as it is."[16]

3. Right Speech

Abstain from lying, gossip, vanity, and hurtful rejoinders. These all create turmoil in one's mind.

4. Right Conduct

The Buddha codified right conduct into a set of specific precepts, including requirements to not kill, steal, engage in hurtful sexual activity, lie, or become intoxicated "to the point of heedlessness."[17] Beyond the specific actions the code forbade, the notion of right conduct was meant to encourage us to avoid actions that would create a disturbance in the mind.

5. Right Occupation

Take no part in any livelihood that involves deceit or exploitation. Examples from the Buddha's time include "trading in weapons, buying and selling human beings, killing animals, selling drugs or other intoxicants, and manufacturing or distributing poisons."[18]

Mental Discipline (Steps 6, 7, and 8)

The remaining three steps—right effort, right mindfulness, and right concentration—give us a set of instructions for cultivating the clear-headedness, presence, and concentration encouraged throughout the Path. While the next chapter of this book offers an in-depth discussion especially of right mindfulness and right concentration, it is important to remember that despite their growing popularity in our present culture, the practices embodied in these two steps account for only one-quarter of the Eightfold Path. Focusing on this popular portion at the expense of the remainder of the Path would yield some beneficial results, such as a calmer mind or fewer reactive behavioral patterns. But this would be short-sighted because these benefits alone will not lead us to achieving beginner's mind and generating strategic insights.

With that proviso in mind, let us move into the world of mindfulness and concentration in chapter 6.

Strategy Lessons from Chapter 5

1. Be mindful and remain present to the current moment.
2. Remain equanimous. Do not be too sad if things turn out badly. Do not be too happy if things turn out well.
3. Do not overanalyze. Emotions will inevitably arise, so acknowledge them. But do not let them affect you and disturb your mind.
4. Acknowledge the Four Noble Truths:
    - Life is full of frustration and discontent (what the Buddha calls suffering).
    - Craving and aversion are the cause of suffering.
    - To eliminate suffering, let go of craving and aversion.
    - There is a path one can follow to eliminate suffering—the Eightfold Path.
6. Follow the Eightfold Path.

6

The Buddha and Mindfulness

This page is intentionally left blank.

This page, too.

The next few pages, as well.

Keep . . .

. . . going . . .

Just a few more.

What did you feel as you encountered the blank pages?

Did you notice your emotions as you flipped through the pages?

Did those emotions change as you encountered the last few pages, which were not blank?

Over the preceding pages, you will have experienced a set of emotional responses as you turned blank page after blank page. Take a moment to consider them.

Perhaps the journey was a bit like a virtual roller coaster ride—your emotions initially rising along a steep slope of curiosity, then plunging down a descent toward impatience, twisting through several cycles of frustration mixed with inquisitiveness, and finally, experiencing the sweet relief of a return to the familiar pace of the text-filled page you are reading now.

Or maybe the experience was more like a Sunday drive along the beach. Here are some blank pages . . . so what?

Admittedly, flipping through a few blank pages is not likely to have set off a dramatic emotional response. Your reaction probably was subtle, remaining below the radar of your conscious awareness. Yet, according to both ancient Buddhist teachings and research by modern psychologists, encountering an external stimulus different from what we anticipated inevitably pricks our emotions and psychology. For only a moment, we asked you to become attuned to the reaction that the blank pages provoked for you, even if it required activating a little more of your self-awareness than usual.

Why start our discussion of mindfulness with this exercise? Because by its very nature, mindfulness is profoundly experiential.

The following pages describe the how and why of the benefits that mindfulness can bring to crafting strategy. By starting this chapter with an unexpected stimulus (the blank pages) and then encouraging you to consider your response to that stimulus, we wanted to give you a brief window into the "what" of mindfulness.

While an intellectual understanding of mindfulness is useful, the value of this understanding comes only when combined with the actions that cultivate mindfulness as a lived experience.

Conceptualizing Mindfulness

Emotions vary from person to person and from moment to moment. But they happen so fast and so continuously that we rarely notice them. Studies in psychology and neuroscience show that humans are efficiency-seeking creatures, and that we make decisions based on old frames, memories. and associations.[1] Our brains are not equipped to handle the constant flood of data and information that flows at us, nor the emotions they trigger, so we activate autopilots and predictable habits in our decision-making process. Despite its efficiency, our use of pre-programmed intelligence based on past data and historical patterns has some obvious limitations. For example, we might expect this approach to run into roadblocks when we try to solve problems of a kind we have not previously encountered. Coup d'oeil (a "flash of the eye"), creativity, a breakthrough solution, or strategic insight—which this book is about—does not result from how our brain normally works, but from how we train the brain to work in a much more nuanced and impactful way.[2] And this is what the practice of mindfulness is about.

By cultivating a capacity to choose our responses, rather than fall prey to instinctual reactions, we can come up with solutions that are appropriate to the specific realities of a new challenge. A recent *Harvard Business Review* article elegantly described this process via a quote from Viktor Frankl: "Between stimulus and response, there is a space. In that space is our power to choose our response."[3]

Frankl, an Austrian neurologist and psychiatrist whose classic work *Man's Search for Meaning* chronicled his experience in Nazi concentration camps, held that the ability to choose one's response to external stimuli is essential to the human capacity to overcome even the harshest circumstances. As Frankl put it: "Everything can be taken from a man but one thing: the last of the human freedoms—to choose one's attitude in any given set of circumstances, to choose one's own way."[4] It is this capacity to choose one's attitude and responses to circumstances that forms the foundation for the practice of mindfulness.

Mindfulness and Strategists

Mindfulness has been embraced by corporations not only because it helps reduce stress and anxiety, but because it promotes the mental clarity critical to resolving challenging strategic problems. While the popularity of mindfulness in business organizations can be traced back to Silicon Valley, today the list of firms that offer mindfulness training to employees and executives cuts across industries and geographies.

For example, according to a recent study:

> The movement began among startups in Silicon Valley and has been implemented by long-established companies across the US and Europe as well as by government bodies. These include Aetna, Beiersdorf, Bosch, General Mills, Goldman Sachs, Intel, Royal Dutch Shell, SAP, Target, the UK's Parliament, and the US House of Representatives. . . .
>
> Among the top executives who meditate and encourage their employees to follow their example, for instance, are Salesforce CEO Marc Benioff, Twitter CEO Jack Dorsey, and Google cofounder Sergey Brin. In fact, attending a meditation class is a popular way to begin the workday at many Silicon Valley companies, including Apple, Facebook, LinkedIn, and Twitter.[5]

Many studies support the benefits of mindfulness, which range from reduced stress levels, more efficient time management, and improved interpersonal communication skills to increased focus and mental stamina, improved sense of mental and physical well-being, and enhanced capacity for making high-pressure decisions.[6] Strategists who regularly practice mindfulness are more likely to be able to quiet their minds and to maintain that clear-headedness longer, thus raising the probability of experiencing coup d'oeil.

There are a number of portals into mindfulness practice. One can engage in movement-based techniques such as yoga, or in meditation as a mental fitness practice, approaching mindfulness with the exercise-oriented strategies used to cultivate physical health. The Mindfulness-Based Stress Reduction program developed by Jon Kabat-Zinn is a form of cognitive therapy. Professional development training programs include Daniel Goleman's emotional intelligence framework and the Search Inside Yourself curriculum developed at Google.

Any of these approaches, and numerous others, can serve as entryways. Although many workplace mindfulness programs remove religious symbolism and language from their practices, the teachings of the Buddha can still be found at the root of quite a few, which is where we will direct our focus. In the following pages, we return to the Eightfold Path to explore the nuances of the Buddha's original teachings on mindfulness.

Steps 6, 7, and 8 of the Eightfold Path: Becoming More Mindful; Creating Beginner's Mind

As we saw in the introduction, our aim in studying Eastern philosophies is to enable and facilitate the beginner's mind that will open us to strategic flashes of insight, or coups d'oeil. The final three steps in the Eightfold Path—effort, mindfulness, and concentration—take us there. Recall that the Eightfold Path was the Buddha's prescription to arrest the suffering caused by selfish desire. Each step on the Path is designed to help immunize practitioners from craving and aversion, the sensations diagnosed by the Buddha as the root causes of anxiety, fear, stress, and other forms of suffering. To accomplish this, the Path helps us cultivate the ability to respond skillfully, rather than automatically, when our senses, thoughts, feelings, and emotions encounter external stimuli. In other words, the Eightfold Path brings us closer to a place of mental clarity and calmness, and further from autopilot decisions and behaviors.

Walking the eight steps of the Path can be understood as an iterative process. The first five steps offer guidance on how to direct our thoughts and actions. The wisdom section on right thoughts and motivations guides us to see reality as it is and to confront our emotions. In the morality section, the third, fourth, and fifth steps suggest favorable physical expressions in speech, behaviors, and actions, including our occupations.

The sixth, seventh, and eighth steps—right effort, right mindfulness, and right concentration, which make up the mental discipline section—describe the mindset with which we must imbue our mental and physical activities if they are to lead us to freedom from suffering. The next section explores these steps in more depth.

6. Right Effort

The sixth step is an indispensable factor in achieving right mindfulness and right concentration. As Joseph Goldstein mentioned in his book *Mindfulness: A Practical Guide to Awakening:* "The mental factor underlying effort is *viriya,* or energy . . . energy can be used for many different goals, both wholesome and unwholesome. . . . Right Effort is the application of energy to four great endeavors . . . to prevent the arising of the unwholesome states not yet arisen, . . . to abandon those unwholesome states that have already arisen, . . . to arouse wholesome states that have not yet arisen, . . . and to maintain and strengthen those wholesome states that have already arisen."[7]

Right effort underscores the importance of perseverance, discipline, and balance as major engines of our ability to handle the negative and positive mind states that are sure to continuously emerge, linger, and eventually subside. In laying out his teaching, the Buddha focused relentlessly on taking action. No matter how profound the thought process and well intentioned the behaviors, arriving at the intended destination requires diligent, persistent effort. Yet, the Buddha recognized that for the Buddhist seeker of *nibbana* (and similarly, for the organization looking to undergo strategic change), effort, energy, and time are limited resources that must be put to use wisely.

Shortly before he passed away, the Buddha said: "I declare to you: all conditioned things are of a nature to decay—strive on untiringly."[8] Not only a reflection of the universal impermanence explained by the Three Marks, his final words were a reminder that this condition of constant, unexpected change should be treated as a catalyst for continued effort, rather than as a cause for distraction or frustration.

Nevertheless, the Buddha warned his disciples to pursue their diligent efforts within the confines of the Middle Way: to neither indulge nor restrain themselves too much.

For organizations operating in competitive, twenty-first-century environments, cultivating this hard-to-achieve balance between diligent effort and appropriate restraint is a strategic imperative. Impactful strategy strikes a balance between awareness and equanimity. Effective strategists are deeply aware of their surroundings, such as the competitive landscape, but also choose to make decisions based on their organizational and individual missions and goals, not in reaction to the behavior of others.

7. Right Mindfulness

If you arrive at your doctor's office looking to develop a full picture of your physical health, she is likely to recommend a battery of tests to better understand your condition. If you ask auditors to pressure-test your company's standards and processes, they are likely to require a range of analyses to understand fully how the organization operates.

Right mindfulness plays a role no different than bloodwork and MRI scans do for the human body and data analytics and monitoring software do for companies. The Buddha recommended mindfulness as a tool that practitioners can use to more objectively and thoroughly understand themselves, their patterns of thought, and their habits. Along with being radically informative, mindfulness also helps us free ourselves from the mind's entrenched habits. As leading Buddhist Zen teacher Thich Nhat Hanh noted: "Habit energy pushes us all the time. That is why mindfulness practice aims at liberating ourselves from habit energy."[9]

In Buddhism, right mindfulness derives its name from the concept of the four foundations of mindfulness. The Mahasatipatthana Sutta—a discourse in the *Digha Nikaya,* a foundational text of Theravada Buddhism—quotes the Buddha as saying that mindfulness involves "contemplating body as body, ardent, clearly aware and mindful, having put aside hankering and fretting for the world; . . . contemplating feelings as feelings; . . . contemplating mind as mind; . . . contemplating mind-objects as mind-objects."[10]

Per this teaching, well-rounded mindfulness is founded on four objects of contemplation: body, feelings, state of mind, and *dhamma.* All four are necessary to establish a comprehensive view of our full selves—including our behaviors, emotions, states of mind, and thoughts. This comprehensive view, in turn, enables us to develop beginner's mind.

CONTEMPLATION OF BODY

To start developing a mindful awareness of the body, Buddhist tradition suggests that you begin with easy-to-observe physical sensations, such as your breath. Feel the air as it passes your upper lip on its way into your nostrils, and again as it goes out. Feel your chest filling, then emptying. This is an easy entry point to mindfulness practice, but it is also exquisitely at the foundation of all mammalian existence: oxygen in, carbon dioxide out.

Once you are grounded in breath mindfulness, you might advance to contemplating the nuances of your physical posture, developing a detailed awareness of how you stand, sit, and move. For example, when you stand up, you might become aware of how you are standing. Contemplate the feeling of your feet on the floor, your hands in your pockets, your shoulders pulled back or slumped forward, and so on.

With time, your contemplation will become more nuanced. In your practice, you might at first focus on sensations such as the temperature of your skin and the touch points between skin and clothes. Eventually, you may begin to direct your focus much deeper inside your body, paying attention to your bones, your blood flow, your heartbeats. Regular mindfulness practice can reveal a detailed awareness of your body even when you simply sit still.

Here is a practical example from the Buddha: "Breathing in a long breath, he knows that he breathes in a long breath."[11] Then breathe in a short breath and be aware that it is short. Tell yourself: "I will breathe in, conscious of the whole body. . . . I will breathe out, conscious of the whole body. . . . I will breathe in, calming the whole bodily process. . . . I will breathe out, calming the whole bodily process."[12]

CONTEMPLATION OF FEELINGS

As mindfulness of the body breeds a state of increased physical calm and awareness, we become more capable of cultivating a deeper, more subtle mindfulness as it pertains to our feelings and emotions. This exploration can begin with a simple question: "Are the feelings I am currently experiencing pleasant, unpleasant, or neither?" Evaluating your feelings through these criteria creates space for a more subtle form of mindfulness to emerge. The goal is to become present to your feelings at each moment. Simple, but not easy. Establishing an awareness of feelings, without any judgment or attachment, requires diligent effort.

CONTEMPLATION OF MIND

The next level focuses on objectively evaluating your current state of mind. Having become conscious of individual emotions, we now consider "the roots of mind and how they color or condition our minds"[13]—the underlying energy that keeps our emotional flywheel spinning. Ask yourself: Is my state of mind calm or turbulent? What causes the turbulence?

The Buddha pointed to three underlying causes of a turbulent mind: lust, anger, and delusion. Know "a lustful mind as lustful, a mind free from lust as free from lust; a hating mind as hating, a mind free from hate as free from hate; a contracted mind as contracted, a distracted mind as distracted."[14] With this mindfulness, an awareness of your own mental energy starts to form at a more subtle level, without judgment or criticism.

CONTEMPLATION OF *DHAMMA*

This is the deepest level of mindfulness practice, and the most difficult to attain. In most translations of Buddhist scriptures, this foundation is translated as "mental objects." However, Analayo suggested in his book *Satipatthana: The Direct Path to Realization* that to avoid confusion, the term *dhamma* is more suitable here because "contemplation of *dhamma* skillfully applies *dhammas* (classificatory categories) as taught in the Dhamma (the teaching of the Buddha) during contemplation in order to bring about an understanding of the *dhamma* (principle) of conditionality and lead to the realization of the highest of all *dhammas* (phenomena): nibbana."[15]

(A note to readers: It is typical of Buddhist philosophical frameworks to have sub-frameworks for clarification and guidelines to execution. The Buddha proffered five categories to direct practitioners during the contemplation of *dhamma:* the Five Hindrances, the Five Aggregates, the Six Internal and External Sense Bases, the Seven Factors of Enlightenment, and the Four Noble Truths, including the sub-framework of the Eightfold Path.[16] We won't explore the first four categories in further depth in this book.)

A practicing meditator experiences profound benefits as she takes each incremental step along her path from the first foundation. She becomes present to all mental, physical, and emotional sensations simultaneously. Furthermore, her awareness extends to an understanding of the holistic nature of her lived experience that is both the cause and the result of the individual sensations.

Contemplation of *dhamma* is the stage of deepest knowledge and awareness. After becoming fully present to bodily sensations, emotions, and state of mind, we have one more powerful tool at our disposal. We can return to the Buddha's teachings, or *dhamma* categories, such as the Four Noble Truths and the Three Marks. Contemplating selections from the teachings offers a balm to help heal tension, turbulence, and suffering.

Like a medicine prescribed to cure disease, the right teaching, applied at the right time in the right dose, allows us to voluntarily let go of the lust, anger, or delusion causing our suffering. We can interpret this state of nonattachment as the presence of beginner's mind, fertile ground for coups d'oeil or flashes of insight to occur.

The four foundations of mindfulness are progressive and interrelated. For example, you may be upset that your work team failed to meet a critical deadline on a high-priority project. As you fume, you may begin to recognize that your tensed muscles and racing pulse (contemplation of body) result from painful, negative emotions (contemplation of feeling). These negative emotions might be linked to an angry attitude (contemplation of mind). Upon further examination, you might attribute your anger to the havoc wrought on the team's performance by an irresponsible member who failed to conduct a critical analysis in a timely fashion. In this example, the first three foundations of mindfulness are showing you the causal chain from an external stimulus (your team member's behavior) to your body's reactions, to your thoughts, to your feelings, and ultimately to your mind.

Consider the anger experienced in this moment. At the deepest and most self-aware stage, a holistic perspective might emerge that reveals an understanding of how your physical tension, upset feelings, and angry mindset are causing you to experience life through a paradigm of anger, and how that paradigm is causing you to interpret new external stimuli in a way that causes these negative sensations to continue to arise. Perhaps you were already angry due to the unreasonable deadline set for the project by your manager, and you could not help but treat your teammate's delayed deliverable as just more fuel for that anger. To see and understand how your body, its feelings, and your accompanying mindset are interacting as a system is the essence of mindfulness of *dhamma*.

Applying appropriate Buddhist teachings, *dhamma*—now used to refer to its definition as the teachings of wisdom—can help you further clear your mind and effectively make critical decisions. For this example, you may turn to the teachings on the causal relationship between external stimuli and internal reactions in order to break the chain of cause and effect and allow your anger to subside. Perhaps there are any number of legitimate reasons for why the team member's analysis was delivered late. In any case, it is more helpful to focus on how to resolve the issue of the delayed final deliverable than to fume about your teammate's missed input.

Or, the right teaching in this case may be Buddha's lessons on impermanence. You realize that your attachment to the expectation of a timely submission of the project is causing you anger but is not bringing you and the team any closer to a solution. You may recognize that you have very little or perhaps no control over your teammate's behavior. But you can act differently to improve the current situation. You can allow your mind to clearly focus on resolving the problem, instead of letting your energy be subsumed by anger. This does not mean your team member is off the hook for his actions. Ensuring that his problematic behavior does not repeat itself is also important, and determining the right course of action to address that is another problem to resolve. In finding the answer, you will again benefit from approaching the problem from a place of clear-headedness rather than anger, no matter how righteous.

How do you find the right *dhamma* to guide you in each situation? Different individuals and circumstances require different *dhammas* or teachings to clear the mind. The first three foundations of mindfulness bring awareness of the body, feelings, and state of mind. At the same time, while contemplating *dhamma* to detach from lust, anger, and delusions, relaxation and equanimity of body, feelings, and state of mind will lead you to the right teaching to lean on.

Emmaus, Pennsylvania, 2008

Back from lunch, the Rodale Press's strategic planning team awaited the next session of their retreat. Senior vice president Lou C. opened by announcing: "I would like to portray our competitor landscape with an interpretive dance."

Rodale Press was unique. Founded by J. I. Rodale, the company pioneered natural gardening in the U.S. with the 1942 publication of *Organic Gardening*, and helped introduce Americans to the notion of wellness with the launch of *Prevention Magazine* in 1950. Originally seen as fringe ideas, both organic gardening and wellness had become firmly ingrained in America by the mid-1980s. As Maria Rodale, vice president for strategy, stated: "Organic is hip, not hippie."

Rodale's well-known publications also included *Runner's World* magazine, as well as books on nutrition and bicycle repair. The company was centered in rural Emmaus, Pennsylvania, where it owned several buildings, some of which housed subsidized cafeterias, and the Rodale fitness center was nearby.

As core values at the company, fitness and nutrition were often on full display. In the cafeteria one might spot individuals wearing bicycling gear or workout clothes. The food selections sported labels with nutritional point values—an omelet was worth twenty-five points, for instance, whereas an egg-white omelet was worth two hundred points. Employees could exchange points for athletic gear to use in their fitness activities, creating a sort of virtuous cycle.

Designed into the center of Rodale's three-story headquarters building was a multistory *kiva*, or Native American prayer atrium, whose sloped walls ended in a glass ceiling that allowed the space to fill with natural light. Many employees and executives availed themselves of this serene space for contemplation, centering, and meditation.

The strategic planning team had spent two months preparing for their retreat. They had conducted extensive analyses of economic forecasts, demographics, reading habits, and emerging lifestyle trends. Financial analysts had studied each product line's profitability and sales history and had benchmarked performance against industry growth data.

Now, next on the agenda after lunch was the competitor analysis taskforce report. Once the team members settled down, their senior vice president announced his intent to dance for them.

Lou walked to the front of the room, stood still, and closed his eyes. Then he began with graceful moves. Focusing on the book division, he proceeded to represent one set of competitors, the large legacy publishing houses, with smooth, fluid movements. Narrating as he danced, Lou explained that these incumbents, such as *Reader's Digest,* appeared satisfied with their market share and were prioritizing a stay-the-course approach over new growth strategies.

Lou then transitioned to the other set of competitors, emerging book publishers such as FiT Publishing and Beyond Words, who were aggressively expanding in a variety of niche genres, including a number of Rodale's core markets. Lou's movements became increasingly aggressive, almost frantic.

Unusual though the communication method was, the strategists in the room understood the message: To which group did Rodale want to belong? The languid incumbents satisfied with the current state of affairs, or the new entrants disrupting the market? The planning team agreed to create more aggressive strategies for their books across a range of niche segments, including bicycling, fitness, preventive health, and gardening.

This example illustrates Rodale's unconventional but often effective approach to strategy-making. In the same spirit, Rodale was among the first American business firms to incorporate mindful practices. The resulting environment gave employees of all ranks the freedom to express their ideas—often, as we just saw, in unusual ways.

This free-thinking atmosphere had allowed the company to successfully reposition existing publications and launch new magazine brands, such as the highly successful creation of *Men's Health* in the mid-1980s.

At that time, Rodale's portfolio included gardening and fitness how-to publications including, in addition to the titles mentioned above, magazines such as *Bicycling* and *Backpacking.* The competitors included two types of publications. The first group, such as *Health, Horticulture,* and *Country Gardens,* focused on highly specific, often somewhat countercultural subject matter and was oriented toward casual hobbyists. The second group was more serious in tone and focused on professionals and committed amateurs, with titles such as *Muscle and Fitness, Spirituality and Health,* and *Psychology Today.*

Rodale's men's health publication faced a major strategic question: how to transform a popular eight-page newsletter containing fitness advice for men into a full-blown magazine. Up until then, the newsletter—subsequently titled *Men's Health Magazine*—provided researched and medically sound tips to men interested in improving their health. This original positioning envisioned *Men's Health* as a wellness how-to magazine for men younger than the fifty-and-older readers targeted by existing offerings, such as *Prevention.* Jeff Morgan, a new member of Rodale with prior experience at a major men's lifestyle magazine, proposed a different competitive positioning. Rather than men's *health,* perhaps the emphasis should be on *men's* health. In other words, it would be a men's entertainment magazine, much in the vein of *Gentlemen's Quarterly* or *Esquire,* rather than simply a wellness magazine.

This was a paradigmatic breakthrough for Rodale. The repositioning of *Men's Health* as a lifestyle magazine marked a new direction for the company. *Men's Health* became one of the leading men's magazines in the world.

MINDFULNESS LESSONS FOR STRATEGY

Mindfulness, when understood as a balance between awareness of the present moment and nonreactivity to the thoughts and emotions that arise within that awareness, can benefit strategy-making both as a mindset for individual strategists and as a cultural value promoted within organizations.

With mindfulness at the heart of an organization's planning process, decisions can come from a fuller and more objective understanding of key external and internal dynamics. In deciding how to approach a strategic challenge, the organization can free itself from the cultural biases and ingrained processes that would tend to lead to incremental and non-innovative strategies.

As the cliché goes, if the only tool available is a hammer, everything looks like a nail. Not dissimilarly, an over-reliance on past experiences tricks us into limiting the range of potential solutions to novel new problems. In interpreting external stimuli and forming responses, mindfulness unlocks room for insightful ideas to emerge. Practitioners can therefore not only distinguish nails from screws, but also determine whether a hammer, a screwdriver, or a drill is the most appropriate tool to use. Indeed, were it not for Rodale's receptivity to such seemingly trivial nudges as the emphasis placed on "men" instead of "health," it might never have launched one of the highest-circulation and most profitable magazines in North America. As important, it is unlikely that many firms would be receptive to one of their executives conveying information through a dance rather than a PowerPoint presentation.

Buddhism does not simply tell us to prioritize this combination of awareness and equanimity. The Buddha's teachings go further, describing a range of distinct skills necessary for the cultivation of mindfulness, with the development of those skills arranged according to an established hierarchy.

Each of the four foundations of mindfulness describes a distinct skill or capability that must be cultivated over time. In this context, mindfulness can be conceived of as an iterative journey that gradually builds the competencies necessary to address the individual parts of the human experience (i.e., emotions, thoughts, physical sensations). Organizational leaders looking to develop a culture of mindful strategy should similarly consider the various types of mindfulness that would be required.

What distinguishes the four foundations from each other is the subtlety of the details that can be perceived at each level. Physical sensations are easier to perceive than surface-level feelings, surface-level feelings are easier to perceive than a broad state of mind, and a broad state of mind is easier to perceive than the paradigm through which we perceive our entire life experience. To that end, strategists should strive to build a culture that continuously drives toward an ever-more perceptive and nuanced understanding of the organization's key objectives, resources, and stakeholders.

In Rodale's case, it was the company's creation of a purpose and mission a few years earlier that lay the foundation for Lou's freedom to act in an unconventional way, as well as to allow the group to entertain a significant shift in the positioning of the new men's health venture without judgment. Rodale's purpose was as simple as it was straightforward: to promote and support healthy and active lifestyles.

8. Right Concentration

In the Buddhist tradition, the qualities of mindfulness can be thought of as necessary precursors for the development of concentration. Right concentration describes a powerful experience in which the individual has directed the entirety of his consciousness toward a single focus, the deliberate development of a higher level of awareness. But without the calm mind developed in right mindfulness, this concentration is impossible.

The *Digha Nikaya* defines right concentration in terms of four levels of *jhana*, a Pali term describing a meditative state of mind. These include (1) a detachment from sense-desires and unwholesome mental states, (2) concentration, inner tranquility, and oneness of mind, (3) equanimity and clear-mindedness, and (4) transcendence above pleasure and pain.[17]

Earlier in this chapter, we used the analogy of diagnostic medical tests for the various forms of mindfulness. To extend the metaphor further, the four levels of right concentration would be medical data such as blood sugar, blood pressure, and cholesterol levels. By monitoring the data over time, doctors can track whether an individual's health is improving or deteriorating. Similarly, each of the four levels of *jhana* provides a description of the various characteristics associated with each level of a concentrated mind. By comparing their experience to each description, practitioners can benchmark and monitor their progress toward a full realization of right concentration.

To benefit from the guidance of the *jhana,* practitioners must remain in alignment with the Buddha's non-attachment principle. The *jhana* enables us to become aware of progress, but growth can continue only if we do not get attached to or crave more of it.

For strategists, this final step of the Eightfold Path unlocks two powerful lessons.

First, for right concentration to have any value, practitioners must align their focus with the other seven steps of the Path. In the same way, any focus that an organization identifies for its strategic initiatives will succeed only if it is grounded in the organization's core values.

Second, as medical doctor and Buddhist teacher Mark Epstein advises, right concentration "offers stillness, not just as respite, but as a way of entertaining uncertainty. In a world where impermanence and change are basic facts of life, the willingness to be surprised gives us one big advantage."[18] In implementing a strategy, an uncertain future and improbable events are near guarantees. The principle of right concentration creates a framework for responding to uncertainty without taking the organization's focus off key priorities or core values.

Once an appropriate focus has been determined, both the individual and the organization looking to develop strategic capabilities must relentlessly pursue their target. Yet, and here lies one of Buddhism's great insights, that concentration cannot be harnessed unless there is first a foundation in mindfulness. Clarity of mind is required for focus to take root.

Two More Lessons for Strategy

1. THE SOLUTION IS INSIDE

> Don't start by trying to change other people. Your first priority should be to find your own quiet space inside so you can learn more about yourself. This includes getting to know and understand your own suffering.
>
> —Thich Nhat Hanh, *Silence*

When faced with existential crises in their respective organizations, neither Sumeth Laomoraporn nor Nok Anulomsombut ventured far in their search for strategic insight. Rather, they looked inside themselves.

The Buddha's teachings on mindfulness encourage us to turn our attention inside ourselves, disconnecting from the external world by closing our eyes and grounding ourselves with observations of breath, body, and mental state. In that deep, empty, and peaceful mind space, creative solutions—manifestations of coup d'oeil—are ready to emerge.

By her account, Patchara (Pat) Taveechaiwattana believed she had finally achieved success when she was promoted to chief marketing officer of Allianz Ayudhya, a leading insurance company in Thailand. Still, this sense of professional accomplishment did little to ease the near constant sense of stress and anxiety that had followed her throughout her career. While Pat believed herself to be tough and competitive—even her most accomplished direct reports trembled as they entered her office—she could not help but wonder if a better path was possible.

Pat had tried a panoply of external solutions to ease what she labeled her "chronic mental suffering," with little success. Finally, at the recommendation of a friend, she took part in a silent Buddhist meditation retreat.

Here, too, the answer was not to be found anywhere external. Pat did not achieve clarity along the retreat's winding walking paths or inside the spartan sleeping cabins. But unlike her previous attempts to ease her state of mind, the mindfulness practices she learned at the retreat encouraged her to look for answers inside herself. Over ten grueling days, she was taught simple exercises—as easy to understand as they were challenging to practice—to quiet the mind and observe the self.

In the days that followed, she began to understand the root causes of her suffering with increasing clarity. Recognizing a frequent mental refrain of "I am not good enough," she traced this nagging sense of unworthiness to her childhood in a Chinese-Thai family biased toward celebrating the accomplishments of her male siblings. Even as she was accepted to Thailand's most prestigious university and climbed the career ladder at several international companies, she continued to be dogged by feelings of inadequacy.

Pat recognized that no job title or accomplishment could stop this mentality from haunting her. But with the help of a diligent mindfulness practice, she started to understand the cause-effect relationship between the experiences of her daily working life and her mindset. Over time, she learned to apply the Buddhist principles in order to gently tame her mind. Focusing on the present moment helped ease her anxiety about her and her company's future. Treating each moment with awareness and equanimity helped her break the habit of assigning a self-critical interpretation to every interaction. Describing the role the laws of impermanence and nonself (two of the Three Marks) play in her mindset today, she said: "Everything in life is very uncertain. Nothing to be held on to. Emotions keep changing. I do not attach too much joy to successes as it will eventually subside. . . . Nothing is in my control. I learn to accept and move on with what happens."

Hoi Ning Mak, an executive for Dong Rong Electronics Ltd., an import-export startup in Hong Kong, described how Buddhism changed Fifi Mak, Dong Rong's CEO, and transformed the business itself:

> Fifi Mak has been a Buddhist for over twenty years, but only in the last ten years has she become a devout practitioner. Previously, she had a very bad temper and was easily irritated, and had a strong attachment to "being right"—she wouldn't let go of a mistake or an opinion easily. She was always in anxiety, vexation, and anger at work, such that her employees and clients were very afraid of her. Since she resumed Buddhism ten years ago, her temperament has changed—she is calmer, more open-minded to critics, and tends to forgive rather than blame. Then we saw changes in the company—the management style transformed from micromanagement to empowerment; employees are happier and feel more sense of belonging; suppliers are no longer enemies but partners; and a new startup in health care was developed with a mission to help people. The entire story is a good illustration of karma—with [right] intention and conduct, you will automatically attract good things happening around you. For example, employees become more productive and tend to stay longer, and business partners are more willing to collaborate because they know you are reliable or aim for a win-win situation. Dong Rong Electronics is doing quite well [in 2019], and Energy Plus Development (our startup) is gaining traction.[19]

As avid meditator and cofounder of Bridgewater Associates Ray Dalio describes in his book *Principles:*

> Many people only see the conscious mind and aren't aware of the benefits of connecting it to the subconscious. They believe that the way to accomplish more is to cram more into the conscious mind and make it work harder, but this is often counterproductive. While it may seem counterintuitive, clearing your head can be the best way to make progress. Knowing this, I now understand why creativity comes to me when I relax (like when I'm in the shower) and how meditation helps open this connection. Because it is physiological, I can actually feel the creative thoughts coming from elsewhere and flowing into my conscious mind. . . . When thoughts and instructions come to me from my subconscious, rather than acting

> on them immediately, I have gotten into the habit of examining them with my conscious, logical mind. . . . Doing this opens further communication between my conscious and subconscious minds.[20]

2. OBSERVE AND EMBRACE REALITY

Essential to practicing mindfulness is the ability to observe and embrace reality as it is. This practice offers a powerful opportunity to understand how we habitually perceive ourselves. For example, even if our intent is to spend some time sitting in quiet contemplation of our breath, sooner or later our mind will inevitably interrupt our concentration with observations about ourselves and the world around us. These comments and criticisms may be part of a subconscious thought pattern that is with us many times throughout each day. But it is often only by making an effort to quiet the mind that we can notice the noise.

This noise—our habitual criticism and judgments—colors how we perceive the world around us. Decision makers who want to find effective solutions must have an objective understanding of the facts. Otherwise, no matter how powerful our analysis of what we perceive, our solutions will be targeted at our misguided understanding of reality, rather than the actual situation at hand.

Recall Ravi Menon and his urgent trip to Switzerland. Replaying his story through the lens of mindfulness, we might imagine the following chain of events. Were Ravi more present to the moment, perhaps he would have noticed his physical reaction to the decline in quarterly sales. Perhaps, even as he was overcome with negative emotions, he would have noticed that it was his bruised ego that lay behind the waves of panic and anxiety.

By engaging Buddhist principles, Ravi potentially could have appreciated the impermanence and uncertainty of his current experience, no matter how unpleasant it seemed in the moment. By accepting this reality, he would have been able to calm his mind and create mental space to consider potential solutions.

Of course, Ravi did not process the experience from this place of mindfulness. Instead, he reacted instinctively, rushing to Zurich in order to tender his resignation. He had to rely on the advice of his boss in order to begin to deal with the problem thoughtfully.

Perhaps you have gone through a similar experience. Perhaps panic and avoidance were front and center. But perhaps next time there will an opportunity to take a more mindful approach.

Minneapolis, Minnesota, April 2019

"Tfweet!" The referee's whistle sounded, and the players slowed to a reluctant halt. The clock showed 0.6 seconds left in the NCAA tournament game. The University of Virginia Cavaliers were trailing the Auburn Tigers by two points.

Hanging over UVA's 2019 basketball season was the previous year's tournament, when first-seeded Virginia suffered a history-making and humiliating loss to sixteenth-seeded University of Maryland at Baltimore County (UMBC) and was eliminated from the tournament. A year later the Cavaliers had soldiered past the Sweet Sixteen, struggled through the Elite Eight, and miraculously reached the Final Four. Now, less than a second remained in the game, and Auburn appeared poised to end UVA's redemptive journey. U.S. Bank Stadium rang with the screams and taunts of the Tigers fans: "UMBC! UMBC!"

With the Tigers leading 60–62, the referee blew the whistle and announced that UVA guard Kyle Guy had been fouled while taking a desperate shot from outside the three-point line.

Guy had three free throws, and he had to sink every one of them to win the game. Shouldering the hopes of UVA fans and the attention of 13 million viewers, Guy—who had publicly struggled with anxiety throughout the season—was under tremendous pressure.

He sank the first shot. The arena went quiet. Then Tigers fans burst into another round of screaming as the referee handed to ball to Guy for his second attempt. "UMBC! UMBC!"

The ball arced, then again swished through the net. The game was tied. UVA fans were in a frenzy while Guy's teammates swarmed around him to exchange high fives.

Would Guy win with his final shot, or would he miss, taking the game into overtime?

Guy returned to the free-throw line, received the ball from the ref, and crouched with his eyes focused on the basket. ESPN's reporting offered a detailed description of the next moments:

> Auburn coach Bruce Pearl called a 60-second timeout. [He wanted] to "ice" Guy at the line. While his teammates gathered together in a cluster on the court, Guy walked away. In that moment, with the biggest shot of his life hanging in the balance, he needed to be alone.
>
> "Yeah, I didn't want to have anything to do with my teammates or coaches at that time," Guy said. "I just wanted to be in my own space. I knew they had confidence in me; I just needed to build up my own."[21]

If you were Guy at that critical moment, how would you deal with yourself, your thoughts, your feelings, and your mind? Imagine yourself in his shoes. Take a moment to observe and feel your body. Gently close your eyes and take a deep breath.

Kyle Guy made the shot. UVA was headed to the championship game.

Strategy Lessons from Chapter 6

1. Establish a purpose and mission to guide your organization's strategies.
2. Search inside yourself for the solution.
3. Simply observe, then accept and embrace reality.

7

Zen

San Francisco, California, January 2007

Dressed in his usual blue jeans and black turtleneck, Steve Jobs strode across the stage at San Francisco's Moscone Center to deliver the Macworld 2007 keynote address.[1] Apple's annual extravaganza attracted tens of thousands of technology enthusiasts eager to learn about the company's latest innovations. Jobs's remarks and dramatic presentation was Macworld's most anticipated event.

Ten years earlier, Jobs had been reinstated as CEO of Apple, a company he cofounded, after having been fired a dozen years previously. At the time of his return, Apple was losing market share, laying off employees, and near insolvency. But over the next decade, Apple would return from the brink of bankruptcy to become a highly profitable Wall Street darling and a dominant brand on the cutting edge of consumer technology. Many of the products that fueled Apple's reemergence—the iMac computer, the OS X operating system, the iTunes online media marketplace, and the iPod music player—had been introduced in one of Jobs's Macworld keynote addresses.

Jobs began his 2007 presentation coyly, describing his excitement at the introduction of "three revolutionary products": an iPod with touch controls, a revolutionary mobile phone, and a breakthrough internet communications device. After several dramatic pauses, Jobs let his audience in on the twist: "These are not three separate devices. This is one device, and we are calling it . . . iPhone."

Jobs walked the audience through the iPhone's innovations: a large touchscreen; a gesture-based operating system; no physical keys save for one button; and web browsing, photos, and video. The iPhone was a dramatic departure from existing high-end cell phones. BlackBerry, which controlled half of world's smartphone market, and other popular smartphones were smaller, with sophisticated physical keyboards.

Media and industry reaction to Apple's new offering was mixed. Executives at BlackBerry remarked: "[The iPhone] has rapid battery drain and a lousy keyboard. . . . It's OK—we'll be fine."[2] Microsoft CEO Steve Ballmer agreed: "There's no chance that the iPhone is going to get any significant market share."[3] A technology journalist at Bloomberg described it "as nothing more than a luxury bauble that will appeal to a few gadget freaks."[4]

By 2008, the iPhone had become the world's best-selling cellular device. By 2010, Apple's total market capitalization surpassed that of Microsoft. By 2013, Blackberry was near bankruptcy, its market share decimated by Apple.

By disregarding established norms and focusing on simplicity, functionality, and user experience, Jobs led Apple in creating a device that had a transformative impact on the high-tech industry, digital communication, and the very nature of human interaction.

Chicago, Illinois, July 1989

In his first head coaching opportunity at the highest level of basketball, Phil Jackson was expected to translate the jaw-dropping talents of young Chicago Bulls star Michael Jordan into team success.

Jordan was recognized as one of the greatest basketball players of his generation. But year after year the Bulls failed to find success in the NBA playoffs. The team's 1987, 1988, and 1989 playoff campaigns had ended in one disappointing loss after another. By the summer of 1989, doubts about Jordan and the Bulls' ability to succeed swirled among fans, the media, and the public.[5]

As the new coach entered what the *Chicago Tribune* described as "perhaps the most pressurized job in the National Basketball Association,"[6] few would have predicted that the Bulls were on the precipice of a historic run of success.

In Jackson's second year, 1991, the team won their first championship. In the following seasons they would repeat time and again, winning six championships in eight years. Jackson left the Bulls in 1998 to coach the Los Angeles Lakers, where he would go on to win five more championships.

On his way to racking up more championships than any other coach in NBA history, Jackson built as much of a reputation for his unusual coaching methods as he did for his teams' successes. Believing winning in basketball depends on more than just skills and tactics, Jackson established a philosophy centered on coalescing team unity, cultivating each player to reach his potential, and preparing players to thrive outside their comfort zones. To develop these qualities, Jackson deployed a range of unconventional strategies drawn from his lifelong interest in a variety of spiritual and philosophical traditions.

The Zen of Steve Jobs and Phil Jackson

Iconoclasts with strongly held beliefs and a willingness to buck orthodoxy, Jobs and Jackson shared similarities in character, leadership style, and life experience that extended beyond their extraordinary successes in their chosen fields. Both came of age in the U.S. in the mid-twentieth century, a place and time characterized by Americans' growing interest in philosophical traditions outside of the Western mainstream. In their teens and twenties, both men became interested in Eastern religious practices. As young men, Jobs (who as a teenager traveled to India to study Buddhism) and Jackson (whose interest in Eastern practices earned him the nickname "the Zen Master" in basketball circles) developed a particular affinity for the Zen tradition of Buddhism, which had a lasting influence on their worldviews. Although Jackson and Jobs were very different leaders operating in different industries, each man's rise to the top of an intensively competitive field was influenced by his commitment to Zen principles.

To be sure, Jobs's and Jackson's successes relied on more than Zen. Their creativity, communication skills, and management abilities underpinned their achievements; and personal qualities such as hard work, competitiveness, ambition, and, no doubt, a dose of good luck also played key roles.

Both men also had a reputation for deploying a variety of less than savory tactics to get results. Jackson was known to spread unwarranted doubts about players' abilities through the media to motivate his teams. Jobs was infamous for a ruthlessly critical style in his personal and professional lives, berating family members and employees alike when they did not perform to his standards.

Yet, embracing Zen principles did lie at the heart of the processes each man used to achieve his greatest accomplishments, including in particular the concepts of nondualism, practical wisdom, and inherent enlightenment. Although Zen principles were not the sole source of Jackson's and Jobs's achievements, and although we are not guaranteed success by deploying them, the wisdom of Zen does hold powerful lessons for strategists looking to improve their decision-making.

Origins of Zen Buddhism

In contrast to the Theravada Buddhist tradition described in chapters 5 and 6, Zen belongs to the Mahayana tradition. In the centuries following Siddhattha Gotama's death in 483 BCE, his teachings spread across Asia. Soon, various sects began to emerge as a result of the interplay between Gotama's teachings and the local belief systems, values, and social norms that had preceded the arrival of Buddhism.

By the second century CE, the two major schools of Theravada and Mahayana had arisen, and within each tradition a rich range of sub-schools developed in population centers across modern-day India, China, Korea, and Japan.

In the midst of this vibrant milieu, the Zen school emerged in China (where Zen is called Chan) before spreading across East Asia.[7] Chan lore holds that the tradition arrived in China in the late fifth or early sixth century CE, brought to the country by the Indian monk Bodhidharma. By the time of Bodhidharma's arrival, China already enjoyed a rich Buddhist tradition, with thousands of temples and hundreds of thousands of monks across the country. A number of regional schools had emerged, with a meditation-oriented version popular in northern China and an approach focused on philosophical discussion flourishing in the south.

Even in this crowded field of competing ideologies, Bodhidharma's teachings stood apart. He rejected the concept of enlightenment as a state to be achieved gradually through scholarly study and diligent meditation. Instead, Bodhidharma described it as a natural quality inherent to each individual. Reaching enlightenment, he taught, was not a matter of developing new skills or cultivating previously unavailable qualities, but an exercise in rediscovering one's true nature.

Bodhidharma's Description of Zen Principles

A brief, four-line passage attributed to Bodhidharma is said to be the original description of Zen's interpretation of Buddhism:

> A special transmission outside the scriptures;
> No dependence upon words and letters;
> Direct pointing at the soul of man;
> Seeing into one's nature and the attainment of Buddhahood.[8]

The insights contained in these four lines have guided Zen students for millennia. Each line reveals an interrelated set of principles that have become the foundation of the Zen tradition:

A special transmission outside the scriptures. With this opening line, Bodhidharma foreshadows Zen's rejection of esoteric rituals, intellectual exercises, and the scholarly study emphasized by other Buddhist traditions. This principle would evolve into Zen's emphasis on in-person pupil-instructor interaction and experiential wisdom as the only authentic forms of Buddhist learning.

No dependence upon words and letters. With the second line, Bodhidharma hints at a realm of knowledge whose qualities exceed the descriptive powers of human language. To achieve liberation, Bodhidharma suggests, requires wisdom that words and letters cannot teach. This provides a foundation for Zen's deemphasis of activities dependent on verbal communication, such as academic learning, theoretical analysis, and reasoned debate. Instead, Zen encourages a focus on wisdom acquired through firsthand experience, such as meditation.

Direct pointing at the soul of man. Bodhidharma emphasizes directly acquired knowledge, implying that the path of enlightenment can be traveled only through firsthand experience. Furthermore, Bodhidharma identifies the soul of man as the object of this experiential learning. To unlock liberation, it is necessary only to study one's innermost self.

Seeing into one's nature and the attainment of Buddhahood. By connecting the attainment of Buddhahood to one's nature, Bodhidharma explains that not only is studying oneself the path to enlightenment, but achieving complete self-knowledge is itself the very experience of liberation. Enlightenment, then, is becoming more deeply aware of who one already is.

With these lines, Bodhidharma discarded scholarly training, ritualistic practices, and study of sophisticated universal laws and instead embraced experiential learning, individual empowerment, and self-reliance. These themes are the foundation for Zen's reputation as an especially practical and action-oriented tradition.

Zen's word for the attainment of Buddhahood is *satori,* a Japanese term that can be roughly equated to the Pali word *nibbana,* Sanskrit "nirvana," and English "enlightenment." As we will see, *satori* is attained through the two practices of contemplating *koans* and engaging in *zazen,* the Japanese word for meditation.

Zen Theory: Nondualism, Experiential Wisdom, and Inherent Enlightenment

Like all Buddhist traditions, Zen aims to free life from suffering by eliminating its causes: desire and craving.

To experience craving we must understand the world from the perspective of dualism. Dualism describes the psychological phenomenon of organizing the world into distinct, separate entities: me versus you, us versus them, mind versus body, success versus failure, and so on. In order to experience craving, the object that we crave must be somehow separate from us (after all, we would not yearn for that which we already embody). In a world without dualism, therefore, craving is impossible. If craving is impossible, suffering too is impossible. If we have rid our life of suffering, we have achieved enlightenment. The goal of Zen, then, is to perceive the world through the paradigm of nondualism.

Language and logic both require dualism. Words are separate entities with distinct definitions linked together by language, and logic relies on establishing relationships between separate ideas. Therefore, we cannot use these tools to bring us to an experience of nondualism. If we exclude all activities driven by the intellectual use of language and logic as viable paths to enlightenment, this leaves available only direct experience and experiential learning.

Zen views nondualism as the true essence of reality. The Zen practitioner's ultimate task is seemingly straightforward: Let go of the ingrained habits of logic and language that are preventing the realization of this truth. If the world is nondualistic, then there are no distinctions between any entities. In other words, we—all people, objects, phenomena—are all one. (We will encounter a related concept when we explore the Tao in chapter 8.) That must mean, by definition, if any being has ever achieved enlightenment, then enlightenment must be present already within all of us and the entities around us. Furthermore, if the seed of enlightenment exists in everything and everyone, every part of our lives must at its core be an experience of enlightenment. It is up to us to do the work of experientially developing an understanding of that already inherent enlightenment.

The ideas of nondualism, direct experiential wisdom, and inherent enlightenment deserve further explanation. The irony here is that we are attempting to explain nondualism with words, which are inherently dualistic. But stick with us.

NONDUALISM

> There is no bodhi tree,
> Nor stand of a mirror bright.
> Since all is void,
> Where can the dust alight?
>
> —Huineng, *The Diamond Sutra*

The notion of nondualism is not unique to Zen or to Buddhism. The concept plays an important role in other Eastern and Western spiritual and philosophical traditions, such as Hinduism and Christianity. Yet Zen is unique in its singular focus on the direct experience of nondualism as the pathway to ultimate liberation.

Huineng, a leading seventh-century Chinese Chan monk whose ideas influenced the tradition's early development,[9] remarked that "whatever can be named leads to dualism. Buddhism is not dualistic. To take hold of this non-duality of truth is the aim of Zen."[10]

Any attempt to describe nondualism verbally, at least per the Zen tradition, is destined for failure. Modern scholars—as did the ancient Zen monks—tend to rely on explanations that focus on what nonduality is not: Nondualism is the absence of the qualities of dualism.

One might be tempted to ask, "What's the big deal?" Why are the Zen teachings so hell-bent on driving students to the experience of nondualism? The answer to these questions takes us back to Zen's deeply Buddhist core. Let us briefly return to the first three of the Buddha's Four Noble Truths:

1. Life is full of suffering
2. Craving and aversion are the cause of suffering
3. To eliminate suffering, let go of craving and aversion

From the Zen perspective, craving and aversion are inherently dualistic. To arise, our desires require an object at which we can direct them, and we must necessarily believe that object to be fundamentally distinct from ourselves. After all, we can only desire the pleasure we do not already possess or hope to escape pain that is possible to avoid. These notions, by relying on distinctions between us and the world around us, necessarily require a dualistic mindset.

Nondualism, therefore, is an answer to truth 3 and Zen's solution to Buddhism's ultimate purpose, a life free from suffering. If craving and aversion require a world filled with polarity, then a nondualist reality would eliminate even the possibility of these emotions and the resultant suffering.

What Is the Sound of One Hand Clapping?

Familiarity with nondualism can help us understand one of Zen's most famous practices, *koan* contemplations. Like the famous "one hand clapping" question,[11] *koans* are a form of riddle or puzzle unique to Zen that are structured to make finding a solution through intellectual reasoning impossible. Instead, finding the answer requires the student to go beyond the dualistic limitations of language and logic.

To today's strategists, Zen's rejection of dualism may at first seem as strange as the seemingly nonsensical *koans* for which Zen has become famous. After all, perhaps no concept is more fundamental to traditional strategic planning than dualism. Whether the goal is to capitalize on new growth opportunities, fend off an existential threat, or address another strategic challenge, the very practice of strategic planning is immersed in dualism.

For example, to address a strategic problem, we must first segment it into its component parts. To define our available resources, we diligently catalog our organization's capabilities. To identify competitive advantage, we study our competitors and compare their strengths and weaknesses to our own. To forecast demand, we divide our customer base into cohorts to understand changing trends in consumer preferences. At every step of the process, we are segmenting, organizing, isolating, and distinguishing—all versions of dualism dressed up in business jargon.

Zen tradition would conceive of traditional strategic planning as an important and necessary step, but one that by itself will not unlock the intuition experience. Dualistic strategic analysis can help us arrive at the data, qualitative understandings, and other information that form the raw materials of a breakthrough insight. But to interpret this information and allow insight to emerge, we need a skill that exists beyond the scope of what dualism and analytical frameworks can offer. Through a kind of alchemy, the individual data, hypotheses, and analyses must synthesize into a single coherent strategy. Strategic intuition is the capability that can help us unlock this phenomenon. Understanding Zen's emphasis on the direct experience of nondualism can help strategists identify pathways toward cultivating this strategic intuition.

Being able to experientially connect to the essential oneness of nondualism is the Zen gateway to enlightenment. A well-known Zen proverb teaches "not one, not two," meaning that practitioners of the tradition should seek to let go of attachment to a sense of the world as composed of separate entities, as well as to a perception of the world as unified. Instead, we must seek out a third position of emptiness that allows free movement between the two perspectives.

This principle was at the core of Phil Jackson's coaching philosophy. As he put it, "[My] primary objective [as a coach] is to bring the team into a state of harmony and oneness."[12] Jackson's view was that by helping his team cultivate unity on the basketball court, he could accomplish more powerful results than even the most effective combination of individual players could achieve. At the same time, Jackson emphasized his players' specialized capabilities and encouraged them to embrace the contributions that each could make. In cultivating this juxtaposition of individual contributions with on-court unity among the players, Jackson connected to a basketball version of the "not one, not two" mentality to maximize his teams' performance.

For example, Jackson's Triangle offensive system was designed to help his players develop nonduality on the court. The Triangle's principles emphasized players' creativity, awareness, and chemistry with teammates. Unlike other coaching systems, the Triangle did not rely on predetermined plays. Instead, it positioned players strategically around the court with the goal of exploiting mistakes by the opposing team. When a player noticed such mistakes, he was encouraged to leverage his own and his teammates' positions on the court to take advantage of the errors. This emphasis on creativity, rather than predetermined actions, unlocked for skilled players a nearly endless array of options. As Jackson described it in one of his autobiographies:

"What attracted me to the Triangle was the way it empowers the players. . . . That stimulates an ongoing process of group problem solving in real time."

Similarly, Jackson would regularly lead his players in meditations for the same purpose. He noted: "I discovered that when I had the players sit in silence, breathing together in sync, it helped align them on a nonverbal level far more effectively than words."[13]

As Michael Jordan told a reporter,

> It helps so much having Phil as our coach. He goes around and burns sage in front of our lockers, and when we're playing bad in practice he'll beat on a war drum to wake us up. You laugh, but that stuff is a part of him. He believes it, the Zen, the poise. It comes from his meditating, gaining the ability to stay in touch with your body and your inner self, calming yourself when tension is all around.
>
> That is something I've learned from Phil. Calming the body. No matter how much pressure there is in a game, I think to myself: It's still just a game. I don't meditate, but I know what he's getting at. He's teaching about peacefulness and living in the moment, but not losing the aggressive attitude. Not being reckless, but strategic.[14]

In the case of Steve Jobs's leadership style at Apple, the influence of nondualism can be understood from a slightly different perspective. For example, traditional Western paradigms of strategic management require us to make difficult trade-offs between competing priorities, such as breadth versus depth, growth versus profitability, or sophistication versus ease of use. One of nondualism's most powerful insights for strategists is the ability to approach these contradictions more creatively. Instead of deciding between several mutually exclusive options, the Zen strategist might attempt a nondualistic approach to solving the problem. Even if logic or conventional wisdom suggests that a compromise is required, nondualism emphasizes the possibility of integrating all possible qualities and capabilities, no matter how seemingly at odds some of them may appear to be. Therefore, no matter how necessary a trade-off may seem at first blush, the Zen perspective opens the door to finding an "all of the above" solution.

Numerous technology companies before Apple had introduced cell phones with increasingly sophisticated features—web-browsing, powerful cameras, and the ability to play music. All these attempts had failed to gain widespread adoption; integrating multiple advanced capabilities in a cell phone seemed to require a user interface that was simply too cumbersome for the average consumer.

Simultaneously, the market was flooded with basic phone models that could make calls, send text messages, and play a few simple games. These products' straightforward user experiences helped popularize the cell phone among average consumers. But their minimal feature set also meant that they were at best only slightly different from each other. As a result, none of the major players in the market had cultivated a powerful brand identity.

Jobs pushed his team to develop a product that bridged two seemingly incompatible qualities: a sophisticated feature set and a streamlined user experience. The team's main job was figuring out a way to make a novel interface feel intuitive and natural.[15]

The powerful creative breakthrough that emerged from this nondualist challenge would manifest as Apple's iOS operating system. With the large touch screen, consumers could operate the device through a user-friendly gesture-based system. Because iOS relied on finger taps, pinches, swipes, and other familiar hand motions, navigating the iPhone instantly felt unintimidating, despite the device's multifaceted capabilities.

The results were revolutionary. The iPhone become a phenomenon that helped Apple achieve record profitability, and the iOS protocols soon became the industry standard. Today, variants of the iOS gesture-based methodology are employed by nearly every smartphone on the market.

The on-court success of Phil Jackson's teams demonstrated the potential of integrating distinct individuals, processes, or parts of an organization—each with unique capabilities—into a unified force working cohesively. Apple's development of the iOS operating system highlighted the power of applying the nondualist approach to seemingly contradictory goals or capabilities. Both are examples of Zen-inspired approaches that, by pushing beyond conventional, dualist perspectives, unlocked the potential for powerful strategic insights.

LIMITATIONS OF INTELLECTUAL KNOWLEDGE AND THE PRIMACY OF DIRECT EXPERIENCE

> The true Way is sublime. It can't be expressed in language.
>
> —Bodhidharma, *The Zen Teaching of Bodhidharma*

> The truth of Zen is the truth of life, and life means to live, to move, to act, not merely to reflect.
>
> —D. T. Suzuki, *Zen Buddhism*

As we have seen, Zen theory contends that language and logic are inherently incompatible with nondualism:

- To function, language must assign each word and phrase a unique definition. Creating distinctions between the meanings of individual words is necessary for communication. However, that process imbues language and communication, at their very cores, with dualism.
- Logic is the process of organizing individual ideas into structured relationships. This capacity to arrange inferences in relation to a conclusion has been one of the great catalysts of scientific, economic, and social progress. Yet, logic too is incompatible with nondualism. Without separate ideas that can be connected through reasoned argument, logic would have no room to exist.

While language, communication, and logic are all incompatible with nondualism, they are also vital ingredients in the process of acquiring, creating, and transmitting intellectual knowledge.

Zen's preference for direct experience, then, is a byproduct of its singular focus on helping students grow closer to a state of nondualist consciousness. Bodhidharma and the Zen masters who followed him were deemphasizing those activities whose very nature required a dualist worldview—such as engaging with intellectual knowledge—and prioritizing behaviors with the potential to unlock nondualist consciousness.

Translating these ideas to a strategy context has several implications. If we are to accept that Zen wisdom contains at least some insights regarding strategic intuition, we now have a clearer understanding of the limitations of traditional planning tools, such as frameworks and data analysis, for helping solve the toughest strategic challenges.

While analytical frameworks themselves cannot create insight, they serve as important components. The example of the Zen teacher's use of language and logic with his students can help us better understand the role of traditional analysis. The teacher must use language and some logic to provide guidance, ask questions, and suggest answers. Of course, the Zen teacher is expected to wield language skillfully to optimize student progress.

Likewise, the teacher's instruction itself will never bring the student closer to enlightenment; only the student's direct experience can do that. And yet, skillful instruction by the teacher can guide the student's efforts in the right direction, increasing the pace at which he or she develops the required direct experience.

Similarly, effective use of research and analysis helps us fully understand the context for a major decision. But, we must expand beyond these tools if we are to come to strategic insights.

Phil Jackson's coaching philosophy illustrates Zen's emphasis on knowledge acquired through direct experience. Like other coaches, Jackson employed a set of traditional techniques, including physical conditioning, offensive and defensive drills, and analysis of past games to develop his players. Yet Jackson believed that what set great teams apart was not players' stamina, on-court skills, or knowledge of opponents' strategy. Rather, he emphasized intangible qualities such as resilience under pressure, present moment awareness, and camaraderie.

Experiential learning was essential to developing these skills, Jackson believed. As he put it: "Most coaches get tied up in knots worrying about tactics, but I preferred to focus my attention on whether the players were moving together in a spirited way."[16] Jackson cultivated this by having his players regularly engage in a variety of unorthodox drills meant to push them out of their comfort zones. His tactics included having the players play in the dark, running a team practice in total silence, and sharing parables drawn from Native American folklore.[17]

Jackson believed that these experiences—more than a film session or the diagramming of a play—would develop the players' instincts and abilities. "My confidence grew out of knowing that when the spirit was right and the players were attuned to one another, the game was likely to unfold in our favor," he explained.[18]

Steve Jobs displayed a parallel embrace of Zen's emphasis on sensory, experiential wisdom over knowledge derived from study or contemplation. Jobs despised the analytical, sequential approach to product and strategy design favored in corporate America, going so far as to ban PowerPoint presentations. He instead preferred to make his decisions by interacting tactilely with potential products. To that end, Apple developed a sophisticated system for quickly creating physical prototypes from digital designs. Team members would then handle these mock-ups and discuss how interacting with the device felt in order to make decisions. Jobs himself embodied this emphasis on experiential learning. Tasked with the multitude of responsibilities expected of a Fortune 500 CEO, he still spent time almost every day in the studio of design chief Jony Ive, handling foam models of products.[19]

The iPhone's iconic physical design and breakthrough operating system came out of this approach. The design team engaged in endless cycles: creating prototypes, handling them extensively, and adjusting the design based on what they learned. Many of the iPhone's key features, including inertial scrolling and the rectangle-with-rounded-corners shape—were as intuitive as they were innovative. How were Apple's designers able to meld innovation and usability so deftly? By pursuing direct knowledge of how users would experience the iPhone throughout its design process.[20]

Parallels to Zen's emphasis on direct knowledge can be observed in Jackson's experiential approaches to developing his players and Jobs's emphasis on physical interaction with potential products. Both demonstrate the power of insight fostered by doing rather than knowledge developed through mere intellectual learning.

ENLIGHTENMENT IS INHERENT IN ALL BEINGS

> To find a Buddha, you have to see your nature.
>
> —Bodhidharma, *The Zen Teaching of Bodhidharma*
>
> Our attention must be directed inwardly to the working of our minds.
>
> —D. T. Suzuki, *Zen Buddhism*

Zen scholar D. T. Suzuki defines *satori* as "an intuitive looking into the nature of things in contradistinction to the analytical or logical understanding of it."[21] Suzuki's description is a reminder of the core Zen belief that enlightenment is already within us, and that achieving it requires no new skills, qualities, or other prerequisites.

This idea may at first appear radical. Even the most self-assured among us can identify at least a few flaws in his or her own habits, mindset, or character. It's tempting to assume, then, that our path to enlightenment can come only by diligently cultivating qualities we lack or working to eliminate our shortcomings.

Zen insists on quite the opposite. A fully formed, already perfect enlightenment rests within each of us just waiting to be uncovered. Considering this notion from the perspective of nondualism will reveal its inherent logic.

We start by reminding ourselves of the absence of any distinctions or separations in a nondualist reality. Next, we consider the notion that enlightenment exists, has existed, or will exist at some time, somewhere in the universe. If we assume both the first and second statements to be true, then we must accept the reality of fully formed enlightenment as an inherent part of our core. In fact, within this construct, each object, each being, and each moment are filled with enlightenment.

Even if we give Zen the benefit of the doubt and attempt to embrace this conclusion at face value, for most of us our experience of daily life hardly reflects a world of universal enlightenment. Even on our best days, are we not prone to at least a few small moments of frustration, stress, or anxiety?

Zen answers this question by returning us to the fundamental tension between the limitless potential of nondualism and the corroding influence of our dualist conditioning. Our education, social norms, and evolution have trained us to engage the world through an inherently dualist set of paradigms. Logic and language, in particular, are important tools that help us solve problems, relate to others, and contribute value. Yet, as we have seen, by their very nature these constructs also breed an attachment to a dualist worldview. That dualism, Zen contends, stops our inherent enlightenment in its tracks. Instead, our mind engages in a relentless pattern of forming distinctions, including the particularly insidious variety that catalyzes our cycles of craving, clinging, and aversion.

Decision makers looking for clues to how organizational strategy can benefit from the notion of nondualism would do well to start here. Zen conceives of enlightenment as an omnipresent quality to whose ubiquity we must become more attuned. A truly nondualist mindset appreciates every moment, decision, and action, no matter how mundane, as filled with the same potential for enlightenment as life's most profound moments. In fact, Zen tradition stresses the normalcy of enlightenment as a constant presence in life's day-to-day activities.

Similarly, strategic decision-making, and the potential for strategic breakthrough, can be thought of as inherent to an organization's every activity. As we highlighted in the discussion of whole-enterprise-driven strategy in chapter 1, to address major challenges we cannot expect creative solutions to emerge only from the strategic planning function or the C-Suite. Front-line employees, back-office staff, and business unit operators all have the potential to provide powerful insights for the entire organization.

The Japanese practice of *kaizen* exemplifies the potential of this "strategy is everywhere" approach. *Kaizen* stresses continuous improvement across the entire organization and requires that individuals at every level identify opportunities for improvement in their areas of expertise. Perhaps most widely popularized by Toyota, this approach enables organizations to quickly address small issues before they spiral into major challenges and allows for the testing of new ideas at a small scale to identify high-potential innovations.

This belief in an omnipresent enlightenment has equally powerful implications at the individual level. Searching for creative solutions outside of the narrow confines of the specific issue at hand strikes at the very heart of strategic insight. Examples include Steve Jobs's college courses in calligraphy and visual arts serving as inspiration for Apple's emphasis on aesthetically pleasing product design, and the coaching insights Phil Jackson drew from the books on Eastern philosophy he devoured in his college years.

Jackson's ability to cultivate extraordinary performances from his teams originated from a profound belief in the inherent capabilities of each player. As he described it: "My approach was always to relate to each player as a whole person. . . . That meant pushing him to discover what distinct qualities he could bring to the game. . . . Many players I've coached didn't look special on paper, but in the process of creating a role for themselves they grew into formidable champions."[22] Whether Jackson was encouraging Michael Jordan to pursue a more team-oriented approach or cultivating the resilience of benchwarmers, his inherent belief in each player's potential time and again unlocked his teams' ability to succeed at the highest levels.

This mindset will position us to actively search for insights, and to invest care, attention, and resources in engaging with the world in a way that allows intuition to emerge. Any part of the organization that is treated as an operational or administrative necessity with no broader importance is likely to behave as such. On the other hand, even if a unit's functions are primarily clerical, management engagement with that unit in a way that consistently encourages strategic problem solving can yield dramatic results.

For example, in many large banks blockchain technology—the innovative data-storage architecture widely believed to have the potential to disrupt a multitude of industries—was first embraced by administrative, cost-center functions responsible for record-keeping and data management. A few of these organizations treated the initial applications of the blockchain as experiments with an emerging new technology, rather than simply a back-office cost-cutting exercise. As the technology has matured, a wide array of financial services applications for the blockchain, many with the potential to generate additional revenue, are being developed. The select group of banks that embraced the opportunity to draw organizational insights from their administrative functions can now leverage those early lessons to capitalize on this emerging growth opportunity.

Doing Zen: *Zazen* Sitting Meditation

At a fundamental level, all individuals who start on the Zen path have set out to achieve direct knowledge of their true nature. We appear to have two options: strengthen our connection to our inherent enlightenment, or weaken our attachment to the dualistic habits sabotaging our connection to that true nature. Of the variety of exercises prescribed by Zen teachers to help their pupils achieve these objectives, two—*zazen* sitting meditation and the *koan* practice described earlier—have stood the test of time to become Zen's most indispensable practices.

Zazen is Zen's essential technique for practical and direct experience to reach enlightenment. The appearance of a practitioner immersed in traditional *zazen*—typically seated cross-legged on a small round cushion, eyes closed, breathing quietly, body completely still—does not scream that powerful, highly experiential, and direct spiritual training is underway. But *zazen* is just such an exercise. Meditators are provided with specific instructions for how to align the mind, body, breath, and emotions, with the goal of directing every part of the practitioner's being to strengthen connection to nonduality and detach from dualism.

Traditional *zazen* instructions place primal importance on the meditator sitting in the lotus position.[23] The lotus is a cross-legged posture in which the practitioner places each foot on the opposite thigh. Instructions are also offered regarding the position of meditators' hands (turned upward and placed together in the lap), spine (straight, but relaxed), eyelids (halfway closed with eyes lowered to the ground), and even tongue (pressed against the upper palate).

Compared to other Eastern meditation traditions, the guidance offered by *zazen* meditation is exceptionally prescriptive. Why this rigorous level of detail? Is it not enough to simply position the body in any physically comfortable, reasonably still position and get on with the work of training the mind?

The specificity is meant to help meditators place themselves in a position that exactly resembles the physical posture assumed by the Buddha when he received his enlightenment. Zen theory holds that by putting his or her body in the same position that Gotama did, the meditator is developing an understanding of the felt experience of enlightenment. In other words, to achieve the experience of enlightenment, the practitioner has to take on the behaviors that have been demonstrated to bring on that experience.

The *zazen* practice holds a powerful lesson for decision makers struggling with how to solve a tough strategic problem. Zen's advice? Assume the answer is already at hand and take the actions that you would take if the solution were readily available. Act as if the strategic insight has already manifested, and those actions will allow the insight to manifest.

Steve Jobs's approach to designing the iPhone serves as an example of Zen's solution-through-action approach. After a few weeks of using a prototype iPhone, Jobs had become dissatisfied with the device's plastic covering, believing that it would scratch easily in users' pockets. With only a few weeks until the product's launch, Jobs informed his design team that the plastic would have to be replaced with a less scratch-prone material.

As Apple's designers attempted to explain that this would be impossible in such a short time frame, Jobs replied, "I won't sell a product that gets scratched. I want a glass screen, and I want it perfect in six weeks."[24] In Jobs's response, we observe the power of acting as if what appeared to be an unsolvable quandary was bound to be successfully resolved.

Jobs, a famously challenging personality, may not have used a particularly amicable tone. However, his commitment to acting as if the solution was not only feasible but necessary led to extraordinary results. Within a few weeks, the team had secured a supplier capable of producing the scratch-proof glass material. When the manufacturer expressed concern about producing the little-used material at the required scale, Jobs employed the same tactic, approaching the issue with a hard-nosed commitment to finding a solution. In short order, the supplier was able to repurpose an existing factory to produce the glass material required by Apple.

Jobs's iron will and perfectionism played crucial roles. But just as important, Jobs acted as if the seemingly impossible had already been achieved. In turn, that approach created a virtuous cycle that led to a solution being found quickly. As we search for a strategic insight to an intractable challenge, it may be tempting to allow the process to paralyze us. Zen teaches that the answer will come by taking action. Act as if the answer is available, and the necessary insights will emerge.

Conclusion

Stripped of the elaborate rituals and esoterica that surround other forms of Buddhism, Zen is a deeply practical interpretation of Gotama's teachings. Grounded in a few central principles—nondualism, experiential knowledge, and inherent enlightenment—Zen offers an action-oriented approach. For strategists, Zen's core tenets translate to a path to strategic insights that encourages us to eschew false dichotomies, prioritize learning through practical experience, and treat each moment of our lives as an opportunity to find a strategic breakthrough.

By means of the Gita and the Buddha's teaching, both Hinduism and Buddhism guide us through an inner journey toward peace and clear-mindedness. In the next section, we will explore how Confucianism and Taoism provide enlightened leadership through our relationships with the world beyond.

Strategy Lessons from Chapter 7

1. Use language and logic to provide guidance, but experientially derived wisdom is key to unlocking insight.
2. Direct your attention inward to the working of your mind.
3. Invest care, attention, and resources in engaging with the world in a way that allows intuition to emerge (i.e., practice *zazen*).
4. Eschew false dichotomies, prioritize learning through practical experience, and treat each moment of your life as an opportunity to find a strategic breakthrough.

PART III

RELATIONSHIPS

While organizational leaders play a key role in catalyzing effective strategy, organizations can reach their full potential only if all stakeholders are actively engaged in creating and executing that strategy. As the following chapters describe, this whole-organization approach is rooted in relational principles centered on how one engages with colleagues, organizations, and societies.

Overview of Part III

As we will see in chapter 8, the Tao is based on humans' natural relationship with the universe, whereas Confucius (chapter 10) positioned each leader within a human rule-driven web of familial, social and governing relationships.

To be effective, strategists need to understand the Tao of strategy and the Tao of their businesses. They need to cut through the flood of distracting stimuli, including the endless streams of data about their business's short-term performance, uncertainties in their personal and professional lives, and information about the economy, industry, and competition. Instead they must focus on "the nature," and act and adjust their strategies in harmony with it.

As described in chapter 9, *chi* is the natural energy flowing in both the human body and the universe. In this chapter, we will draw mind-centering lessons from aikido, Tai Chi, and acupuncture, with specific focus on the martial art of *Ki-Aikido*. We will explore applications to the corporate world, and, as with Sun Tzu, we will see that the best fight is the one avoided. However, when required, one can choose to embrace conflict and succeed by absorbing or deflecting the actions of an aggressor.

Confucius shifts our attention from the individual strategist to the structure of organizations and societies. The philosophy of Confucius suggested that social order resulted from moral foundations of humaneness, justice, etiquette, wisdom, and trust. Similarly to the societies in which they are embedded, organizations need to be built and run with these five values at their core to effectively operate and implement strategy. Just as social order is maintained by values embedded in individual members of a society, so too must strategists ensure that all stakeholders know and are aligned with the organization's culture and values.[1]

8

The *Tao Te Ching*

Fame or integrity: which is more important?
Money or happiness: which is more valuable?
Success or failure: which is more destructive?

—Lao Tzu, *Tao Te Ching*

I have occasional delusions of adequacy.

—Tara Brach, "Awakening from the Trance of Unworthiness"

If you're radically uncertain about what to do, doing nothing is often the best option.

—Joseph C. Sternberg, "The Dismal Overreachers"

In this chapter, we transition from the inward, intra-psychic focus of Buddhism, mindfulness, and Zen to the organizations and societies in which we live. The *Tao Te Ching* takes us through the realm of nature and our relationships with fellow human beings.

Los Negros Island, Papua New Guinea, 1944

The campaign to capture the Japanese-held Admiralty Islands during World War II would serve as a key inflection point in the Pacific theater, helping the Allies establish crucial air and naval footholds in the region. The campaign launched in the early hours of February 29, as U.S. Navy warships started to bombard the eastern shore of Los Negros Island. By mid-morning, the beaches had largely been cleared of the surprised Japanese troops, who had expected the attack to come from elsewhere on the island.

After the ships' guns finished pummeling the beaches of Los Negros, the Seabees—the navy's construction battalion—boarded their landing craft, already loaded with bulldozers, scrapers, and backhoes. The Seabees' primary mission was to scrape away the existing landing strips built for lightweight Japanese "Zero" fighter aircraft and replace them with longer and deeper tarmacs to accommodate the navy's heavier fighters and bombers. These new four-thousand-foot-long airstrips would support the Allies' island-by-island assault on Japanese territory. The Seabees' secondary mission was to build barracks, showers, kitchens, mess halls, and a command post for the soldiers and airmen who would follow.

Before they could reach the airstrips, the Seabees had to clear the beach, upon which hundreds of Japanese soldiers had died from the destroyers' artillery. Under heavy fire from forces positioned farther inland, the American engineers bulldozed a hundred-yard-long trench parallel to the ocean to bury the fallen enemy combatants.

It took eight days for the Seabees and the accompanying Marines to subdue the remaining Japanese troops and pacify the island. Sixteen days later, the runways and an advance base camp for seventeen thousand soldiers were complete, and the Seabees were able to treat their fellow Americans to pancakes and hot showers. The exhausted Marines, especially, benefited from the Seabees' motto in action: "We can do the difficult immediately. The impossible takes a little bit longer."

The landing strips had been a bigger challenge than expected. Ripping the shallow tarmac surface out of the ground was easy. But lengthening the landing area necessitated the removal of several banyan trees.

Banyan trees have a deep root structure, and the roots of all proximate trees are intertwined, making the removal of any one tree nearly impossible. Try as they might, the Seabees could not budge the thick trees with their bulldozers.

Their solution: Use readily available artillery to blast the trees out of the ground.[1]

The *Tao Te Ching*

The banyan trees and their web of roots can serve as a metaphor for the concept of the Tao (pronounced "dao"). Commonly associated with the Chinese philosopher Lao Tzu, Taoism holds that all of creation is interrelated, that everything we do immediately impacts others, and that the world would be in an ideal state if all human activity was in harmony with nature. We will return to a definition of the Tao in a moment.

The *Tao Te Ching* (pronounced "Dao de Ching") was written as a guide for Chinese rulers. As we will see in chapter 10, Confucius—perhaps China's most influential philosopher—advised rulers by focusing broadly on the formal structuring of society, ethical government, education, and rituals. By contrast, Lao Tzu focused on how individual leaders should think and behave.

The *Tao Te Ching* is a deceptively short collection of eighty-one two- to three-paragraph passages or "chapters." Each chapter contains instructions for living and leading, along with thought- and dialogue-provoking questions, such as the one quoted at the beginning of this chapter ("fame or integrity . . . ?").

While versions of the *Tao Te Ching* published across the centuries have ordered the chapters in various ways, for the purposes of this book we have classified the eighty-one passages thematically, and will offer a few as illustration as we draw lessons from them. (All references are to chapters in the Stephen Mitchell translation.) The passages are of four types: the Tao and its meanings (thirty-three chapters); *wu wei,* the art of "not doing" (twenty-one); leadership advice (thirteen); and general philosophy (fourteen). As we pass through these four themes, we move from the abstract to the concrete.

WHAT IS THE TAO?

The word "Tao" shows up seventy-six times in the *Tao Te Ching,* and each time its meaning is slightly different.[2] Literally, Tao means "the way" or "to guide." *Te* refers to the power of the Tao, and the Chinese word *Ching* means the work has canonical status.

Lao Tzu describes the Tao as the driving power of all nature and the ordering principle behind all life.[3] The Tao cannot be easily perceived by human senses, nor is it easily defined. The opening passage of the book states:

> The Tao that can be told
> is not the eternal Tao.

The Tao cannot be understood through logic, but only through experience, feeling, and intuition. The book says the Tao is inexhaustible, older than God, birthing both good and evil, never born, never dying, and present for all. All things are born from the Tao, but it creates nothing. The Tao flows everywhere and in all things. The Tao is the center of the universe, and in the end, all things flow back to the Tao.[4]

As a modern scholar described it: "The Tao is a semi-metaphysical concept [that] describes an invisible, natural order about the Universe. It is a nameless force that not only represents the flow of the Cosmos, but which is found in every one of us."[5]

A number of metaphors attempt to explain the Tao. It is a well that is never used up (4), the "great mother" (6), it's "smaller than an electron" and cannot be seen (32), and it is like the pot we shape from clay whose emptiness holds whatever we want (11). "We hammer wood for a house, but it is the inner space that makes it livable" (11).

Lao Tzu instructs us to follow the ineffable Tao as our guide for behavior, rather than the Confucian-style rules, roles, and codes of conduct that we will see in chapter 10. (Confucius did, however, encourage rulers and subjects to live in accordance with the Tao.) If all humankind lived in harmony with the Tao, we would have a world of peace, serenity, goodness, authenticity, gentility, and beauty.

For Lao Tzu, control of our desires is a cornerstone of living in alignment with the Tao. He does not eschew success, but he stresses that any material achievement must be pursued responsibly. Like the Buddha, Lao Tzu recognizes the need for citizens to support their households. But impulses that might injure others should be reined in, and we should recognize that the pursuit of fame, power, and wealth beyond our basic needs is inherently a zero-sum game and a futile endeavor.

The Chinese concept of yin and yang underlies much of Lao Tzu's philosophy, emphasizing the notions of cyclicality, constant change, and balance (see fig. 9). Yin and yang reflect Easterners' acknowledgment of, and comfort with, fluidity, impermanence, and constant cyclicality. By contrast, Westerners—particularly in the naturally abundant lands of Europe and North America—tend to perceive time as moving inexorably forward in the direction of progress. Fueled by their nation's youth, U.S. citizens especially tend toward exuberant optimism: "Onward and upward!" "Go west, young man!" Moonshots, manifest destiny, and the like.

But seasoned executives who have lived through economic cycles are more sober. Adam Westerfeld, vice president of production at ICI Australia's commodity chemicals division, explained to us how young MBAs can easily panic when they see the inevitable downturns in demand for commodity chemicals such as chlorine and soda ash. As Westerfeld said:

> We know that the cycle is fifteen years from peak to peak and trough to trough. If we hire a young salesperson soon after a trough, his or her experience will lead them to think that our business is on a steady upswing. For seven years, anyway. But when the inevitable downturn comes, dismay and alarm are common, especially since the amplitude of our price swings are higher than demand [quantity] swings. We older-timers usually stay calm and work with our customers and futures contracts; but even with intellectual foreknowledge, we can expect our younger associates' emotional swings to mirror those of our industry.

In effect, Westerfeld and his associates were demonstrating the long-term horizon and impermanence taught by both Lao Tzu and the Buddha:

FIGURE 9. Yin and yang

> If you realize that all things change,
> there is nothing you will try to hold on to.
> If you aren't afraid of dying,
> there is nothing you can't achieve. (74)

What Westerfeld described as an old-timer's perspective can also arise naturally from the principles of Eastern philosophy. In Taoism, especially, everything is bound to return to its starting point. The world is always changing, moving from one state to another, such as from summer to winter and day to night. These states have complementary properties, and each succeeding state arises from its predecessor, as represented by the yin/yang symbol in figure 9. Opposites such as good and evil, light and dark, active and passive are phases in an endless cycle.

> The Tao doesn't take sides;
> it gives birth to both good and evil. (5)

Although the opposing sides of the yin/yang are in tension, they complement and balance each other. The yin is night, soft, negative, and passive; yang is day, hard, positive, and active. The black and white dots in each of the symbol's halves signify that each invades the other and takes up space within it. The curves in both sides represent how they flow into each other. In the end, both sides find themselves resolved by the circle that encloses them. That is the nature of the Tao.

While elaborated as a sophisticated philosophy and represented in a profound symbol, the Tao manifests as a cultural Asian attitude about time and the relativity of core values. At the risk of oversimplifying, we might summarize the time attitude with phrases such as "there is a season," "go with the flow," and "this too shall pass." How this translates in business terms can be seen in the typically longer planning horizons of Eastern corporations, as we saw in the Komatsu case in chapter 3. Value relativity is manifested in seeing the world not in either/or dichotomies, as many Westerners might (something is good or evil, an opportunity or a threat), but as possibly either, both, or neither. A thing simply is.

WU WEI

> I unplugged my brain.
>
> —Julian Alaphilippe

> I have always felt I enter a sort of trance when I'm performing [as a singer]. That trance is so critical to my success on stage.
>
> —Jennifer Jasinski

The notion of doing-not doing or action in inaction can be puzzling until you recognize it as what athletes describe as "being in the zone." As Tour de France cyclist Julian Alaphilippe described, the athlete experiences a heightened sense of proprioception and makes the right moves.[6] It is as if the movement happens by itself, without effort or deliberate exertion. When Miyamoto Musashi described emptiness as a battle condition (chapter 2), he was referring to his ability to disengage from any conscious attempt to control his moves. This disengagement was possible because Musashi had studied and practiced his moves to the point of exhaustion in order to achieve mastery. In other words, the samurai combat maneuvers became second nature.

Similarly, Lao Tzu advises us to let go, be patient, and let things take their course. For example:

> Do you have the patience to wait
> till your mud settles and the water is clear?
> Can you remain unmoving
> till the right action arises by itself? (15)

and

> Open yourself to the Tao,
> then trust your natural responses;
> and everything will fall into place. (23)

Although the literal translation of *wu wei* is the art of "not doing," its intent is to advise that one should not do anything extraneous, and should act thoughtfully rather than impulsively:

> Act without doing;
> work without effort. . . .
>
> Confront the difficult
> while it is still easy;
> accomplish the great task
> by a series of small acts. (63)
>
> Prevent trouble before it arises.
> Put things in order before they exist. . . .
>
> Rushing into action, you fail. (64)

It is not that Lao Tzu encourages his students to avoid pursuing great achievements or to stand by idly as opportunities slip past. Rather, he is explaining that to take advantage of opportunity and achieve meaningful impact, it is often necessary to engage in a series of incremental tasks, rather than hoping to change the world with a single, dramatic action.

As perhaps the first proponent of exploiting emergent strategy (chapter 1), Lao Tzu said:

> The Master allows things to happen.
> She shapes events as they come.
> She steps out of the way
> and lets the Tao speak for itself. (45)
>
> True mastery can be gained
> by letting things go their own way.
> It can't be gained by interfering. (48)

In other words, don't fight nature; be spontaneous, natural, and flowing. Stop trying so hard! *Wu wei* is action without friction or conflict.

Although *wu wei* is somewhat abstract in nature, it is the foundation for Lao Tzu's advice on leadership.

LEADERSHIP, NOT CONTROLSHIP

> We simply hire thoroughbreds and let them run.
>
> —Bob Jaedicke, dean, Stanford Graduate School of Business

> My job is to just get out of the way.
>
> —Bob Harris, dean, Darden School of Business

> In my company, CEO means "Chief Enabling Officer." I try to empower my team to make as many decisions as possible, but it is hard to do. When you empower someone, you are reducing your power at the same time. And when you give it, it is very hard to take it back without ruining the relationship.
>
> —Fernando Fernandez, CEO, Unilever Brazil

Lao Tzu's leadership philosophy can be described as one of minimal intervention, of getting out of the way. In a particularly incisive passage on leadership in the *Tao Te Ching,* he said:

> When the Master governs, the people
> are hardly aware that he exists.
> Next best is a leader who is loved.
> Next, one who is feared.
> The worst is one who is despised. . . .
>
> The master doesn't talk, he acts.
> When his work is done,
> the people say, "Amazing:
> we did it, all by ourselves!" (17)

Above all, Lao Tzu advocates letting go and avoiding the urge to control:

> If you want to be a great leader,
> you must learn to follow the Tao.
> Stop trying to control.
> Let go of fixed plans and concepts
> and the world will govern itself. (57)

and

> Whoever relies on the Tao in governing men
> doesn't try to force issues. . . .

The Master does his job
and then stops.
He understands that the universe
is forever out of control. (30)

As Michael Puett and Christine Gross-Loh put it in *The Path:* "True power does not rely on strength and domination. Strength and domination render us incapable of relating to others."[7] Taoism seeks attunement with others and with nature, not dominance. In *The World's Religions,* Huston Smith wrote: "When the British scaled earth's highest peak, the exploit was widely hailed as 'the conquest of Everest.' [By contrast, Zen master] D. T. Suzuki remarked: 'We orientals [*sic*] would have spoken of *befriending* Everest.'"[8] Indeed, Frank Lloyd Wright was inspired by Taoism's ecological approach: "Taoist temples do not stand out from their surroundings. They nestle against the hills, back under the trees, blending in with the environment."[9]

We end this section with one of our favorite passages:

Governing a large country
is like frying a small fish.
You spoil it with too much poking. (60)

GENERAL PHILOSOPHY

Lao Tzu has either guidance for or provocation around a number of topics, including the quest for success, the danger of comparing oneself with others, competition, humility, moderation, serenity, the power of soft over hard, and the metaphor of flowing water. We will mention a few of these as examples. (The power of soft over hard will be covered in the next chapter, on energy as a source of strategic force.)

Social Comparison

"Success is a goal without a satiation point," notes Smith in *The World's Religions.*[10] Modern society's metrics for success, such as material wealth, prestige, and influence, are often measurable only in relation to others. Because inevitably there will be someone richer, more admired, or better connected, the comparisons may lead to dissatisfaction and feelings of envy, low self-esteem, and even depression.

The second quotation at the beginning of this chapter is Tara Brach's humorous dig at how easy it is for us to self-denigrate.[11] Brach, a Buddhist scholar and clinical psychologist, says that underneath our need to gain acceptance and status is "the trance of unworthiness, a chronic feeling that we are deficient."[12]

Lao Tzu offers a few passages that warn us of the dangers of comparison and help with its effects:

> If you look to others for fulfillment,
> you will never truly be fulfilled.
> If your happiness depends on money,
> you will never be happy with yourself.
>
> Be content with what you have. . . .
> When you realize there is nothing lacking,
> the whole world belongs to you. (44)
>
> If you realize that you have enough,
> you are truly rich. (33)
>
> Chase after money and security
> and your heart will never unclench.
> Care about people's approval
> and you will be their prisoner.
>
> Do your work, then step back.
> The only path to serenity. (9)
>
> Must you value what others value,
> avoid what others avoid?
> How ridiculous! (20)

Humility

Taoism preaches the "three treasures" of compassion, moderation, and humility. For many successful people (as deemed by modern standards), the latter is often the most difficult to embrace. As billionaire media mogul Ted Turner famously said: "I wish I were humble. Then I would be perfect."

By contrast, the Tao emphasizes what we might call the *wu wei* leadership style:

> All streams flow to the sea
> because it is lower than they are.
> Humility gives it its power.

If you want to govern the people,
you must place yourself below them.
If you want to lead the people,
you must learn how to follow them. (66)

The argument for humility is that it requires you to set your ego aside. After that, there is nothing to chain you to your previous course of action, opening the door to flexibility and emergent strategy.

The idea of a humble leader living within moderation speaks volumes about that person's credibility and authenticity. Sam Walton was famous for driving an old pickup truck around Bentonville, Arkansas, where Walmart is headquartered. Warren Buffet lives in the modest Omaha, Nebraska, home that he purchased sixty years ago. Indeed, in *Good to Great,* Jim Collins identified the CEOs of "great" companies as displaying a humble, often self-effacing, quiet, and reserved leadership style.[13]

Lao Tzu characterizes the humble leader as able to learn from mistakes:

A great nation is like a great man:
When he makes a mistake, he realizes it.
Having realized it, he admits it.
Having admitted it, he corrects it.
He considers those who point out his faults
As his most benevolent teachers. (61)

Some cultures value modesty and are wary of standing too tall. In Australia, a familiar refrain is "the tall poppy is the first one cut down." As Lao Tzu says:

He who stands on tiptoe
doesn't stand firm. . . .
He who tries to shine
dims his own light. (24)

When you are content to be simply yourself
and don't compare or compete,
everybody will respect you. (8)

Along with humility comes reticence to speak unnecessarily:

Those who know don't talk.
Those who talk don't know. (56)

> Express yourself completely,
> then keep quiet. (23)

Moderation

We will share a single passage on moderation:

> Fill your bowl to the brim
> and it will spill.
> Keep sharpening your knife
> and it will blunt. (9)

Suffice it to say, moderation and balance are core values permeating the Tao.

Water

We conclude this chapter with perhaps the most powerful metaphor for *wu wei:* flowing water. Water does not fight the obstacles it encounters; it flows around them. In Chinese thought, water is the emblem of the *yin:* the flowing source of the universe.[14] Water supports objects and carries them effortlessly on its tide. It adapts itself to its surroundings and flows to the lowest places. It wears down rock, which it rounds to conform to its flow. It works past barriers and under walls and doors.

> Nothing in the world
> is as soft and yielding as water.
> Yet for dissolving the hard and inflexible,
> nothing can surpass it.
>
> The soft overcomes the hard;
> the gentle overcomes the rigid.
> Everyone knows this is true,
> but few can put it into practice. (78)

This is, of course, the same imagery that Sun Tzu used in describing how to maneuver fluidly in battle.

Be Water is the 2020 ESPN documentary about martial arts legend Bruce Lee. Born in San Francisco and raised in Hong Kong, Lee is considered to be the most influential martial artist of all time.

Lee used the water metaphor to describe his approach to both martial arts and life. As Lee explained, "Empty your mind, be formless, shapeless—like water. Now you put water in a cup, it becomes the cup. . . . Now water can flow or it can crash. Be water, my friend."[15]

Strategy Lessons from Chapter 8

1. Strive for empathy, frugality (non-excessiveness, non-greed), humility (non-arrogance), and continuous improvement.
2. If you're radically uncertain about what to do, doing nothing is often the best option.
3. Have the patience to wait until your mental mud settles, the water is clear, and the right action arises by itself.
4. If you want to be a great leader, stop trying to control. Hire thoroughbreds and let them run.
5. Stop comparing yourself to others or seeking their approval; otherwise, you'll never be fulfilled and will always be their prisoner.
6. Be content to simply be yourself. Respect will follow.
7. Be fluid like water, flowing around obstacles and conforming to the terrain ahead of you.

9

Energy as a Strategic Force

Tai Chi. Acupuncture. Aikido. What do they have in common? They all channel the human body's natural energy toward health, grounding, and mental clarity. Strategists too can overcome obstacles and discover new insights by channeling this energy.

Minneapolis, Minnesota, 2019

In chapter 6 we saw the start of one of the most inspiring comeback stories in sports history, when UVA's basketball team won in the last 0.6 seconds of an NCAA semifinal game. In every one of its tournament games, UVA had seemed destined to replay the previous year's humiliation. Indeed, the team kept losing by wide margins, but always came back to win in the final seconds.

A tied score at the end of the championship game itself sent UVA and Texas Tech into overtime, where UVA prevailed 85–77. For the first time in school history, the Cavaliers were crowned the NCAA national basketball champions.

"Redemption!" proclaimed headlines around the country, often accompanied by stories about UVA's resilience. News commentators frequently use the word "resilience" to describe the quality needed for recovery from defeat. We all encounter adversity at some point in our lives. Resilience is the capacity to rebound from and triumph over such ordeals or traumas. Popular TED Talks, best-selling books, and think pieces in prestigious magazines discuss the role of resilience and perseverance in achieving fulfillment and success.

Eastern philosophy offers a second, complementary strategy, what we might call eliminating the need for resilience. How? By channeling energy in such a way that we—or our organization—are less likely to be knocked off balance in the first place.

The Eastern philosophers we have encountered so far have taught us to stay balanced by following the Middle Way with perseverance, discipline, and a focus on the relational. The *Tao Te Ching* (chapter 8), for example, centered on our connection to, and harmonious relationship with, nature. The Eastern inclination toward relationships rather than individualism, and toward harmony instead of separation, manifests itself in the practices of managing and channeling energy.

This energy has several names in and outside Asia: *chi* in China, *ki* in Japan, spirit (Europe, the Americas, the Middle East), *ubuntu* (South Africa), *vodou* (Haiti and Nigeria), and *prana* (India). In this chapter we introduce you to *chi* (pronounced "chee"). We start with a brief discussion of acupuncture and its release of the natural energy coursing through *chi* channels in our bodies. Then we move to the "internal" or "soft" martial arts of Tai Chi and *Ki-Aikido,* which will serve as analogs for handling external and internal challenges coming from all directions. Because the Chinese art of Tai Chi is already familiar in the West, we will focus here on the Japanese martial art of aikido.

The concepts presented in this chapter are by their nature metaphysical. Some parts may appear abstract, and the concepts' relevance to the business environment may seem elusive. Therefore, we provide a range of examples throughout. Much as in the game of Go (chapter 3), in our experience lessons come alive in the doing rather than in the reading or telling. Our aim is to distill lessons that are sufficient to coax you into trying them for yourself.

Energy at the Personal Level: Western Science and Eastern Medicine

Joyce Bolger, a medical doctor, stared in disbelief as her patient came waltzing down the clinic's hallway. Six months earlier, Bolger had informed Helen that her leg and back pain was beyond cure—no medication would be effective, and surgery was not a viable option. "What's the secret?" Bolger asked her laughing, prancing patient. "Acupuncture!" declared Helen.

After extensive investigation, Bolger closed her thriving internal medicine clinic and moved to San Francisco to study two schools of Chinese acupuncture. One school treats the energy, or *chi,* flowing along the vertical meridians of the body; the other treats the circular flows. In Bolger's acupuncture practice, she draws from both modalities and also treats her patients with full knowledge of their medical histories and conventional (Western) medications. Her practice is decidedly holistic.

When Bolger visited our MBA class, a physicist in attendance asked her: "As a Columbia-trained scientist, how do you reconcile your Western empirical brain with Chinese medicine and its treatment regimens? That is, how do the two coexist in your mind? Did you have to deny the former in order to embrace the latter?"

Bolger answered: "It's rather straightforward. If you consider the human body at its fundamental, microscopic, level you encounter pure energy in the form of atoms and molecules in motion. That's all we are—energy. And that is what Chinese medicine treats—energy channels or meridians, along which travels *chi*, your life energy force. Acupuncture merely unblocks the *chi* that has been prevented from flowing, allowing it to transport away pain and anxiety and restore your health and wellness. Seeing energy as the common denominator allows me to embrace both traditions."

"Interestingly," she told the class, "when U.S. president Richard Nixon visited China in 1972 to establish diplomatic relations, his entourage included American physicians. While visiting hospitals and healing centers, these M.D.s witnessed the positive results from acupuncture and embraced the idea that one can treat energy flows along the body's meridians. Upon their return to America, they instructed their labs to dissect cadavers in order to locate the meridians—with predictably disappointing lack of success."

Chi or *ki*, like *nibbana*, is hard to explain empirically. Although it can be released through treatment, it can be neither seen nor touched. But, like the intangible Western notions of spirit, enthusiasm, motivation, beauty, and revulsion, it exists.

How does this inform strategy? The answer lies in the use of *chi* in dealing with your ability to center (as you do in mindfulness) and to redirect an opponent's attack or energy.

Energy at the Interpersonal Level: Martial Arts and *Ki*

The aikido master boarded the ferry with his four students, headed downriver to Kawasaki, Japan. A group of ruffians boarded at the next stop and sat across from the group. Their leader stood up, approached the master, and challenged him to a fight. When the master demurred, the ruffian said, "You are acting cowardly in front of your own devotees!" Unruffled, and after deflecting a few more provocations, the master said, "I will accept your challenge, but not on this boat with so many people who might get hurt. I invite you to get off at the next stop, and I will deal with you there." "Agreed!" said the ruffian, and sat down with a triumphant nod to his gang members.

At the town of Hamura, the ruffian and his gang disembarked. When they turned to escort the master off the ferry, the master leaned out from the side of the boat with the ferrying pole in hand and pushed the boat away from the dock. As it drifted away, he waved goodbye to the nonplussed gang.

Thus is the martial art of *Ki-Aikido.*

Ki-Aikido: Universal Mind in a Practical World

> Your mind should be in harmony with the functioning of the universe; your body should be tuned to the movement of the universe; body and mind should be bound as one, unified with the activity of the universe.
>
> —Morihei Ueshiba, *The Art of Peace*

> Let us have a Universal Mind that loves and protects all creation and helps all things grow and develop. To unify mind and body and become one with the Universe is the ultimate purpose of our study.
>
> —Kōichi Tōhei, *Ki Sayings*

We encountered "harmony with the universe [nature]" in the previous chapter on the Tao.[1] The concept of universal mind and its variants, such as "one mind," have also had a long history in Eastern thought. We encountered an extensive application of it in Zen Buddhism (chapter 7), where it is described as nondualism. For the great ninth-century Zen master Huang Po, universal mind was the foundation of all being. Per Zen tradition, nondualism or universal mind is part of our deepest nature. Although always right before us, it is obscured by our self-centered strivings and attachments. When through years of meditation and spiritual discipline we are able to shed the obscurations of ego and desire, universal mind blazes forth. This actualization of nondualism is the path to the state that English speakers refer to as enlightenment, Zen Buddhists call *satori* (Japanese), the Buddha described as *nibbana* (Pali), and Chinese Buddhists call *dhyana.*

Zen received strong support from the military Shogun government in twelfth-century Japan and has since enjoyed a close relationship with the country's military and martial arts traditions. As a result, Zen principles undergird a number of Japanese martial arts.

The samurai sword-fighting techniques described by Miyamoto Musashi in chapter 2 serve as an example. Musashi emphasized striking an equal balance between technique, tactics, and philosophy, as well as cultivating skill across a range of military and artistic disciplines and avoiding excessive preference for any one style of combat over others. Each of these teachings bears the hallmarks of nondualism.

Manifestations of Zen values—including the integration of principle and technique, the universal and the particular, and body and mind—are evident in aikido. Takuan Sōhō, one of the great Zen masters in seventeenth-century Japan, is known for his spiritual tutoring of some of Japan's most famous swordsmen, including Musashi. In his essay "The Mysterious Record of Immovable Wisdom," Sōhō writes:

> The mind that does not stop at all is called *immovable wisdom*. . . . The function of the intellect disappears, and one ends in a state of No-Mind-No-Thought. If one reaches the deepest point, arms, legs, and body remember what to do, but the mind does not enter into this at all. . . . This is an example of the behavior of people who have reached the depths. . . . While hands, feet, and body may move, the mind does not stop anywhere at all, and one does not know where it is.[2]

They may seem esoteric, but Sōhō's lessons for professional swordsmen incorporated an acute sense of application to the real world. He goes on:

> There is such a thing as training in principle, and training in technique. . . . Even though you know principle, you must make yourself perfectly free in technique. And even though you may wield your sword well, if you are unclear on the deepest aspects of principle, you will likely fall short of proficiency. Technique and principle are just like the two wheels of a cart.[3]

Principle and technique, although two wheels of the same cart, are nonetheless distinct, and the swordsman needs both. True technique emerges from the universal, immovable mind, the state of no-mind-no-thought. Here, in fact, is the basis for Musashi's style of swordsmanship, which he termed *gorin no sho,* the sword of no-sword.[4]

What we find in the Japanese martial arts, particularly with respect to the way of the sword, is a continuation of this integration of principle and technique, the universal and the particular, and body and mind. This evolution comes to its culmination in Morihei Ueshiba's art of aikido.

THE ORIGIN OF AIKIDO: LOVE AND HARMONY

In Japanese, the term aikido can be broken down into the words *ai* (joining, unifying, combining), *ki* (spirit, or energy), and *do* (way or path). In effect, aikido means "way of unifying energy," referring to methods of controlling an attacker's attempts to harm with minimal effort and minimal harm to the attacker.[5] Morihei Ueshiba's genius was to synthesize his martial studies, philosophy, and religious beliefs into a defensive art that protects the attacker from injury.

Ueshiba was born in 1883 on Honshu, Japan's largest island, where as a youth he studied various forms of martial arts. In 1915, he encountered the legendary master Sōkaku Takeda, a hard and dangerous man. Ueshiba was totally taken by Takeda's martial prowess and studied with him day and night for more than a month,[6] during which he perfected *aiki-jutsu,* meaning techniques for harmonizing *ki*. In 1919, Ueshiba established his own *dōjō* for teaching *aiki-jutsu*.[7]

In 1925, a visiting naval officer challenged Ueshiba to a *kendo* match (*ken* means "wooden sword"). Ueshiba agreed but remained unarmed, which infuriated the officer. Attempting to teach the upstart a lesson, the officer repeatedly attacked Ueshiba, who easily and deftly avoided the officer's sword. Finally exhausted, the officer conceded defeat. What happened next was a defining moment of Ueshiba's life:

> Following the contest, Ueshiba went out into his garden to draw water from the well and wash the sweat from his face and hands. Suddenly, Ueshiba started to tremble and then felt immobilized. The ground beneath his feet began to shake, and he was bathed with rays of pure light streaming down from heaven. A golden mist engulfed his body, causing his petty conceit to vanish, and he assumed the form of a Golden Being. . . . The barrier between the material, hidden, and divine worlds crumbled; simultaneously Ueshiba verified that the heart of *budō* [the Way of the Warrior] was not contention but rather love, a love that fosters and protects all things.[8]

Six years later Ueshiba opened a *dōjō* in Tokyo. His fame quickly spread, and the *dōjō* attracted students from the Japanese military and other martial arts schools. Soon, his powerful *dō*, or way, came to be known as Ueshiba's aikido, the way of harmony.

Aikido is a defensively oriented martial art. The aikidoist does not attack, but responds decisively to an attack with either a throw or wrist control—the latter often ending in a pin or immobilization. Aikido technique is not about leverage, as in judo, but is designed to utilize the energy, or *ki*, of the attack in a manner that turns that energy to the detriment of the attacker. The technique is not meant to be fatal, but it can result in broken bones or even fatality depending on the vigorousness of the response and the ability of the *uke*—the one who takes the fall—to handle the resulting throw. Consequently, training in *ukemi*, taking falls, is an integral aspect of aikido training.

THE DEVELOPMENT OF AIKIDO: UNIFYING BODY AND MIND

Kōichi Tōhei began his study of aikido with Ueshiba around 1940. Ueshiba's technique was strong, relaxed, and flowing, but bewilderingly complex. Tōhei struggled to comprehend what Ueshiba was actually doing.[9] He eventually removed the veil shrouding the mystery of Ueshiba's actions through his studies with another individual, Tempū Nakamura,[10] who received his M.D. from Columbia University and taught and practiced medicine in the United

States and Canada. Nakamura was not satisfied with Western materialist approaches to health care and sought an alternative perspective, eventually going to India to study yoga. Upon his return to Japan, he began to teach that mind and body are not two different entities but one unified system. Mind was the source, and body was the current—or simply, it is mind that moves the body. Our daily actions serve to isolate our mind from our body, as when we are angry or frustrated, or when we abuse our body in an effort to get ahead or cope with life's daily grind. Nakamura taught that only through the (re)unification of mind and body can we fully release and effectively utilize our *ki.*

KI AND *KI-AIKIDO*

The concept of *ki,* which translates most simply as energy or spirit, was derived from the Chinese notion of *qi* or *chi.* In Japanese, however, it carries a range of meanings depending on its context.[11] It is similar in this respect to the English word "spirit." We speak of spirited action, the human spirit, team spirit, and the Holy Spirit—meanings that range from the mundane to the sacred. The term *ki* carries this same range of meanings. When Ueshiba, Nakamura, or Tōhei spoke of *ki,* they meant something both natural and profound. *Ki* is that which animates not only our individual existence, but also the very existence of the universe. Through mind and body unification, we join our *ki* with the *ki* of the universe. A fundamental property of the universe,[12] *ki* is neither created nor destroyed. But it can be mobilized, and this is the central purpose of unifying mind and body.

Tōhei *Sensei* (teacher) was able to fuse the teachings of Ueshiba and Nakamura into a single comprehensive system, which he termed *Shin Tōitsu Aikidō,* "aikido with mind and body unified," which is usually shortened to *Ki-Aikido. Ki-Aikido* is based on principles and ideas deriving from both the martial art of aikido and the Japanese system of yoga taught by Nakamura. Because of its focus on the expression of *ki* over physical strength, *Ki-Aikido* is often regarded as a "soft" style. This is, in fact, a point of pride for *Ki-Aikido* practitioners. When a person is thrown according to one of the "hard" styles, he or she may feel it for days afterward. When thrown by a practitioner of *Ki-Aikido,* however, a person often cannot tell exactly why or how it happened, and it almost never results in lasting negative side effects.

Both Ueshiba and Tōhei recognized that mind and body unification was the key factor allowing individuals to join their *ki* with that of the universe. Part of the genius of Tōhei's development of *Ki-Aikido* was that his methods for instructing mind and body unification enabled even a beginner to directly experience that unification.

Six Principles of *Ki-Aikido*

Tōhei distilled his method into a set of six simple yet profound rules, which he termed "Principles of Mind and Body Unification." These principles constitute both a practical psychology of being in the world and a concise model for the realization of universal mind. They are both physical and mental in nature:

1. Keep one point.
2. Relax completely.
3. Keep weight underside.
4. Extend *ki.*
5. Take the *ki* (of the situation) to the one point.
6. Universal action: Let action manifest naturally.

The first four principles form the foundation for the manifestation of universal mind. Numbers 1 and 4 (keep one point, and extend *ki*) are principles for the mind; numbers 2 and 3 (relax completely, and keep weight underside) are principles for the body. Numbers 5 and 6 are principles for action.

1. CENTERING—KEEP ONE POINT

> In Buddhism, we should start from our essence of mind. . . . In all preaching, stray not from the essence of mind.
>
> —HUINENG, *The Diamond Sutra*

> If you can understand the mind, everything else is included. . . . Unless you see your mind, reciting so much prose is useless.
>
> —BODHIDHARMA, *The Zen Teaching of Bodhidharma*

While serving in the Japanese military in World War II, Tōhei was deployed to Japanese-occupied China, where he realized that he could calm the fears and anxieties brought on by combat by focusing on a point about two inches below his navel in the center of his torso.[13] He called this his "one point," and maintaining concentration at this center became the foundation of his ideas about mind and body unification.

There are several ways to think about your one point. In a standing position, your one point is roughly equivalent to your physical center of gravity; however, it is foremost a point of mental concentration. As Tōhei discovered, focusing on the one point is the best way to calm the mind and relax the body.

How would an individual's one point, so easily understood as a physical location in the body, apply to an entire organization? In business, the one point would be the equivalent to your organization's basic purpose. For example, whenever he visited any of Dollar General's (DG) five thousand stores, CEO Cal Turner Jr. would reinforce DG's mission of providing limited-income buyers with the lowest price for basic consumables such as clothing, cleaning supplies, and home health products. Turner kept a list of DG's values and mission on a laminated card in his breast pocket and would pull it out when he met with store managers, who had the same card in their pockets. Any new hire, any merchandise purchase, and any new store location had to stand up to these basic values. By making frequent reference to DG's values, by writing stories and examples for the firm's monthly newsletter, and by identifying with his customers by shopping for his own clothes at DG, Cal was reinforcing DG's one point. Holding this one point allowed DG employees across rural America to behave according to the company's values with limited supervision or control systems. Dollar General had reached the state of no-mind-no-thought, where "one reaches the deepest point[;] arms, legs, and body remember what to do, but the mind does not enter into this at all."[14] In other words, DG and its employees were on a values autopilot that freed them to face challenges without needing to go up the chain of command for directions.

Consider another example. Aston Martin's one point was "automotive art," expressed in each supercar with "beauty, power, and soul." When we visited the spotless Aston Martin factory in Gaydon, England, we spoke with Jasper, a former yacht builder, who was attaching a large swath of stitched leather over the interior of a passenger door. He paused in his work and greeted us with a smile. When we asked him how he felt about working for Aston, he said: "I have reached the pinnacle of my profession. I am crafting part of a vehicle that will not only be one of the world's most beautiful, but it will be appreciated by whomever sits in it, looks at it, feels it, and smells it. Meantime, I get to look around me and see dozens of breathtaking Aston Martins at various stages of creation. We are small enough that we can all see each other and their work, and, when a finished car comes off the line, the end-of-the-line associate fires up the engine and we all get to hear the glorious symphony."

We later asked the same question of one of the seamstresses stitching together the swaths of leather that Jasper would install. She answered: "When a driver sits in his Aston, he is coddled in my handiwork. My stitch is slightly different from those of the other five seamstresses. Each car has over two hundred thousand stitches in the leather interior, and each of us can identify whose work—Doreen's, Briana's, or mine—is in those seats, doors, and dashboards of any of our beauties by a quick look inside." Aston Martin, on the whole, was acting as one body—a body that had identified its one point.

In another example, we turn to Wall Street in the mid-2000s, when Standard and Poor's Global Ratings headquarters sat across from the famous "Charging Bull." Inside was a remarkable group of young analysts known for their integrity and analytical horsepower. Their intelligence rivaled that of their counterparts at the investment banks across the street, but the S&P analysts preferred the collegial, almost academic, 9-to-5 lifestyle of their work. They also held inordinate power over the institutions that they rated. Indeed, at least one client CEO complained about the "humorless arrogance of that power-obsessed kid sitting in my office" when S&P conducted diligence on the CEO's company.[15]

Rating a bond was a committee activity that involved quantitative assessments of an issuer's business and creditworthiness. It also involved qualitative assessments of the issuer organization and its leadership. A certain "feel" was required; it was said that S&P CEO Leo O'Neill could walk into any institution's factory, headquarters, or customer service center and within five minutes predict what its bond rating would be. (Leo's integrity kept him from sharing his prediction before the rating committee finished its work and published its rating.)

S&P's one point was absolute integrity, both in the rating process and in personal behavior. The firm resisted issuers' pressures to speed up the process so that they—the corporation, municipality, or financial institution, for example—could access the funds they needed by getting their bonds to market as quickly as possible. Standard and Poor's had to balance the fact that although the bond-issuing institution paid the bill, the true customer was the investor. S&P took the time needed to guarantee that investors knew how much risk they were taking when buying these bonds. (We will come back to S&P and the crash of 2008 in a moment.)

Now, back at the *dōjō:* The *sensei* is in front of you, telling you to stand with feet shoulder-width apart and focus on that physical spot two inches below your navel. The way to keep your attention centered on the one point is through the practice of *ki* breathing, where you breathe in slowly, taking your breath all the way down to the one point, hold it there momentarily, and then breathe slowly out. Of course, anatomically, you breathe in and out of your lungs. Nonetheless, you experience your breath as if it actually does move to and from your center. This occurs because *ki* breathing involves breathing with the diaphragm rather than the chest. This allows for deeper, more relaxed breaths, producing a paradoxical state of energized calm. When practicing *ki* breathing, you experience how keeping one point can result in the full expression of all four principles of mind/body unification. Tōhei taught:

> Breathe out so that your breath travels infinitely to the ends of the Universe, breathe in so that your breath reaches your one point and continues infinitely there. . . . At night when all is quiet and calm, do this alone, and you will feel like you are the Universe and the Universe is you. It will lead to the supreme ecstasy of being one with the Universe. At this moment, the life power that is rightfully yours will be fully activated.[16]

How does an organization keep the one point? As we saw with Dollar General, Cal Turner visited stores constantly to spin the flywheel and keep spreading and instilling the message.

But an institution can lose the one point.

At Standard & Poor's, there were five divisions, four of which were based on client industry groups—corporations, municipalities, financial institutions, and insurance companies. The fifth division was different—it was based on products. This division, the Structured Finance group, specialized in rating new issuances of sophisticated financial products, such as mortgage-backed securities. Because of these products' complexity, the group's associates were required to possess sophisticated quantitative skills beyond those required in S&P's industry groups. As a result, Structured Finance was considered the most elite group in the firm. Its analysts were the highest paid, and they were considered the most intellectually capable and the most likely to be offered lucrative job opportunities at Wall Street's major banks. S&P's other analysts aspired to join the group.

Yet, infamously, it was S&P's Structured Products team that missed the disaster brewing in the mortgage-backed securities (MBS) market in the lead-up to the 2007–8 global financial crisis. In the mid-2000s, mortgage-backed securities, a type of debt security that bundled large numbers of individual home mortgages, grew increasingly popular with the Wall Street banks that issued them and the investors who purchased them. The credit-worthiness of an MBS depended on the ability of individual borrowers whose mortgages were bundled in it to make their loan payments. By diversifying the risk of default on a mortgage across the thousands of loans bundled into an MBS, these instruments, their issuers argued, were a low-risk way for investors to benefit from the interest paid by home-loan borrowers.

But financial markets greatly underestimated the inherent risk. As housing prices declined nationwide in 2006 and 2007, large swaths of borrowers went into default and prices for mortgage-backed securities began to collapse. This decline in the MBS market played a major role in setting off the devastating global financial crisis and economic recession of the following years.

Investigations of the financial crisis's causes identified S&P's Structured Products team as a key culprit in the MBS market's implosion. In the years preceding 2007–8, S&P consistently issued strong AAA ratings to MBS securities backed by high-risk mortgages. The firm was found to have overvalued the benefits of diversification advertised by issuing banks, and it had not thoroughly investigated the individual mortgages on which the MBS creditworthiness relied. The overly optimistic ratings offered a false sense of security to unsuspecting investors and contributed to the growth of a bubble in the MBS market.

What drove S&P's elite Structured Products division to lose sight of the firm's core value of ratings integrity and miss the negative signals in the MBS market? Perhaps it was arrogance on the part of the analysts, the group's isolation from the rest of the firm, or the influence of the issuing banks who funded the ratings process. Regardless of the cause, S&P had lost its one point.

Takata Corporation is another example. Based in Tokyo, Takata started as a manufacturer of child seats, seat belts, and seat covers for automobiles, as well as parachutes. Its mission was focused on driver and passenger safety. Its one point was expressed on plaques hung on the walls of factories, the headquarters building, and distribution centers: "Eliminate fatalities." The firm's expertise lay in fabrics and plastics, which extended logically to airbags. In the late 1990s, Takata started sourcing its airbag inflators from a Mercedes Benz joint venture in Vance, Alabama. Unfortunately, an untraceable flaw in the detonator caused numerous fatalities in Takata-equipped Hondas, Toyotas, and other automobiles.[17] Having outsourced a critical component to a supply chain member over which it had no dominion, Takata lost control of its one point.

Identifying, proclaiming, and knowing an organization's one point is critical, but it is not enough. Unlike a human, an organization does not and cannot go to sleep at night. It does not regenerate through rest. Just as we need to work at keeping our values at our centers, so do our organizations. It takes work, perpetual vigilance, and constant reinforcement. Aikido philosophy can help us do that.

2. RELAXATION—RELAX COMPLETELY

> The *Inward Training* teaches that deep breaths are more than simple breaths; we breathe in energy that helps us to soothe ourselves, calm negative emotions, and relax.
>
> —Michael Puett and Christine Gross-Loh, *The Path*

Each of us carries around a certain degree of tightness and tension in our body. This tension can be a chronic consequence of our lifestyle or a situational response to circumstances. Whatever the origin, tension is always detrimental to our short-term ability to act and our long-term health and well-being.

In *Ki-Aikido* there are two main forms of relaxation, which can be termed nonactive and active. The nonactive form is sometimes called "dead" relaxation, although this characterization is somewhat misleading. Nonactive relaxation is equivalent to going limp or lying down. This might be appropriate as we lie on the couch after a long, hard day, but it serves no other functional purpose. Active relaxation, on the other hand, is always beneficial. Its practice can keep that long, hard day from being so draining and debilitating.

Active relaxation entails letting go of all the tightness and tension in our body but not the active energy coursing through us. Active relaxation of the arm relaxes the musculature but allows the arm complete freedom of movement. The experience of active relaxation is one of calm readiness. To relax completely, therefore, is to rid our mind and body of all tension and create a state with the potential for experiencing and responding to any circumstance. "Relaxation is truly an elixir of life. . . . The true method of relaxation . . . enables us to meet each day with a spirit like that of a mild spring breeze."[18]

It is an interesting characteristic of relaxation that people often think they are relaxed when they are not. People who carry a large amount of chronic tension throughout their body find it especially difficult to relax completely. A little bit of relaxation can feel inordinately large, since they are judging it relative to their usual state. For some people, we have found that complete, active relaxation produces a powerful emotional release. They had no idea the degree to which they had bound up mind and body in a shell of tension.

A way to think about corporate relaxation is to consider firms that are constantly reaffirming their values and rewarding those who keep them. In this case, relaxation does not imply laziness, lack of urgency, or a slowing of the pace necessary to compete. Instead, it means eliminating the distractions to smooth operations and the stressors that inhibit flow and creativity. It even means eliminating anger—the recipe for both employee and customer turnover.

Amer Group in Helsinki, Finland, includes four divisions: automotive, tobacco, fashion, and sporting goods, each of which works independently when facing customers and competitors. The auto dealerships and Marlboro cigarette factories have no reason to "find synergies," nor do the Marimekko design and McGregor Golf businesses. But the executives from all four businesses convene quarterly to celebrate successes and to advise each other when one faces challenges or difficulties. These are not meetings where the CEO beats up on the company presidents and their staffs. Rather, they are intended to provide mutual support and suggestions for corrective actions when things are not going as planned.

The two-day quarterly meetings begin with an evening of round-table dining and a visit to the sauna. The next full day of meetings ends with squash and tennis, a group dinner with blinis and hearty toasts with frozen vodka, and a group sauna.

Why the sauna? Finland, where the sauna was invented, boasts 5 million people and a million saunas. Many of them are in homes, where the Saturday family ritual is likely to include fifteen minutes in the sauna. Finns are not demonstrative, showing neither affection nor anger. A pair of eight-minute sessions in a sauna is so enervating, however, that it is difficult to hold on to negative emotions. The sauna is a means to family harmony without the need to talk things out. This holds true for corporations such as Amer Group, as well. During its quarterly meetings, a recording of piano and cello concerts plays throughout dinner, at coffee and lunch breaks, and in the sauna. CDs are distributed to the participants to take home so that they can recall the meetings with pleasure and calm.

When Amer built its new headquarters in Helsinki, the plans included a sauna-in-the-round in the basement. Executive meetings are held there from time to time, during which men and women sit in a circle on teak benches, facing the heated rocks and water bucket in the middle. (An interpreter told the senior author: "When our meetings include Americans, we erect a visual barrier between men and women. You Americans are so ashamed of your bodies!") Sometimes Amer uses the sauna as a competitive advantage. When Amer was negotiating to acquire McGregor Golf, the Finnish executives invited the McGregor team to the sauna immediately after the Americans had deplaned from their ten-hour trip. When some of the travel-weary McGregor people grumbled, their CFO turned to them and said, "C'mon, guys. We have an advantage here. After all, we pretty much live in a sauna in Athens, Georgia, anyway. Buck up." The gathered group came to a meeting of the minds sooner than expected.

Much like Rodale Press and its central meditation room in chapter 6, Amer Group provided a literal relaxation spot for its employees. And both Rodale and Amer conducted their business review sessions as opportunities for mutual assistance, with accompanying comradery and relaxed respect. As a result, both companies engaged in an active form of relaxation, which facilitated the flow of *ki* internally.

3. GROUNDING—KEEP WEIGHT UNDERSIDE

The meaning of the *Ki-Aikido* concept of "keeping weight underside" is most straightforward when we consider Tōhei's characterization: "In a natural state, the weight of objects is naturally underside. Therefore the physical expression of living calmness is that the weight of every part of our body is also underside."[19] A sailboat metaphor can clarify this. The underside weight of the keel of the boat keeps it upright. If this were not the case, the boat would tip over.

Bodily tension usually manifests itself in the torso and creates a condition *Ki-Aikido* describes as "weight upperside." In this state, the person is unstable and easily taken off balance. By letting the weight of all parts of the body be underside, not only is the body relaxed, but it also feels naturally and effectively grounded.

Next time you are at the beach, stand in the shallows with the waves breaking against you. You will immediately be able to tell the difference between weight upperside and weight underside. If the former is the case, even small waves will knock you over with ease. In the latter state, you will remain stable as the waves sweep past.

The grounding of weight underside is one of the critical factors that allow the *Ki-Aikido* practitioner to receive the energy of an attack by neither fighting the energy nor giving in to it. It also creates a solid foundation from which to move in any direction as needed.

This gets more complex when the practitioner is in motion. On the one hand, moving with proper weight underside creates a stable, powerful action. On the other, dancers often balk at this idea because they are taught to be light and to float as they move. During a lift, the weightlifter certainly does not want the lifted object to be heavy and the weight underside. So what is the answer? Does this case argue for the weight being upperside?

The answer is no, but this requires a more sophisticated understanding of weight underside. Grounding is not equivalent to the notion of being rooted. The *Ki-Aikido* practitioner standing with weight underside is not rooted to one spot but is more akin to floating. In effect, he or she floats on the surface of the ground as a boat floats on the surface of the water. This carries over directly to movement as well. Grounded movement is actually a form of floating. This becomes clearer when we understand that at this point "keep weight underside" effectively merges with the fourth principle—extend *ki*, which we will come to in a moment.

In a strategic context, keeping weight underside can help organizations avoid being knocked off their feet by competitive pressures and unforeseen challenges. Strategists first need to identify the capabilities, principles, or behaviors that—like keeping weight underside for a *Ki-Aikido* practitioner—help the organization remain resilient in the face of opposing forces and provide the grounding necessary to pursue ambitious initiatives. These weight underside pillars can range from organizational core values or products or services in which the organization has a core competency to a geography in which it has a competitive advantage. Initiatives can then be developed that leverage these principles and ensure that the organization's strategy keeps weight underside.

EdCon of Johannesburg, South Africa, was a mass retailer much in the style of Walmart. Its expansion through acquisition had a simple principle: Stay south of the Equator. Christo Klaasen, EdCon's head of strategy, told the authors: "We've built a solid foundation in south and middle Africa and understand both the logistical challenges of our vast geographic areas and the needs of our emerging-economy customers. The large northern retailers—Tesco, Carrefour, Walmart—are not interested in our markets, yet. But when they look in this direction, we will be so ensconced and well-networked that we will be immovable." With this one point in hand, EdCon searched the Southern Hemisphere for likely business combinations. It identified Coles and Meyer in Australia, Makro in Argentina and Brazil, and Supermercados Disco in Uruguay and Argentina. EdCon then assembled a list of conversations-to-be-had with several of these "underside" firms.

4. ENGAGEMENT—EXTEND *KI*

> When you still yourself, you are getting close to the Way. . . . After you have gained a sense of stillness, walk into the room. You immediately sense the room and all the people sitting there in all of their complexity. . . . Without saying a word, with just a glance, you have quietly taken the measure of the people around you.
>
> —MICHAEL PUETT and CHRISTINE GROSS-LOH, *The Path*

It is sometimes stated that this principle should be "*ki* is extending." This is because, according to the perspective of *Ki-Aikido,* we are always extending our *ki,* whether we realize it or not. When a person walks into a room, his or her posture, movements, and facial expression have an immediate impact on others present. They perceive that person's energy—his or her *ki*—as negative (angry or upset), neutral, or positive (happy or relaxed).

The point of this principle is not to regard *ki* as something that can be turned on or off like a current, because our *ki* is always extending. Rather, the critical points are that we have control over what kind of *ki* we extend (positive or negative, for example), and we have control over the direction in which that *ki* is extended. We can send our energy in a single focused direction or in all directions simultaneously, our *ki* forming an energy sphere with our one point at the center.

This is best understood experientially through proper practice. One further point, however, is of critical importance. In any situation, the central value of the spherical extension of our *ki* is that it completely engages us with our situation. The extension of our *ki* becomes coextensive with the opening of our awareness. In the midst of an attack, fear and anxiety tend to result in our pulling in our *ki,* dissociating ourselves from the situation. When this is the case, we cannot process the information required to adequately resolve the issue. The full extension of our *ki* awareness, however, makes it possible to fully connect to our world and receive all the information needed to move forward.

As Jennifer Jasinski, a Liberty Mutual executive and participant in one of our aikido sessions with instructor Jonathan Doner, explained to us:

> Jonathan kept telling us to "get bigger" and "take up more space" to extend our *ki.* This was reminiscent to me of strategic intuition. In the metaphor, space equals openness and *ki* equals knowledge. By taking up space and extending our *ki*—leveraging our innate energies—we are enabled to act more effectively, in the same way that keeping an open mind and filling it with knowledge enables us to pull from different experiences to act more intuitively in strategically challenging situations. In conflict resolution, this openness allows you to be comfortable with different outcomes, rather than focusing on one singular solution. In Jonathan's example, the first solution that came to mind was to use force to push someone away. The proposed solution was instead to actually bring the person with us, rather than push them away. Jonathan's depiction of this reminded me that in many situations, the untrained mind thinks of one solution that, when forced, likely will not work. Instead, I should practice openness and extending my *ki* to explore, or even happen upon . . . other solutions.[20]

By the time Walt Disney died in 1966, his company had become a conglomerate of theme parks, movie and television studios, merchandizing outlets, and resorts. None of these industries was particularly attractive on its own. Theme parks are capital intensive at one end and as come-and-go as a county fair at the other. Movies depend on blockbusters from which the actors take a large share of the profits. And merchandizing relies on fads—Frisbees, strange dolls, and Happy Meal trinkets. Still, Disney made money in all of them. How?

The answer lies in Disney's one point surrounding Mickey Mouse. The cartoons and other movies created characters that children encountered at the theme parks, where parents might pay fifteen dollars for a felt cap with thin plastic ears that cost fifty cents to make. The TV shows kept the characters alive, highlighted Disneyland and Disney World, and promoted the latest movies. The half-life of the movies themselves was several generations, as parents and grandparents took children to see the same *Snow White* they had themselves seen as children. And the cartoons involved no expensive actors or elaborate sets to eat up profits. What drove this profitability across so many "unattractive" industries? The characters. Mickey Mouse and his cohorts comprised the one point that drove expansion into Disney's various businesses.

Disney Development Corporation, Disney's new business innovation unit, met in Los Angeles in January 1994 to explore expansion opportunities. Its charge was to find new businesses within as-yet-unexploited capabilities. The assembled group was diverse in terms of race, ethnicity, and gender, but otherwise homogenous in several ways. The men were clean-shaven. Hair length extended no farther than to the tops of men's ears and women's shoulders. All were dressed in what might be called Land's End smart casual. Not a word of profanity was uttered.

The group went through several rounds of analytical work, such as industry and competitor analyses. To help discover Disney's hidden and unexploited capabilities, the group invited a few non-analytical, Taoist-leaning Imagineers to join in.

Then an earthquake hit—6.4 on the Richter scale. As the freeways buckled outside, the participants dove below the tables and desks. Whiteboards flew off their easels and chairs flipped over. When the dust began to settle and participants reassembled around the boardroom table, one of the Imagineers asked, "Why don't we simulate the experience we just had as an attraction at Disney World?"

A lively conversation ensued, during which they discussed other resort-type destinations and the immersive activities they provided. They zeroed in on the Chautauqua Institute in New York state, where visitors engage in a variety of learning programs and classes. The Imagineer mused: "Why not have a school at Disney World where we teach what we know about animation and robotics to children?"

By the time the group broke to tend to possible earthquake damage at home, the participants had in hand the blueprint for the Disney Institute at Disney World, which expanded beyond all expectations to become what is now the Disney Animation School, a nationwide education program available to public schools and colleges. In other words, Disney got bigger and took up more space as it extended the *ki* from its animation one point.

5. HARMONIZATION/ACCEPTANCE—TAKE THE *KI* (OF THE SITUATION) TO THE ONE POINT

> Can you balance your life force and embrace the One without separation?
>
> —LAO TZU, *Tao Te Ching*

The previous four principles form the basis for mind and body unification, and their proper application creates the condition of universal mind. The final two principles concern what we might term universal mind in action. No matter how well we have embodied the first four principles, all can be lost in an instant if either the fifth or sixth principle is violated.

To describe the fifth principle, we use two terms—harmonization and acceptance—because each captures an important aspect of this principle's significance. As we have noted, aikido translates as "the way of harmony," and this relates to Ueshiba's vision of aikido not as a method for winning fights but as a means for creating peace and harmony among human beings.

Philosophy aside, our specific aim is to create the optimal conditions to take any action that might be called for. As noted above, this begins with *ki* extension. By extending our *ki,* we fully engage with our situation and therefore fully connect ourselves with its process. But this is only half the story. Full engagement means harmonization, and in this case, harmonization means full acceptance of the *ki* or energy of the situation. We extend our *ki* from our one point into the world, but then we must take the *ki* of the world back to our one point. Only then are we prepared to act.

Acceptance of the energy within a situation can be very difficult. If a person is trying to hit me, what does acceptance mean? Does it mean I let him? No, it means that I fully accept that he is trying to hit me and that I am fully attentive to his actions such that I am completely aware of the blow's trajectory. Only when these two conditions are fulfilled am I ready to effectively handle the situation. Acceptance means seeing and comprehending the true nature of a situation. Harmonization means using this information to fully and completely draw the situational energy to our center.

We saw this in chapter 6 when Rodale Press was facing tough competition to its men's health newsletter. At the time of Rodale's strategic planning session, Americans' enthusiasm for health and fitness was skyrocketing. *Sports Illustrated* was the highest-circulation magazine in the country, and Rodale's newsletter was being challenged by alternative sources of health information. It was in this context, in a company whose executives routinely practiced morning meditation, that the strategy group harmonized with each other, embraced Lou C.'s unusual interpretive dance, and discovered the innovative strategy for *Men's Health*. In other words, having taken the *ki* of the situation to their one point with harmony and acceptance, they were ready to move on to the next step of letting the strategy play out—or, in other words, allowing the appropriate implementation to manifest itself naturally.

6. UNIVERSAL ACTION—LET ACTION MANIFEST NATURALLY

> Let your mind be in a state such as that of the illimitable void, but do not attach it to the idea of vacuity. Let it function freely. Whether you are in activity or at rest, let your mind abide nowhere.
>
> —HUINENG, *The Diamond Sutra*

> When you feel sleepy, you retire; when you are hungry, you eat, just as much as the fowls of the air and the lilies of the field.
>
> —D. T. SUZUKI, *Zen Buddhism*

In a classic text, Adele Westbrook and Oscar Ratti provide a detailed analysis of the interaction between the conditions of attack and the aikido techniques appropriate for response.[21] Their basic analysis includes 18 attack conditions and 35 classes of response for a total of 630 attack/response combinations. Is this universal action? Not really. These are examples of the distillation of a flowing, continuous process into a discrete, analytical framework. Tōhei said: "The techniques of [aikido] change constantly; every encounter is unique, and the appropriate response should emerge naturally. Today's techniques will be different tomorrow. Do not get caught up with the form and appearance of a challenge. [Aikido] has no form—it is the study of the spirit."[22]

Tōhei also said: "Like the eye of the typhoon, which is always peaceful, inner calm results in great strength of action. Calm and action are exactly one. Only when we keep one point and unify mind and body can we . . . perform to the utmost of our ability."[23]

Applied to an organizational context, the principle of universal action describes the possibility of strategy emerging spontaneously as the natural result of effective organizational structure, appropriate understanding of available resources, and a keen awareness of the market environment. This is the set of conditions that brings about a state ripe for the manifestation of strategic intuition.

Charlottesville, Virginia, 2018

Imagine that an aggressive person shoves the palm of his hand toward you. To protect yourself, you put your own palm up against his. The result is that, as you both exert energy, both palms move upward together toward the sky. Such is the escalation that takes place when two are arguing, competing for the same space, or attacking one another's current market. Think of the start of a price war, a new entrant, or a competitor coming into your territory. How should you respond without raising the stakes in the game?

One exercise often used to introduce aikido to the Strategic Intuition and Eastern Philosophy class at Darden is to have the participants pair up and face each other. One is told to brace herself and stand her ground firmly. Then her partner gives a hefty shove to one of her shoulders. Typically, she will be pushed off balance and will take a step backward to steady herself and keep from falling. But if instead she centers with her feet at shoulder width, focuses on her one point below her navel, lowers her center of gravity (grounding), extends her *ki* to the space around her, relaxes completely, and accepts her partner's shove against her shoulder, then her shoulder—not her foot—will slide backward and to the side as her waist twists, and her opponent's hand will continue past her into the air. Meanwhile, she will have stood her ground by flexing, while her opponent is now off balance as his hand carries him and his energy past her. (If she wanted to, she could now push her opponent down to the floor by pressing against his exposed back while he is recovering his own balance.) As one of our students said: "With respect to uncontrollable circumstances in life, the *Ki-Aikido* lesson taught me that I must be malleable and accepting of the external energies of the world rather than coming into direct conflict with them. As we saw in our combat exercises, there is a huge difference in attempting to control your opponent as opposed to merging your energy with theirs to move fluidly together in painless harmony."[24]

This philosophy may be challenging for a Western executive to embrace. Our culture prizes power, force, assertiveness, and attack. Consider the violent sport of American football. The game entails explosive collisions of powerful giants, with the goal of stopping the ball thrower or carrier by tackling him. Similarly, Western-bred boxing is a fight of force on force. Boxers meet incoming punches with punches, and the more powerful boxer wins. By contrast, in the Chinese Tai Chi and the Japanese *Ki-Aikido*, "practitioners never meet incoming hits with forceful returns. Instead, they always try to deflect incoming hits and then return with a seemingly soft but powerful push. These arts both demonstrate the Chinese philosophy of *yi-rou ke-gang* (use the soft and gentle to overcome the hard and strong)."[25]

We saw in chapter 3 how Komatsu applied Go principles and avoided direct confrontation with Caterpillar by going where CAT was not. There is more to the story. CAT had tried more than once to enter Komatsu's markets by establishing sales offices in, for example, Tokyo. Komatsu was not to be distracted. It focused on its one goal at the time—quality—and metaphorically extended its *ki* by including the Ministry of Economy, Trade, and Industry in its orbit. It brought its weight underside domestically by inspiring its employees to share in its goal. By encouraging Japanese government regulations that stymied CAT's market entry, Komatsu was able to accept CAT's foray without engaging in direct confrontation, while allowing CAT to thrust its energy into Japan without causing damage to either party.

Meanwhile, Komatsu continued to build up its capabilities. When Komatsu finally moved outside of Japan—extending its *ki* globally—it did so by pushing its own metaphorical ferry away from the industrialized West, where CAT was operating, and moving casually down to the mouth of the river, where CAT was not.

In the following chapter, we will encounter Confucius, who sought to channel leaders' energy into skillful governance of filial, institutional, and societal relationships.

Strategy Lessons from Chapter 9

1. Center yourself and keep your one point.
2. Before making a decision or taking an action, relax completely.
3. Keep grounded, with your weight underside.
4. Extend your energy—your *chi*, or *ki*—to the world around you.
5. Don't force things. Let action manifest naturally.
6. Embrace conflict, and succeed by absorbing or deflecting the actions of an aggressor.

10

Confucius

Detroit, Michigan, 2006

"Culture eats strategy for breakfast," declared Mark Fields shortly after being named head of Ford Motor Company's American division, a role in which he would be tasked with focusing Ford's massive North American operations.[1] In making the case for cultural change, Fields was quoting a popular aphorism most often attributed to Peter Drucker, one of the twentieth century's leading business consultants.[2]

Influential as Drucker may have been, he was not the first pioneering management consultant to champion the primacy of culture as the sine qua non of successful strategy. For example, Confucius, who spent his life advising city-state rulers throughout China, put culture at the center of some of history's most significant theories of organizational leadership, values, and structure.

"The great teacher," "the bedrock of Chinese civilization," and "Asia's most influential thinker" are just a few of the honorifics regularly bestowed upon Confucius. While "management consultant" is rarely seen on this list, the label is, as we will see, surprisingly apt.

There is a crucial shared notion at the heart of the theories expounded by Confucius and the modern approach to management espoused by Drucker and many others—the concept that is neatly summarized by Drucker's description of culture "eating" strategy. For a strategic initiative to succeed, it must be culturally aligned with the values of the organization.

We have seen this principle at work elsewhere in this book. For example, as described in chapter 1, Arthur D. Little's attempt to focus its health-care practice in a dedicated unit was foiled by the existing culture of distributing incoming opportunities to whomever was interested and had the time.

For Confucius, this principle manifests in the essential relationship between governance and social order. At the core of his philosophy is a belief that to govern effectively, leaders require a societal structure that enables them to pursue campaigns designed to better their state's political and economic fortunes. His teachings are devoted to offering instruction on establishing such a social order.

Confucius's Biography

Confucius was born in 551 BCE into a family of noble lineage that had fallen on hard times. As a young man, he studied ancient Chinese values and governing methods dating back hundreds of years. He would devote the remainder of his life to promulgating the resulting philosophy—a wide-ranging set of theories on personal behavior, social order, and good governance. As a professional bureaucrat, political advisor, and wandering teacher, Confucius spent decades attempting to influence the feudal rulers of Chinese city-states to adopt his principles.

Though Confucius largely failed to influence the aristocratic lords and ruling class of his era, by the time of his death in 479 BCE he had become a respected historian of Chinese antiquity and teacher of ancient rituals. It wasn't until several hundred years later that his theories began to gain widespread traction with China's rulers, eventually becoming the official state ideology in the second century BCE and continuing to play an important role in Chinese society up to today.

CONFUCIUS'S HISTORICAL CONTEXT

Confucius lived and taught during an era of intense military conflict and political turmoil known as China's Spring and Autumn period (approximately 771–476 BCE), an epoch that corresponded to the world's Axial Age. Foreign invasions and internal power struggles had dramatically weakened the ruling Zhou Dynasty, and the deterioration of its unifying political, moral, and cultural force gave way to competition between feudal rulers of rival states.[3] Confucius attributed the social uncertainty and political turmoil of his age to increasing moral decay within society and the corruption he observed among the feudal rulers. In his history of the period, *The Spring and Autumn Annals,* Confucius uses the term *ba,* or "tyrant," to describe these feudal lords.[4] His description of the ruling class as tyrannical, rather than simply powerful or ambitious, illustrates Confucius's view that the rulers' authority came through force rather than merit.

Disillusioned, Confucius turned to the study of classic writings of the early Zhou period several hundred years earlier, a time marked by political stability and social harmony. He believed these teachings had the potential to facilitate a more stable, peaceful world order than that of his own time.

Major Themes in Confucius's *Analects*

A prolific author, Confucius compiled and edited several tomes of canonical writings from Chinese antiquity, but he made no effort to record his own teachings based on this ancient wisdom. As he said about himself: "I am a transmitter, rather than an original thinker. I trust and enjoy the teachings of the ancients" (*The Analects*, 7:1).

Fortunately, Confucius's teachings were documented by his disciples after his death, much as Socratic thought was encapsulated in Plato's writing. The text traditionally treated as the principal source of Confucius's thoughts is known as *The Analects,* a guide for moral behavior for individuals, families, societies, and governments.[5] Through these guidelines, Confucius aimed to help return Chinese society to the sense of orderliness and stability that had prevailed in past eras.

The Analects consists of twenty chapters offering parables, proverbs, and adages arranged in an order that at times can seem random. (References here are in the form of chapter:verse and unless noted are from Thomas Cleary, *The Essential Confucius.*) *The Analects* is also wide-reaching, addressing topics including individual ethics, proper familial relationships, and governing philosophy. These two qualities—an apparent lack of logical structure and the breadth of topics—have earned *The Analects* and Confucius a reputation for inscrutability.

However, below that opaque surface *The Analects* offers an elegant framework designed to help individuals, families, organizations, and societies enjoy more stable and prosperous lives. These ideas, some of the most influential in human history, have been the subject of hundreds of years of scholarship in China and beyond.

The following is an overview of a generally accepted understanding of the five core themes of *The Analects:* self-cultivation, continuous learning, the values of a noble person, societal roles and codes of conduct, and precision in language.

THEME 1: INDIVIDUAL SELF-CULTIVATION AS A GATEWAY TO SOCIAL HARMONY

> Don't worry about having no position; worry about that whereby you may effectively become established. Don't worry that no one recognizes you; seek to be worthy of recognition. (4:14)

> If leaders are courteous, their people will not dare to be disrespectful. If leaders are just, people will not dare to be intractable. If leaders are trustworthy, people will not dare to be dishonest. (13:4)

Confucius's philosophy of education, veneration of family, and respect for authority permeates many Asian cultures, including those of Japan, Korea, Vietnam, and China. The core assumption of his teachings is that social progress can be achieved only through individual self-development.

This might seem counterintuitive, since the connection between self-development and improvement at the level of society may not be obvious. The key lies in understanding how Confucius went about defining individual identity. He did not abide by the commonly held Western view of the individual self as independent and self-contained. Rather, Confucius saw human beings as social creatures whose identities were derived from and expressed through their interactions with and conduct toward others. Much as in the game of Go (chapter 3), where individual pieces have no power or meaning except in their connections with other pieces, in Confucianism there is no distinction between the individual and the interpersonal. Consequently, self-cultivation must necessarily be a relational exercise, and to improve your character you must address how you treat those around you. If all members of a society, at every level of socioeconomic and political status, cultivate virtuous qualities through ethical interpersonal behavior, then the character of the society will improve.

Translating this insight to a modern organization suggests that effective culture—the kind that allows the organization to benefit from the manifestation of strategic intuition—is defined by how the organization's leadership, employees, clients, and other stakeholders treat each other. And to improve culture, leaders must model, encourage, and reward upstanding interpersonal behavior on the part of their management teams and others associated with the organization.

Accomplishing this requires clarity about what these virtuous characteristics are and what actions help us cultivate them in ourselves and others. This is laid out in themes 2 through 4.

THEME 2: BECOMING *JUNZI* THROUGH CONTINUOUS SELF-DEVELOPMENT

> Be an exemplary man of learning, not a trivial pedant. (6:13)

> If you like humaneness but don't like learning, it degenerates into folly. If you like knowledge but don't like learning, it degenerates into looseness. If you like trust but don't like learning, it degenerates into depredation. If you like honesty but don't like learning, it degenerates into stricture. If you like bravery but don't like learning, it degenerates into disorder. If you like strength but don't like learning, it degenerates into wildness. (17:8)

Much of Confucius's philosophy focuses on defining the behavior, thoughts, and beliefs of an ethical person. *Junzi* was the term Confucius used to describe a person who had attained these virtuous qualities. Throughout *The Analects,* Confucius defines how a *junzi* is to perceive the world, behave in various scenarios, and interact with others.

While *junzi* can refer to a noble person or a gentleman, it can also be translated to mean the son of the ruler, or prince. To Confucius, the son of the current monarch and heir to the throne had a special obligation to cultivate and model moral qualities. Living a life of virtue would help the *junzi* develop the inner peace necessary to become an effective ruler. Furthermore, by displaying these exemplary behaviors, the *junzi* would encourage his subjects to also lead virtuous lives. In explaining to a feudal lord how one can lead without relying on violence, Confucius said: "If you desire good, the people will be good. The nature of the *junzi* is like the wind, the nature of the inferior man is like the grass. When the wind blows over the grass, it always bends" (12:19).

One of Confucius's breakthrough distinctions was to not limit becoming a *junzi* to those of high birth. He broadened the meaning of the term to include anyone who reached a state of high virtue through honorable behavior and thought. Nobility became an earned, meritocratic value rather than a birthright bestowed upon a select few. For Confucius, *junzi* was a status available to anyone living a life aligned with the Tao. Such a life, in turn, was defined by a set of virtuous qualities. The process of cultivating these qualities, which he described using the term *xue,* was the very purpose of human life.

Xue, directly translated, can be understood as "learning." For Confucius, *xue* represented much more than just intellectual training or formal education. *The Analects* describes *xue* as a continual cycle of study, action, and self-reflection undertaken over a lifetime. Recounting his own experience, Confucius described his *xue* as a decades-long journey of incremental progress: "At fifteen my heart was set on learning; at thirty I stood firm; at forty I was unperturbed; at fifty I knew the mandate of heaven; at sixty my ear was obedient; at seventy I could follow my heart's desire without transgressing the norm" (2:4).[6]

THEME 3: THE VALUES OF A NOBLE PERSON

> Exemplary people understand matters of justice; small people understand matters of profit [self-aggrandizement]. (1:16)
>
> Cultivated people consider justice foremost. When cultivated people have courage without justice, they become rebellious. When petty people have courage without justice, they become brigands. (17:23)

Throughout *The Analects,* Confucius offers anecdotes, answers questions, and reflects on his own experiences in an effort to clarify the behaviors and attitudes of the *junzi.* Taken in aggregate, his parables offer a set of five virtues that when cultivated can unlock one's *junzi* nature.

Ren

The foundational idea of Confucianism, *ren* is often translated as "benevolence," "compassion," "love," "humaneness," or "goodness." *Ren* refers to the energy present when a virtuous person engages in any interaction with another. In fact, embodying *ren* is the defining characteristic of a *junzi,* and attaining *ren* is the ultimate purpose of *xue* learning.

Ren, then, can be understood as an all-encompassing ethical energy that imbues all moral behavior. Confucius explained that when "a *ren* man wishes himself to be established, he sees that others are established, and, when he wishes himself to be successful, he sees that others are successful" (6:30). In a later passage of *The Analects,* he is even more succinct. Asked by a student about the meaning of *ren,* he replied, "Love others" (12:22).

Li

To identify an individual imbued with *ren,* we observe his or her actions. Because *ren* itself is a personal trait rather than a behavior, Confucius introduced two principles for translating *ren* into action: *li* and *yi.* Often translated as "propriety" and "righteousness," these concepts are designed to help guide individual behavior in a wide array of scenarios.

Li, or propriety, refers to knowing and abiding by established rituals and codes of conduct (described in theme 4). In addition to significant life events such as births, weddings, and funerals, Confucius's teachings extended ritualistic codes of conduct to a much more quotidian scale.

Confucius portrayed our daily lives as filled with opportunities for ritualized behavior. In every interaction, individuals are subject to socially agreed-upon norms depending on their relative social status, age, gender, and other personal qualities. Confucius argued that individuals have a responsibility to understand and align their words, thoughts, and actions to these codes of conduct.

This practice, *li,* reaffirms the link in Confucian philosophy between individual self-development and the cultivation of an effective broader social fabric. If a society has defined clear social norms that are rooted in treating everyone with *ren* compassion, we can develop our own *ren* qualities by following these norms and thus exhibiting *li.* In a more practical sense, an organization is destined to function more effectively if all its members are aware of, agree upon, and abide by a clearly established set of norms and behaviors for any given scenario.

Yi

Typically translated as "righteousness" or "judgment," *yi* describes the ability to take *ren* actions in the absence of clearly established norms. Comparable to the Western notion of right versus wrong, *yi* is taken to mean both the qualities that are inherent to all ethical actions and our ability to identify and act on behaviors that exhibit those qualities.

"The *junzi* puts *yi* first" (17:21). While embodying *ren* (compassion) is the defining characteristic of a *junzi*, knowledge of *yi* allows the *junzi* to judge which actions best embody *ren*.

Two of the cornerstone qualities of *yi* are reciprocity, as embodied in the concepts of yin and yang, whose opposite polarities require each other (see chapter 8), and the golden rule, expressed by Confucius as "do not impose on others what you yourself do not desire" (12:2).

Zhi

Zhi refers to the concept of practical wisdom. Confucius said: "What you know, you know, what you don't know, you don't know. This is *zhi*" (2:17). For Confucian self-development to be possible, engaging in the practice of *xue* (learning) is not enough. Not only must we be able to learn new information, we must translate that knowledge into skillful action. *Zhi* is the enabling infrastructure that allows the *junzi* to act on his learning and thus develop in himself all other virtuous qualities.

Xin

Traditionally translated as "integrity" or "trustworthiness," *xin* describes the importance of aligning one's words and actions. To explain the importance of *xin*, Confucius referenced, as he often did, the practices of Chinese antiquity: "The ancients were hesitant to speak, fearing that their actions would not do justice to their words" (4:22).

Confucius understood *xin* as the practice of fulfilling one's commitments to others. This principle is crucial to Confucius's philosophy for how it influences both actions and words. Acting in accordance to *li* (propriety) and *yi* (judgment) requires us to exhibit trustworthiness. Furthermore, *xin* requires that we speak thoughtfully, so as to avoid even accidentally making statements by which we cannot abide. Throughout *The Analects,* Confucius repeatedly stresses deliberate speech as an integral part of *junzi* behavior. As in the Tao's admonition to express oneself completely and then keep quiet (chapter 8), "the *junzi* desires to be halting in speech but sharp in action" (4:24).

Confucius was adamant that achieving *junzi* status requires all five virtues to manifest, and that neither individual self-development nor social progress is possible if any of the five are lacking.

THEME 4: SOCIETAL ROLES AND CODES OF CONDUCT

> Have leaders be leaders, have administrators be administrators, have fathers be fathers, have sons be sons. . . . Of a truth, if leaders do not lead, administrators do not administer, fathers do not behave as fathers, and sons do not behave as sons, then even if there were grain, how could I eat of it? (12:11)

Confucius's emphasis on the importance of prescribed roles and codes of conduct is one of the most tangible hallmarks of his teachings. Abiding by commonly agreed-upon notions of appropriate behavior is at the heart of Confucian virtue, and defined societal roles are the mechanism by which these codes of conduct are delineated.

In *The Analects,* Confucius outlines five relationship archetypes: between a ruler and his subjects, a father and son, a husband and wife, an elder brother and younger brother, and between two friends.

For each category of relationship, there is a hierarchical definition that assigns higher and lower status to each participant. Based on relative status, specific responsibilities and rites are prescribed to both members of the relationship. For example, while a subject has clear responsibilities vis-à-vis his relationship to his king, the king is equally obligated to abide by a defined set of behaviors with respect to his subject. The one exception is the relationship among friends, which is considered to be an interaction among equals, although this relationship too comes with prescribed expectations of behavior.

A shared understanding of respective responsibilities, and each participant's commitment to abiding by those responsibilities, was for Confucius the foundation of a stable social order. By specifying the nuances of rites and rituals within each relationship, he clearly defined the appropriate attitudes, behaviors, and actions, creating a paradigm where *li* (propriety) would foment social stability.

THEME 5: PRECISION IN LANGUAGE

> If terminology is not correct, then what is said cannot be followed. If what is said cannot be followed, then work cannot be accomplished. If work cannot be accomplished, then ritual and music cannot be developed. If ritual and music cannot be developed, then criminal punishments will not be appropriate. If criminal punishments are not appropriate, the people cannot make a move. Therefore, the *junzi* needs to have his terminology applicable to real language, and his speech must accord with his actions. (13:3)

Throughout *The Analects,* Confucius emphasizes the importance of accurate and consistent communication, which he refers to as "the rectification of names." Confucius placed primal importance on the principle of aligning the labels assigned to people and objects with their respective function or behavior. This emphasis on using accurate language can be thought of in relation to *li* (propriety). After all, appropriate action is determined based on the role each individual plays in a relationship, and that role is often ascertained based on the label affixed to the individual's social standing. If the individual is mislabeled, then identifying appropriate behavior is that much more challenging. Therefore, the rectification of names is a crucial prerequisite to developing *li* (propriety) and *yi* (judgment),

For example, consider the following experience of Dole Foods in Honduras.

La Ceiba, Honduras, 1974

The Dole Foods labor unions had presented a package of demands that included providing gloves to the stevedores who worked in the refrigerated holds of the banana boats. Although the company routinely provided work tools, such as wrenches and machetes, it was against policy to provide uniforms or other clothing. Honoring this request might set a precedent. Also, buried in the package was a demand for "the seventh day." The request was simple: If a worker toiled a full sixth day of the week, a common practice during harvest season, he would be awarded a full additional day's overtime pay.

The dilemma facing Luke Robinson, Dole's head of human resources, was that one tool typically employed by negotiators was unavailable: There is no word in Spanish for "compromise." There is *compromiso,* which means a mutual commitment (co-promise), such as a date, an appointment, or even a betrothal. But the notion of finding a middle ground in a conflict is not in the vocabulary.

What do you do if the language in which you are communicating does not embody a crucial concept? Confucius might have counseled Robinson to use his *yi* (judgment) to identify an alternative approach if the precise (rectified) word was unavailable.

Drawing on his years of experience negotiating in Latin America and his command of Spanish, Robinson instead relied on the Spanish notion of *dar y recibir,* roughly translated as "give-and-take," to find a solution. The demand for gloves, which had great symbolic value to the workers, had initially been tabled as "too radical a departure from existing policy." When the workers presented their demand for additional pay, Robinson explained the need for *dar y recibir,* a concept all involved were familiar with. Returning the discussion to the earlier request for gloves, Robinson offered to make the case for the equipment to headquarters, though it would be a tough sell. In exchange, the workers would have to drop their demand for the seventh day. The creative solution helped clear the path to a more forthright dialogue and eventually an amicable agreement satisfying to both parties. By replacing a vague concept of compromise unfamiliar to his counter-parties with the tangible *dar y recibir* between competing priorities, Robinson leveraged the principle of rectification of names to bring about a productive dialogue.[7]

Lessons for Strategists

CULTURE IS CREATED THROUGH LANGUAGE

Language is one of a culture's most salient features. Language is a system of sounds that contain meaning, and a language's vocabulary reflects a culture's underlying values. Examples include the aforementioned lack of a word for compromise in Spanish, the lack of a word for disobedience among Australian aborigines, and the lack of a term for privacy in Russian.[8] Conversely, Greek has several words for love, such as *agape* (universal love toward others), *filia* (deep friendship, as among brothers in arms), and *eros* (sexual passion). And just as words have the power to convey meaning, they have the power to limit behavior (by, for example, an absence of expectation for privacy in many Russian-speaking cultures) or expand it (through the many ways to love in Greek).

Walt Disney Productions uses language to reinforce a culture of customer care and wholesome behavior. Employees at Disneyland and Disney World are "cast members," customers are "guests," and theme park rides are "attractions." Use of profanity is prohibited within the corporation. Joe Ruggiano, who joined Disney after a career in sports management in New York City, confided to the senior author that "my biggest challenge in moving here was dropping most of my New York street vocabulary. It's been two years, and I still have to catch myself."[9]

When the Darden School of Business added academic research to its mission, it stretched faculty members beyond their traditional priorities of teaching and engaging with practitioners through executive education and consulting. To highlight the newly raised bar for the faculty, the school adopted the term "triathlete" to describe what was now a tough role to fill in a profession that typically rewards pure research. Darden was able to extend its range of rewarded activities by branding successful faculty members with a performance designation that they bore proudly.

CULTURE IS CREATED THROUGH INTERPERSONAL BEHAVIOR

Experienced leaders are typically adroit at diagnosing the presence of cultural challenges. Capable managers are likely to have developed a strong understanding of their business and their people. As a result, most are effective at recognizing the major roadblocks holding their organizations back, ranging from poor morale and fear of failure to lack of innovation.

Developing actionable solutions to address these challenges, on the other hand, is often far less intuitive. Leadership teams frequently struggle to identify an effective plan to handle a thorny cultural issue. How can a business losing share to a more nimble competitor become more agile or innovative? What can a nonprofit do to improve efficiency and allay apprehensive donors? Where should an organization concerned about employee turnover focus in order to deal with declining morale? The impact of a cultural challenge is often broad, influencing how business is done, customers are served, and value is created. As a result, descriptions of the problem at hand can become suffused in generalities. Discussions around culture often start and end with a focus on ill-defined notions of workstyles, attitudes, and perceptions. Leaders are left feeling at a loss to find specific, tactical answers to vaguely defined problems.

The Confucian perspective offers a potential solution. For Confucius, culture is the sum of individual actions. One way to interpret this teaching is by asking ourselves, "What particular interpersonal behaviors are causing our culture to manifest in this fashion?"

While the question may seem straightforward, finding an answer that meets Confucius's rigorous criteria is often not an easy task. After all, in questions of culture we know Confucius is interested only in specific actions.

Identifying a high-level trend or a general tendency is not enough. While it's helpful to recognize that bureaucracy is stifling innovation or poor communication is creating tension, we still have not provided a satisfactory answer. Instead, we must follow "the chain of why," repeatedly asking why something occurs and each time getting more specific in our answers. The process can be laborious and time-consuming, but the rewards are often worth the effort.

If we articulate our cultural concerns in terms of specific actions, we empower ourselves to seek out the resources necessary to either promote the missing actions we desire or disincentivize problematic behavior.

For example, a corporation losing market share to competitors' new products and services may decide to increasingly emphasize innovation as an organizational value. Leveraging the Confucian paradigm, the company's strategy team may analyze competitors, review research by industry experts, or hold employee focus groups. The resulting findings could lead the team to identify existing behaviors that limit the organization's capacity for innovation (for example, risk aversion or excessive punishment for failed experimentation) or innovative behaviors that are absent from the culture (cross-functional collaboration, agile product development, and so on).

Drilling a level deeper, the team might identify specific examples—a meeting gone awry, an employee reprimanded for an unsuccessful experiment, a missed opportunity due to a lack of information sharing—in order to catalog the actions that need to be addressed.

Armed with this precise inventory, the company would be well equipped to identify the new hires, process changes, technology, or other resources that can spur the desired behaviors and help manifest the resulting cultural qualities. Of course, simply understanding the problem in detail does not guarantee a successful outcome, but it does improve the probability of finding solutions that address it.

We encountered Andy Palmer in chapter 2. Prior to his appointment as CEO of Aston Martin in 2014, Palmer spent twenty years in Japan. Confucianism has been practiced in Japan since approximately 300 AD and has influenced a number of corporations, including Nissan, where Palmer had risen to the No. 2 position. When he took the helm at Aston Martin, Palmer wanted to rev up the energy in the executive suite. Among other initiatives, he engaged a prominent global consultancy to take his senior management team through a truth-telling exercise. The executives paired up, and each member of a pair had five minutes to describe to his partner which of the other's behaviors annoyed him or, worse, made it difficult for him to function effectively in his role. After ten minutes, each member paired up with another individual and repeated the exercise. Through the exercise, the participants unearthed culture-bound behaviors that were causing conflict. A German was told that his directness came across as abruptness; a Brit heard that his reserved nature was perceived as aloofness; and an American learned that his informality was seen as overly intimate. The exercise revealed that the executives' assumptions of discourtesy or lack of respect were unfounded, and that their expectations of and reactions to each other were instead based on their respective cultures. They were able to reach a level of understanding that resulted in more cohesion as an executive team.

As we pointed out in this book's preface, such actions will look familiar to anyone engaged in modern change-management practices. Our point isn't that Confucian principles are new. Quite the contrary: Many of our so-called modern management principles can be traced to the wisdom of the ancients.

In another example, in the early 1980s the Chinese company Orient Overseas Containers acquired Houlder Offshore, a capital-intensive British firm specializing in the manufacture and delivery of mobile offshore drilling platforms. Houlder typically would rent the platforms to oil exploration companies in the North Sea off Scotland. The deep waters and high waves of the North Sea required massive rigs that could extend their legs to the seabed far below in order to provide a stable drilling platform. Being mobile, the rigs were classified and registered as ocean-going vessels. Because they were huge, could be used in extremely hostile environments, and required experienced deep sea divers to anchor, Houlder's rigs were among the most expensive in the world to operate. They could be rented for around USD600,000 per day, whereas less elaborate permanent platforms for shallower, stable waters such as the Gulf of Mexico would rent for a fraction of that cost.

Soon after the merger, Orient Overseas leaders and Houlder senior executives held a strategy session in the Cotswolds Hills of south-central England. Houlder was the Rolls-Royce of drilling rigs and had a corporate culture to match, including expensive company cars (Jaguars), splendid offices, and generous expense accounts. But Houlder's business model was optimized for a regime of oil prices exceeding USD75 per barrel (prices adjusted to 2020 dollars). In the late 1970s, when prices peaked above USD120 per barrel, Houlder prospered enormously. But an oil glut was on the horizon. The forecasts presented in the strategy session indicated a significant probability of prices falling below USD65 per barrel. There was universal acknowledgment among executives at the retreat that Houlder's strategy had to become more cost-conscious. This would require an almost complete shift from a culture supported by premium pricing to one built on cost control.

When the executives returned to London, they initiated a number of changes, both symbolic and procedural. The Jaguars were replaced by Opels. Office temperatures were lowered one degree in the winter, and all lights were extinguished after hours. These moves were visible, immediate, and sent a clear signal. But more important, Houlder redirected its capital into research and development, yielding new products in marine equipment plus a suite of services that capitalized on the firm's existing capabilities in ship design, offshore project management, floating asset analytics, and expert and advisory services in naval architecture and marine engineering.

TO CHANGE ORGANIZATIONAL CULTURE, ENCOURAGE INDIVIDUAL SELF-DEVELOPMENT

If culture is the product of interpersonal behavior, Confucius teaches us, then transforming culture is the process of refining individuals' behavior as it relates to their interactions with each other and their stakeholders.

For example, IBM began its transition to professional services by engaging in a USD50 million program to train the field sales force in strategic thinking.[10] The purpose was to transform these individuals from IT salespeople into business consultants to their clients. Accustomed to "pushing iron," as they referred to their legacy role of selling computer hardware, the highly competent field personnel were being groomed to identify and solve customer problems. The key was to have them become capable of interacting with chief executives, not just chief technology officers. IBM now derives the majority of its revenues from management consulting.

DEFINE AND COMMUNICATE CODES OF CONDUCT

Whether the strategist seeks to eliminate undesirable behaviors or promote desirable ones, Confucius teaches that clear guidelines under the new cultural paradigm are a prerequisite. As he made clear in his emphasis on *li* propriety, as well as the principle of precision in language, individuals cannot be expected to act in alignment with new cultural requirements unless agreed-upon, clearly defined expectations are communicated. Having defined the actions that are associated with the desired culture, leaders must communicate what these behaviors would look like in action.

Asking the organization to be more innovative, for example, would not be particularly helpful. Clearly defining behaviors that create a culture of innovation is a useful first step. But it is also necessary to interpret and explain how those behavioral principles would manifest into specific actions.

In the mid-1990s, the Australia Department of Agriculture (ADOA) identified a number of strategic threats to its traditional business model. The environmental trends forecast, shown in table 3, indicated that its skills, capabilities, and organizational culture were at risk.

In order to identify the new capabilities and behaviors the department

TABLE 3. Environmental trends forecast, Australia Department of Agriculture

Trend	Implication
1. Change in trade pattern • decrease in exports	1. Greater involvement in international marketing by the department • need new skills
2. Technological changes • increasing communication and information • increasing farm production	2. Affects way we're organized and managed, skills of staff, research priorities • do we need to be here at all?
3. Changing political climate • reduced clout of DOA	3. Survival—Reduced resources from government • need new sources of funds • must develop skills to market our services
4. Increasing public demand for accountability from government	4. Greater scrutiny over research, which will drive down morale of scientists. Greater response to priorities required. Greater legal liability.
5. Changing dietary patterns • less red meat • fewer dairy products, carbohydrates • fewer sweets • more fruit, grains, vegetables, poultry, fish	5. Change in priorities • organization of department will change • conflict between research priorities

would need, ADOA leadership engaged in a simple exercise to make explicit their current codes of behavior. Each member of the team was assigned a set of instructions:

> Every institution has some unwritten rules that guide its behavior. In order to surface ADOA's, write down the ten most important explicit or implicit decision rules driving the organization. That is, produce a list of what you consider to be ADOA's "ten commandments" underlying your strategy and culture. Assume that, immediately upon issuing these commandments, you and the rest of the leadership team will be isolated on a desert island for two years. You should feel confident that these guidelines will provide sufficient direction for the organization's actions and decisions, such that

all decisions taken in your absence will be regarded as having been made as if you had been here (not as you *wish* they were made).

Australians can be brutally honest. The team produced the following list:

1. Build and maintain good external relationships, especially by providing sound technical information.
2. Respond rapidly to emergencies (e.g., bush fires, exotic diseases).
3. Feel free to disagree openly.
4. Maintain departmental uniformity for the sake of uniformity.
5. Blame central agencies for problems, legitimately or as an excuse.
6. Minimize expenditures on technical training (live for the present, not the future).
7. Claim that the organization is responsive to change.
8. Service the rural community at all times.
9. Don't involve operational managers in corporate decision-making, or advise them of the reasons for decisions.
10. Morale is of secondary importance to compliance with management (you'll do what you're bloody told).

With their environmental forecast in front of them, the team then answered the following questions:

1. Which of these commandments are so foundational to our mission that they should be nurtured and preserved as bedrock going forward? (They listed items 1, 2, 3, and 8.)
2. Which of these commandments are beyond our control and we shouldn't waste our energy attempting to change them? (They identified item 4—maintain departmental uniformity—as it was based on a set of requirements mandated by the central government in Canberra.)
3. Particularly with respect to the future we forecasted, which of these existing commandments must we change? (As one would expect, they listed items 5, 6, 7, 9, and 10.)

In the following months, ADOA leadership launched a series of strategic initiatives that would drive a change in their now explicit code of conduct. For instance, they started a program that would belie the "claim" that they were responsive to change and that instead would actually initiate and embrace change. They began a series of monthly meetings that included operational managers in key decisions, and—this is important—they postponed any major decisions that were not urgent until these inclusive meetings were held. One of most strategic changes was to lobby for funding and implement a comprehensive training program in communications and marketing, as well as a recruiting program for PhD scientists in nutrition, botany, and zoology. Perhaps most important, codes of conduct were developed for employees at each level of the organization, providing clear guidance to each individual for how to align his or her behavior to the organizational "ten commandments."

INFUSE BEHAVIORAL STANDARDS WITH VIRTUOUS TRAITS

In defining the codes of conduct, Confucius would encourage strategic leaders to ensure that the new behavioral standards being promoted would cultivate core Confucian virtues in members of the organization. Designing behavioral standards in a way that is aligned with Confucian virtues ensures that the organization's culture can benefit from the cycle created when these virtues are at the heart of action.

Ren (compassion) ensures that the organizational culture reflects a humane attitude among stakeholders toward each other. *Li* (propriety) ensures continued commitment to codes of conduct. *Yi* (judgment) ensures that when a new situation arises where codes of conduct fall short, individuals are equipped to make decisions aligned with organizational values. *Zhi* (wisdom) creates the habits and capabilities that allow individuals to translate lessons learned from experience into improved performance. Finally, *xin* (trustworthiness) plays a crucial role in creating a culture of trust that ensures that individuals feel comfortable fulfilling their stated responsibilities because they are confident that others in the organization will fulfill theirs.

Each organization is unique. Its values do not and should not have to mirror those set out by Confucius, explicitly or even implicitly. Yet, for the actions prescribed by the code to inspire the desired organizational culture, the values these behaviors promote must be aligned.

LEAD BY EXAMPLE

While Confucius emphasized the importance of each member of a society or organization in creating culture and social order, he did not shy away from the importance of hierarchy. As we witnessed in our discussion of the term *junzi*, leaders, whether they be executives or feudal rulers, play a particularly important role in transforming how others in the organization behave. A leader's role does not stop with creating codes of conduct imbued with virtuous qualities. Exemplifying a commitment to that code is also a prerequisite.

During the tumultuous years of the American Civil War, Abraham Lincoln, a gracious leader known for his good humor and equanimity, had little patience for excuses from his military commanders. Many times he demoted publicly well-regarded senior officers for what he perceived as a pattern of avoiding responsibility. With the fate of the United States hanging in the balance, he could not tolerate blame-shifting. But Lincoln also powerfully demonstrated this virtue through his own example. Diaries of his advisors and confidants, as well as newspaper records from the time, attest to Lincoln's willingness to take complete responsibility for the Union's losses in battle. Even when historical records reveal that commanders had acted against his advice, Lincoln, both publicly and privately, treated every military defeat as his personal failure. This quality, a willingness to hold himself to an even higher standard than he expected of others, contributes to history's treatment of Lincoln as one of America's greatest presidents.

A century later, Mahatma Gandhi's actions similarly exemplified this principle. As historian Keshavan Nair observed: "In the history of public leadership, there has never been an individual as committed to a single standard in public life as Gandhi. He believed and acted on the belief that leaders have the responsibility to set an example of conduct."[11]

Macon, Georgia, 2004

Southeast Paper in Macon, Georgia, manufactured newsprint from 95 percent recycled paper and employed physically and intellectually disabled workers wherever possible—for example, at the conveyor that separated glossy magazines from the paper trucked in from recycling centers. Many employees were trained to perform the job above them so that they could step in temporarily should their boss be absent. While filling in, each of these trained employees was paid at his or her supervisor's pay level.

Southeast Paper encountered a tough challenge in 2004: Its paper was tearing on the printing presses of some of the daily newspapers it supplied. As a corrective action, CEO Rod Granger took groups of paper-machine workers to customer pressrooms in Atlanta, New Orleans, Dallas, and other cities with large daily-paper circulations to allow them to witness their product in action and interact with the press operators. Once the field training was underway, Southeast redesigned its quality assurance process with the help of the machine operators. In addition, Southeast took delivery of a new football-field-long machine that would allow the company to better control quality. Granger recognized that for the initiative to be a success, leadership's commitment to a quality product had to be reinforced throughout the plant.

After the machine was installed and the new quality processes were in place, Granger set up a lawn chair at the end of the line where he sat every day for a week to observe the output and assure and encourage the operators.[12]

What values was Rod Granger modeling? Among others: environmental consciousness, social responsibility, valuing of workers, quality standards, customer focus, and hard work and dedication to both the product and the people.

Bangkok, Thailand, July 2018

Tevin Vongvanich was president and CEO of PTT Group, a Fortune Global 500 company in the energy sector. Speaking with the authors a few months before his retirement, Tevin reflected on his career at PTT and his leadership principles. As a Thai, Tevin grew up with exposure to Eastern wisdom and had even been ordained as a Buddhist monk in India. His higher education, however, was acquired in the West; he had earned master's degrees in chemical and petroleum engineering in the United States. Tevin told the authors that while he used a Western approach to making decisions, he executed them in an Eastern way.

Normally, decisions at PTT were made by the executive committee. Despite being time consuming, this process worked for the company. For Tevin, a key investment of his time was managing the culture, value system, and stakeholder expectations. His twenty-first-century challenge was that younger generations of employees had been educated and raised with more Western values. Similar to other large corporations in Thailand, PTT had to gradually transform the legacy culture of older employees—who valued relationships, seniority, and years of experience—to the one embraced by the incoming generation of younger employees—who treasured individualism, equality, and intellectual capability. The challenge was to do this while retaining both younger and older talent and ensuring collaborations between the two populations.

Tevin understood this was not about being right or wrong. Rather, he focused on understanding differences, developing acceptance, and respecting and trusting one another. Because a new corporate culture would require time to implement across the organization, Tevin established a business unit that hired mostly young talent educated in Western countries and gave those employees the flexibility to bring in new technology and ideas to energize PTT Group. By combining a short- and a long-term solution for this cultural challenge, Tevin allowed time for different generations to adjust to one another, while leveraging each group's particular strengths. As Tevin put it: "We created a bureaucratic solution—a separate unit—to protect the new wave from our [traditional] bureaucracy."

Conclusion

Confucius, in setting out a set of principles to guide the social order of a state, created a framework for how modern organizations can create and maintain a culture conducive to successful strategic management.

Confucius's key teachings—his emphasis on individuals as interdependent entities, on specialized rituals defined by roles, on social order as the product of commitment to carrying out these rituals—translate neatly to the structures used to organize the large public- and private-sector institutions that twenty-first-century strategists are charged with leading.

Ironically, it was Peter Drucker who was responsible for articulating many of the principles that undergird the modern, large-scale organization. In his seminal works of the mid-twentieth century, he helped formulate the notion of a modern organization as an agglomeration of individuals working in many specialized functions and tasked with specialized responsibilities. Under a certain light, Drucker's framing appears to have a striking resemblance to an updated version of Confucius's conception of the social order.

Perhaps Drucker's and Confucius's shared emphasis on culture is more than just coincidence. Despite having lived more than twenty-five hundred years apart, the two organizational theorists appear to have developed an aligned belief in the principles that undergird any large-scale human endeavor. At their essence, these enterprises, whether they be an ancient Chinese society or a multinational corporation, are the product of individual humans interacting at scale. Creating an environment that allows for such interaction to occur harmoniously, Confucius and Drucker seem to agree, is the key that unlocks the potential for leading these entities successfully.

This concludes our treatment of Eastern philosophies, their relationship to each other, and their guidance to strategists and institutional leaders. In chapter 11, we will draw lessons derived from all the philosophies covered in this book.

Strategy Lessons from Chapter 10

1. Don't worry that no one recognizes you; seek to be worthy of recognition.
2. Be an exemplary person of learning, not a trivial pedant.
3. Learn new information, then translate that learning into action.

4. Build the enabling infrastructure that allows your people to act on their learning.
5. Create a culture through skillful use of words and language.
6. To change organizational culture, encourage individual self-development.
7. Define and communicate codes of conduct throughout the organization.
8. Infuse behavioral standards through your own virtuous traits.
9. Lead by example.
10. Ensure that all stakeholders know and are aligned with your organization's values.

PART IV

LESSONS FOR STRATEGISTS

Strategists should lead a jazz band, not an orchestra. The leader of a jazz group is whomever is soloing at the moment, with the support of the other musicians. The leader of an orchestra is not the conductor, but the composer who wrote the original score. Just as in jazz, adaptability and creative teamwork are essential for a successful organization and the leader at its helm.

Overview of Part IV

Chapter 11 unveils four action directives and twelve underlying principles for strategists.

The afterword suggests that readers taking the route laid out in this book will have learned that they can control only their own decisions and actions, not everything that happens subsequently. Make an informed decision while accepting the inevitability of surprise. Lay out detailed but flexible plans. Inspire followers. Issue directions. But stuff happens. This doesn't mean giving up when things go wrong or letting up on effort. It means we should accept that there are things over which we do not have control, and we will gain clarity of mind when we free our egos from emotional investment in outcomes.

Our goal for readers is that they will progress from "this is new, somewhat unfamiliar, and provocative" to "now I understand how to cultivate strategic intuition. Among other things, it means that this book is merely the first step in a journey."

11

Strategy as a Call to (in)Action

We have explored the philosophies and methods of conventional strategy, Asian warfare, the game of Go, the Bhagavad Gita, the teaching of the Buddha, Zen, Taoism, energy (*chi*) as a strategic force, and Confucius. Examining them collectively, they reveal twelve lessons or principles that underlie four action directives for strategists: Build a foundation for strategizing, prepare the mind to accept insights, adjust your lens to recognize strategy as it emerges, and take decisive action (see table 4).

Action Directive I: Build a Foundation

PRINCIPLE 1. PREPARATION IS THE SINE QUA NON FOR SUCCESSFUL STRATEGIZING

Sun Tzu was a proponent of exhaustive preparations: "The general who wins a battle makes many calculations in his temple before the battle is fought."[1] Preparation—the study of our enemy's capabilities; self-knowledge of our strengths and weaknesses; and extensive scenario planning—allows us to take advantage of opportunity and avoid falling prey to unexpected challenges.

Mountain View, California, January 1985

Sun Microsystems founder and CEO Scott McNealy was still removing sand from his office in Silicon Valley. For his thirtieth birthday the previous November, his coworkers had placed a set of Callaway golf clubs in the middle of a sand trap they had trucked in the night before. He swept a few grains from his desk as he pondered the question the senior author and his colleague had just posed: "Scott, we are investigating how executives make strategic decisions in extremely fast-changing industries. The analytical tools that we teach in our MBA programs assume that (1) you have the data you need to process through those tools, and (2) that you have the time to process them.

TABLE 4. Twelve strategy principles revealed by Eastern philosophy

Build a foundation	1. Preparation is the sine qua non for successful strategizing. 2. Build a foundation on the continuous pursuit of knowledge.
Prepare the mind	3. Cultivate beginner's mind. 4. Presence of mind perpetuates coup d'oeil. 5. Let go of the illusion of control by embracing detachment and acceptance.
Adjust the lens	6. Strategic discovery is a function of fluidity and receptivity. 7. Impermanence is the only reality. 8. Circularity and iteration complement linearity. 9. Self-discipline trumps self as an illusion.
Take action	10. Resolve is fundamental to mobilization. 11. Timing is everything. 12. Good strategy is about balance, the Middle Way, and moderation.

[McNealy had received his MBA from Stanford four years prior.] What do you do in this [microcomputer] industry, where you have neither? What should we be teaching our MBAs to be able to survive and even thrive in this high-velocity environment?"[2]

Speaking at triple speed, McNealy responded: "My first instinct is to tell you to have each student play an intense video game where he must maneuver with lightning speed before Big Blue[3] comes flying in from off-screen and goes ZAP! and annihilates you!" To illustrate, McNealy's right hand swooped in from overhead to grab his extended left fist. He continued:

> Seriously, though? I would teach them how to study, study, and study their competitors until they know them like the backs of their hands. Here at Sun, we know what Hewlett Packard is going to do before they do. We know their people, their technology, their values, and their propensities. We have people here who are experts on HP, on IBM, on Apple, on Compaq. We will often recruit from our classmates who went there to join us. Homework, homework, do your homework! Read, read, read anything you can get your hands on about them. Play golf and squash with them. Go to the favorite lunch joints around here and just listen to the conversations coming from the other tables.
>
> The point is, we don't take a timeout to do analyses at the time the need arises. We've already done them. We know in our bones what they are

likely to do in any given circumstance. The key is knowing them. We do our homework 24/7.

McNealy was extolling the value of the strategy tools he had learned at Stanford: Do the homework, use the frameworks. Those are necessary, but not sufficient. One must already have a foundation of prior preparation in order to survive in a fast-paced environment of innovation, startups, and constant new entrants.

Principle summary: Strategy requires extensive preparation. Do your homework and analyses well before you need them.

PRINCIPLE 2. BUILD A FOUNDATION ON THE CONTINUOUS PURSUIT OF KNOWLEDGE

The senior author and his colleague were meeting with Bill Joy, head of research and development at Sun Microsystems and guru of the UNIX operating system. The two were anticipating a conversation with Joy about rival computer operating systems. (The personal computer business was just beginning to accelerate. There were approximately a hundred microcomputer startups at that time, employing a variety of operating systems such as DOS [now Windows], P/CM, and UNIX.) To their surprise, Joy led them through a wide-ranging dialogue touching on supply chains, marketing channels, strategic alliances, and the mechanics of going public and pricing stock options.

Joy's breadth of nontechnical knowledge was astounding. A polymath and daily meditator, he was revered by the scientific community as one of the leading minds in the development of UNIX. When the senior author recounted this story to scientists at a conference at Bell Labs (where UNIX was created), the Bill Joy fans present were amused but not surprised. One of the conference attendees noted that Joy, like many of Bell's preeminent researchers, was an extraordinary technical specialist not in spite of, but because of his deep knowledge across a wide range of subjects, many only tangentially related to his nominal field of expertise.

As we have learned from Musashi, Confucius, the Buddha, and Sun Tzu, wide-ranging knowledge provides the fertile ground from which coup d'oeil and strategic insight spring. There is no formula for how one prepares to become a corporate leader and strategist, but many accomplished CEOs point to the breadth of knowledge they were exposed to while growing up as important training. For example, Indra Nooyi, CEO of PepsiCo from 2006 to 2018, recalled her childhood: "I grew up in Madras. We never lacked for anything, but we didn't have much. It was a good, conservative Brahmin family, deeply steeped in learning and education. That was the only focus. The expectation was you would get, at a minimum, a master's degree. If you got a PhD, you're better off. We were the ultimate nerds. The only difference was, in my case, I decided to be a nerd in some ways and branch out in other ways. I played cricket. I climbed trees, I played the guitar, I did all those wild and wacky things."[4]

As we saw with several executives—Naresh Kumra, Narayana Murthy, Sumeth Laomoraporn, Nok Anulomsombut—preparation and diverse knowledge undergird a strong foundation for strategic thinking.

One of the senior author's MBA graduates[5] explained: "We have spent countless hours in preparation for being expedient problem solvers and sound business leaders. While it may not be comfortable, at the end of the day it's important that we be confident in our ability to perform at our highest level when we're not over-thinking or over-analyzing, when we're allowing our preparation to take control, essentially when we're 'doing but not doing.'"[6]

While breadth of knowledge is key, we must also be purposeful in training our minds, dedicating ourselves to learning constantly, and maintaining a powerful focus. These are learned skills, and training our minds, including learning to separate our actions from emotional responses (see principle 5 on detachment), is crucial in this regard.

As specified in the samurai regimens in *The Book of Five Rings,* deep training is essential to becoming free from self, a key stumbling block that any warrior must overcome. In Musashi's capstone chapter on the "void" or emptiness, he describes the highest level of samurai mastery, where everything unnecessary, such as extraneous techniques or other "decadence" that may have contaminated one's strategy, has been removed through disciplined training (see principle 9).

Underlying Musashi's *Book of Five Rings* are hundreds of years of Zen Buddhist cultural tradition. As a pair of our MBA students observed: "At first glance, the tea ceremony, calligraphy, and *sumiye* painting have little to do with the fencing abilities of a master swordsman. However, it is these rituals and interests outside of one's profession that allows for the serenity necessary to solve difficult strategic problems. For modern business executives, it is not enough to be at the top of your craft—without balance there will be burnout, and limited ability to achieve a strategic breakthrough."[7]

Confucius also emphasized the importance of studying a broad range of subjects as a key pathway to achieving a greater self. The same pair of MBA students noted: "In Confucian teachings, it is not enough to be an expert at your profession. Proper manners and proper culture are necessary in order to be an upright citizen. There are a great deal more of applicable teachings that a modern strategist might find helpful, including fostering reciprocity and trust, being humane, favoring principle more than personality. In many ways he was a proponent of a liberal arts curriculum that builds the whole person and develops culture. To be a complete person, one must be cultured *and* have strong character."[8]

Principle summary: Practice and preparation allow us to separate our actions from our emotions, while wide-ranging knowledge provides fertile ground for experiencing coup d'oeil and strategic insight.

Action Directive II: Prepare the Mind

PRINCIPLE 3. CULTIVATE BEGINNER'S MIND

How do we enable coup d'oeil to take place? One of the most critical practices for an executive is to disengage from preconceptions.

"Trapped by the emphatic success of the past" is how Geoff Lewis, strategy consultant and professor at Melbourne Business School, described the curse of market dominance by such large Australian firms as BHP and ICI Australia. There is the danger both of ascribing all success to one's own efforts and of having too much accumulated experience in an industry.

Indeed, in a controversial piece in the *Harvard Business Review*, David Gray argued for the addition of a "Chief Ignorance Officer" to the C-Suite.

> Unlike knowledge, which is infinitely reusable, ignorance is a one-shot deal: Once it has been displaced by knowledge, it can be hard to get back. And after it's gone, we are more apt to follow well-worn paths to find answers than to exert our sense of what we don't know in order to prove new options. Knowledge can stand in the way of innovation. . . . Nescience [lack of knowledge] is fruitful when managers want new ideas. Yet the impulse is always to fill the vacuum with ready knowledge, which makes us feel that at least we're getting somewhere. The trick is to delay this thrust into knowledge, to shelter nescience as long as possible. . . . We cannot know ahead of time what will serve as inspiration. . . . To constrain our horizons to the current state of awareness is to destroy the possibility of unexpected novelty.[9]

The benefits Gray ascribes to nescience hold many parallels to the Eastern concept of emptiness. Emptiness in the Eastern sense can be understood as the capacity to observe worldly phenomena without preconception. In

Musashi's time, there were many fighting *dōjōs* that taught specific techniques, with each claiming superiority. He defeated the masters of each *dōjō* in combat because he chose not to rely on a single stance or technique. Approaching every fight from a place of emptiness, Musashi could choose the posture and technique best suited to defeat a particular opponent.

Satori, the Japanese word for sudden enlightenment, is the Zen Buddhist key to unlocking truly original breakthroughs. As two students in our course described it: "Each *satori* requires irrationality, intuitive insight, authoritativeness, affirmation, sense of beyond, impersonal tone, feeling of exaltation, and momentariness. The key components here are irrationality, exaltation, and momentariness. The innovation is irrational in that it cannot come from intellectual or logical analysis—it is new. Exaltation, because like the coup d'oeil it brings incredible clarity to those with the genius to harness the insight. And finally, momentariness. The insight must be acted upon, and expeditiously, or it will be seized by another or fade away."[10]

Principle summary: Beginner's mind is key to achieving insight breakthroughs. In Western practice, paralysis by analysis is too often the result of extensive research into historical data. By approaching strategy with beginner's mind, we can clear our heads of any "this worked before" bias. New developments do not fall into the trap of being mistaken for history repeating itself, and true breakthroughs are possible.

PRINCIPLE 4. PRESENCE OF MIND PERPETUATES COUP D'OEIL

If a cluttered desk means a cluttered mind, as the saying goes, what does an empty desk indicate?

A Westerner might smile at this question, but an Eastern philosopher would react quite differently. As we've just seen, those with beginner's mind are more likely to experience coup d'oeil than those with cluttered, distracted minds.[11] Often, those who meditate or practice yoga develop the calmness and presence of mind that benefits strategic thinking.

The analog in Western strategic thinking is focus. We encourage strategists to not only determine a goal, but to stay focused on that goal with a single-minded vision that excludes all other developments. Similarly, many of the Eastern thinkers we encountered promote the importance of focus. Sun Tzu listed a number of strategies "whereby the ears and eyes of the host may be focused on one particular point."

Yet the Eastern philosophers also encourage a broader present moment awareness. In addition to emphasizing the value of thorough preparation,

Sun Tzu's advice that "if you know the enemy and know yourself, you will need not fear the result of a hundred battles" teaches the value of full present moment awareness. To achieve victory on the battlefield, you must maintain awareness of yourself, your enemy, and your terrain simultaneously. While the Buddha's teaching was focused on a broader, nonmartial context, he similarly underscored a wide present moment awareness, free of a single attached focus on a given point, as the key to achieving *nibbana.*

"Strategists are miserable" was the way Safina Zhou, a Chinese executive and MBA, described our information-overloaded reality.

> In the lumpy and dim world, strategists have to keep wrestling with endless changes and uncertainties to navigate their organizations. They first need to be extremely analytical and cautious to put together all the factors that impact their organizations. . . . But they will never be able to get all the pieces they need. In most conditions, before collecting all the information, they need to move on and choose the direction for their organizations. With great courage, the strategists pick that direction and notify the whole organization to navigate toward the direction that the strategy mandates. The direction may be wrong; then the strategists need to look at the alternatives again, thinking about whether they need to start over or just redirect toward another direction, if the ship did not sink in the meantime. The direction may be right, but only for a while, as we all know that the fundamental rule of the world is that it is always changing.[12]

The worst nightmare of a strategist is not the change itself, but the speed with which the cycle described by Zhou takes place. As David Brooks argues in describing a "rebellion against the quickening of time": "The internet has accelerated our experience of time, and [our leaders have] upped the pace of events to permanent frenetic. There is a rapid, dirty river of information coursing through us all day . . . [and] your reaction to events has to be instant or it is outdated."[13]

The question is, how do we slow things down in order to act with clear presence of mind? Many executives have practiced the mindfulness exercises described in this book, as we've seen in the stories of Nok Anulomsombut, Sumeth Laomoraporn, Pat Taveechaiwattana, Steve Jobs, and Bill Joy. Another accepted path is through the arts—music and the visual arts are the go-to attention arrestors for many. For example, David Brooks describes Nihonga, an expressionist art form from Japan, where one "grinds colored minerals like malachite and azurite into fine particles and then layers them on paper. Each layer takes time to dry, and [artist Mako Fujimura] may use

60 layers in a single work. Nihonga is slow to make and slow to see. Mako once advised me to stare at one of his paintings for 10 to 12 minutes. I thought it would be boring, but it was astonishing. As I stood still in front of it, my eyes adjusted to the work. What had seemed like a plain blue field now looks like a galaxy of color."[14]

Pebble Beach, California, 1982

He sat at the front edge of the Asilomar stage, his sandaled feet folded in yoga posture. The podium behind him had just been vacated by a well-known promulgator of "lateral thinking." As he spoke to the mesmerized group of about two hundred well-dressed executives, the bearded, twenty-seven-year-old Steve Jobs preached about the central role that product design plays in business strategy. The audience included such luminaries as Art Gensler, the legendary architect of the Shanghai Tower and headquarters buildings for corporations such as Pixar, Coca-Cola, and Facebook, and Alan Fletcher, designer of the Mercedes-Benz logo. (The senior author, who was scheduled to follow Jobs to lead a discussion on the same topic, did not know at the time who the young hippie-looking man was.)

A decade or so earlier, Jobs had adopted what would become a lifelong passion for Eastern philosophy. He eventually took a spiritual journey to an ashram in India and studied Zen Buddhism. A Zen monk presided over his wedding to Laurene Powell, and Jobs met almost daily with a Zen teacher. At his funeral in 2011, which he had carefully orchestrated, all were given a copy of a book that he had reread annually: Paramahansa Yogananda's *Autobiography of a Yogi.*[15]

As Jobs told his biographer: "If you just sit and observe, you will see how restless your mind is. If you try to calm it, it only makes things worse, but over time it does calm, and when it does, there's room to hear more subtle things—that's when your intuition starts to blossom and you start to see things more clearly and be in the present more. Your mind just slows down, and you see a tremendous expanse in the moment. You see so much more than you could see before. It's a discipline; you have to practice it."[16]

Seattle, Washington, December 2018

When Satya Nadella became head of Microsoft in 2014, the personal computing pioneer had been derided for years as a relatively "sleepy" tech giant that had missed big innovations like the smartphone and cloud services. In the years following his ascension to CEO, Nadella led Microsoft through a cultural transformation and a period of historic growth, with the stock price nearly tripling between 2014 and 2018.

We often hear of successful business executives who are "level-headed" or "cool under pressure," and whose swings of emotion are of low amplitude. How does one get there?

The Bhagavad Gita encourages us to follow our dharma in order to achieve internal constancy and peace. Only when we have a still mind are we able to make correct decisions in the midst of confusing externalities.[17] Confucius teaches us the need to be purposeful in taking time to reset. This can be especially applicable in today's increasingly frenetic world.

Nadella is a prime example. Although he does not openly associate himself with any religion, he begins each day with a simple mindfulness practice. In an interview with Michael Gervais, one of his coaches, he described the process:

1. Take a deep breath (should last about twelve seconds) while lying in bed.
2. Name something (mentally) that you are thankful for.
3. Make one intention for your day, and visualize it.
4. Put your feet on the ground, and feel your feet.

He said this practice "grounds" him and allows him to get in touch with himself and the world around him. He also tries through practice to "build more muscle around having confidence in myself so that I am capable of confronting my own demons and avoid hubris."[18]

As Bill George, CEO of Medtronic, explained: "Often times, my most creative ideas come out of meditation."[19] That is, flashes of insight come only after he is present and serene. When the mind is free, it is better able to take disparate examples from leaders' past experiences, learning, and history to create something new.[20]

Principle summary: Insight is achievable only through clear thinking, which requires one to develop methods for clearing one's mind. It is difficult, if not impossible, to have strategic insight during moments of duress.

PRINCIPLE 5. LET GO OF THE ILLUSION OF CONTROL BY EMBRACING DETACHMENT AND ACCEPTANCE

The Bhagavad Gita teaches us that "sages call a person wise when all his undertakings are free from anxiety about results."[21] And as Pat Taveechaiwattana, CMO of Allianz Ayudhya in Bangkok, told us: "You can be captain of your ship, but don't insist on commanding the sea."

Rio de Janeiro, Brazil, 1987

The analyst pressed "send," and the Monte Carlo–driven model spit out a profit number and a probability range. The resulting net present value was presented to the board as justification for building a billion-dollar Esso refinery in northern Brazil. L. J. B., the CEO of Esso Brasil, surveyed his senior executive team, and together they decided that he should go to Exxon's New York headquarters in Rockefeller Center with the recommendation and a request for capital.

But L. J. B. tabled his travel plans. Instead, he reconvened his team two weeks later and instructed them to build the case for not making the investment. After much deliberation with his team, and armed with the two opposing arguments, he then went to New York convinced that his request for funding was solid.

Today's strategic decision makers are often highly skilled at data analysis, wielding a variety of tools to identify trends, forecast projections, and draw insights based on historical performance. We would posit that these techniques, while useful in analyzing the past, also promote an attitude that we have come to call "the illusion of control." The Esso Brasil CEO had instructed his team to build a scenario in which Brazil's military dictatorship was deposed, triple-digit inflation returned, and other U.S.-based oil companies were making the same set of decisions as Esso. With this approach, L. J. B. forced himself and his team to relinquish the assumption that the firm was in control of events. Once the decision was made, however, L. J. B. and his team were prepared psychologically for whatever might come. "We have done our part as rigorously as possible," he said, and whatever might happen would happen.

Often, companies' press releases and reports to shareholders focus on achieving specific earnings expectations, hitting revenue targets, or similar rhetoric. The Gita warns against this type of thinking: "You have the right to work, but never to the fruit of work. You should never engage in action for the sake of reward, nor should you long for inaction."[22] Instead, once they do their work, leaders must step back and let the results follow.[23] For Western leaders, adopting this perspective can be particularly challenging because many of the metrics used to measure leaders judge the result, not the actions.[24]

For example, in June 2019 the University of Virginia released details of head football coach Bronco Mendenhall's contract extension. There was no change to his base salary of $500,000, but his supplemental compensation would increase annually. "From $2,750,000 [in 2015], it will increase [in 2020] to $4,500,000. Next year, it goes to $3,500,000 and $3,650,000 the following year." Mendenhall would receive a $50,000 bonus for an appearance in the ACC championship game, $200,000 for winning a conference title, $500,000 for an appearance in the college football playoffs, and $1 million for a national championship.[25]

Mendenhall's compensation structure is prototypical of Western goal-setting and reward systems. But what is the alternative?

Steve Jobs declared in 2011: "Apple's goal isn't to make money. Our goal is to design and develop and bring to market good products. . . . We trust as a consequence of that, people will like them, and as another consequence, we'll make some money. But we're really clear about what our goals are."[26]

Tokyo, Japan, 2012

Kazuo Inamori, the Japanese founder of Fortune 500 companies Kyocera and KDDI, was ordained as a Buddhist monk after his retirement in 1997. In 2010, he was appointed CEO and chairman of Japan Airlines (JAL). Japan's flag carrier was in the midst of bankruptcy and saddled with enormous debt. Accepting no salary, and with no previous experience in aviation, Inamori turned JAL into the world's most profitable airline in two years. His willingness to help JAL and his management approach were based on his belief in right understanding, purpose, and conduct. He believed that decisions based on these Buddhist principles would, by being benevolent, comprehensive, and correct, inspire others to support the organization.

Inamori expressed concern for his employees' welfare and empowered them with trust and freedom to make decisions. To customers, he emphasized service and safety. Inamori's success lay in being clear about what was important to revive the business—right mindfulness—and in putting people before profits.[27]

But it is not a choice of one or the other. In 2000, GE CEO Jack Welch wrote in his annual report that he evaluated his leaders on a 2 by 2 grid. One dimension was "makes the numbers—yes or no," and the second was "lives the values—yes or no." Those with two "yesses" were rewarded, and those with two "nos" were counseled out. The executives who "live the values but don't make the numbers" were given further training or reassigned to a division where their skills were better suited. Executives who "make the numbers but don't live the values" were coached on their behavior and given a limited time to change. If no change in behavior was forthcoming, the manager was discharged. This grid encapsulated a simple idea: The numerical results are not sufficient. As many of our philosophers might argue, attention to the process is equally, if not more, important.

In sports, superstar athletes such as NFL quarterback Tom Brady and tennis phenom Serena Williams frequently describe an obsession with practice, conditioning, diet, and other seemingly mundane, repetitive rituals as the key to their success. This passion for process, rather than outcomes, can also be observed in the examples of celebrity comedians—such as Jerry Seinfeld, who netted nearly a billion dollars from his eponymous TV show, and Joe Rogan, who has earned tens of millions from one of the world's most popular podcasts—who return to the stage in small comedy clubs night after night to practice their stand-up material. It is the work they love, not the rewards.[28]

Principle summary: While difficult to cultivate, a focus on process, rather than results, is key to helping organizations reach their ultimate potential. To promote this attitude, leaders can deploy metrics that evaluate how outcomes were achieved, not just whether they met expectations. This approach will also help leaders engage in the coup d'oeil cycle by enabling them to maintain their presence of mind regardless of results.

Action Directive III: Adjust the Lens

PRINCIPLE 6. STRATEGIC DISCOVERY IS A FUNCTION OF FLUIDITY AND RECEPTIVITY

The senior author arrived home from work and noticed his five-year-old daughter on the porch with her palette and easel and a painting in progress. He asked, "What are you painting, Marie?" She answered, "I don't know yet. I haven't finished."

The Eastern view is that all strategy is emergent. Execute with resolution (principle 10), and go where it leads you. As the Tao proclaims: "A good traveler has no fixed plans and is not intent on arriving. A good artist lets his intuition lead him wherever it wants. A good scientist has freed himself of concepts and keeps his mind open to what is."[29]

A metaphor underlying this book is that of strategy as a jazz performance. Indeed, exquisite jazz comes from practice, musicianship, having no preconceived score, being present in bandmates' solos, and accepting the notes that emerge in the moment. Rather than the pages of sheet music that dictate a symphony, all the jazz performer has is one or two pages of lyrics, melody, and chord structure. That is the intended strategy. Everything else is invented on the spot, emergent in harmony with one's colleagues.

Several of the philosophers discussed in this book employ water as a metaphor. Sun Tzu said: "Military tactics are like unto water; for water in its natural course runs away from high places and hastens downwards. . . . Water shapes its course according to the nature of the ground over which it flows;

the soldier works out his victory in relation to the foe whom he is facing."[30] Similarly, Lao Tzu noted: "Nothing in the world is as soft and yielding as water. Yet for dissolving the hard and inflexible, nothing can surpass it. The soft overcomes the hard; the gentle overcomes the rigid."[31]

The metaphor of water can be applied to martial arts, including the ones explored in this book. Bruce Lee, whose starring roles in a series of 1970s blockbuster films made him one of history's most influential martial artists, often advised: "Empty your mind, be formless, shapeless—like water."[32] In chapter 9, we explored this principle in relation to defensive martial arts, attributing their superiority in conflict to the fact that "the soft and supple will prevail."[33]

Principle summary: Creating a strategic plan is a critical exercise. It helps the participants clarify currently available resources, understand the market, define goals, and prioritize the variables that will enable or prevent success. Once the planning is done and it is time to act, the effective strategist must constantly survey the landscape for newly available resources, changes in the environment, and unforeseen challenges. Targets also must be adjusted accordingly. Sticking too rigidly to a planned course of action puts us at risk of failure, or at the very least of losing out on unanticipated opportunities. This does not mean that we lose sight of long-term goals at the first unexpected turn of events. Rather, we are willing to adjust our path to these goals based on changing circumstances.

PRINCIPLE 7. IMPERMANENCE IS THE ONLY REALITY

Many Westerners see the future as a continuation of the past, with its course changed primarily via human intervention. In other words, as long as cause-effect truths are teased out, the world is predictably stable.

Many Eastern cultures, by contrast, perceive the world as constantly evolving, bending to the laws of dharma and karma, influenced by the interactions between yin and yang, forces of dark and light, growth and decay. The role of the individual is to conform to these laws, accept outcomes as beyond one's control, and blend with fellow humans through calm harmony. The path to this harmony is gained by freeing one's mind of preconceptions, relinquishing ego and attachment to outcomes, and allowing truths to emerge from action.

Which view prevails? That is perhaps the wrong question. A better line of inquiry might be, "Which view promotes long-term strategic thinking?" As to longevity, we note that we used General Electric as a positive example in the introduction of this book. GE pioneered an extraordinary number of management principles, techniques, and philosophies that became best practices studied in MBA programs and implemented in corporate boardrooms. GE was one of the original members of the Dow Jones Industrial Average when it was created in 1886. By 2018, GE was the only one of the original group still part of the DJIA. Yet, after a string of underwhelming results across its business units, GE too was removed from the DJIA in 2019.

To underscore the impermanence inherent to business affairs, it is enough to study the fates of many of the companies touted as outperformers in classic business texts. Despite the popularity of *In Search of Excellence* by Tom Peters and Robert Waterman and *Built to Last* by James Collins and Jerry Porras,[34] many of the companies held up as paragons have subsequently fallen from their pedestals. These books' halo companies include Atari, Wang Labs, and Kodak (*In Search of Excellence*), and Motorola, Ford, General Electric, and Hewlett Packard (*Built to Last*). While some of the organizations continue to operate—and even thrive—today, all have experienced significant periods of underperformance since the publication of the books.

Ultimately, as a Darden student said, "the success or failure of our enterprises are mere dots on an infinitely long and detailed tapestry on which very few singular firms stand out."[35] For many Eastern philosophers, this reality is accepted as the natural state of affairs. (See the next principle on circularity.) For Western strategists, recognition of this reality should invite a humility that will open the door to new strategic insights brought by serendipitous moments of coup d'oeil.

Principle summary: Change is not only constant, but a reality that strategists must incorporate into their expectations.

PRINCIPLE 8. CIRCULARITY AND ITERATION COMPLEMENT LINEARITY

Kingsley Liu, CEO of Casey Companies, led this book's senior author and his wife, Maggie, to the altar of Man Mo Temple, where they would experience the fortune-telling power of *Kau Cim* sticks. It was 1984. Liu, a Stanford Business School graduate now running a major real estate and luxury goods enterprise in Hong Kong, was intent on having his guests "see China through the eyes of a Chinese." Maggie and Jay knelt at an altar, and each shook the *Cim* bucket, a bamboo cylinder holding a hundred wooden sticks with *Kangi* characters emblazoned on them, until a stick fell to the floor. They took their sticks to the monk sitting nearby, who told them the story associated with each stick and translated it into their fortunes. The monk interpreted Jay's stick as foretelling of great wealth accumulated over time. Maggie's stick was interpreted as "wealth is likely to dwindle."

Jay did not like this at all. "Why should our fortunes be so opposite?" he asked. "Why should one of us accumulate wealth while the other sees it whittled down? It doesn't seem right!" With a wan smile, the monk answered simply, "Yin and yang."

The yin and yang symbol features prominently in Eastern thought. It represents the reality of life as cyclical and subject to the alternating forces of opposites, such as dark and light or male and female. For the many Westerners who understand world events as progressing linearly, such a notion is difficult to grasp. Many Eastern cultures, on the other hand, see harmony and balance in the cyclical nature of life. As Liu explained to us, everything balances, eventually. "Yin (the dark and passive) alternates with yang (the light and active). Yin and yang only exist because of each other, and when the world is in a yin state, this is a sure sign that it is about to be in a yang state."[36] Indeed, from this perspective, the monk's prediction was a rational explanation of the inevitable—the presence of wealth means poverty is around the corner.[37]

To illustrate this principle further, we need only turn to the Buddha's Eightfold Path, perhaps one of the most widely known of the teachings shared in this book. Western descriptions of the Path typically describe a sequential list of steps 1 through 8.[38] In English translations each of the steps begins with the word "right": right understanding, right purpose, right speech, right conduct, and so on.

However, in this context the word "right" should not be interpreted to mean "correct" or "not wrong." With "right," a limited English translation, Buddhism means to evoke a sense of truth, alignment, and shared purpose. The eight steps are aligned with each other and with *dhamma.* Rather than a sequential list, Buddhist literature typically depicts the Eightfold Path as spokes on a wheel. Not only are the steps of the Path not to be experienced sequentially, but each step relates to and supports every other one.

Similarly, in Western culture, particularly in the world of business, strategies are often viewed as a set of predetermined benchmarks to be achieved in a specific order. Even Western strategists admit the flaw in this approach. As Bryan Quinn, former professor at Dartmouth's Tuck School, put it: "To cast your strategy in concrete is to assume that new information has no value."[39] Carl von Clausewitz pointed out that no matter how meticulously a battle plan has been crafted, a soldier enters the "fog of war" as soon as the first shot is fired in his direction,[40] implying that strategies often go awry when they encounter the unpredictable nature of business cycles, competitive dynamics, geopolitics, and other forces. While Western strategists have looked to counter the shortcomings in their linear approach by creating additional optionality,[41] Eastern philosophers seem to have eliminated the need for these supplementary tactics altogether.

Instead, strategy informed by Eastern philosophy might take a more iterative, circular approach, with a focus on aligning oneself with the natural order of things, rather than generating progress toward an endpoint. As Ravi Menon told us in Singapore, when he prepares to make a decision his mind revolves in circles, his ideas follow that circular pattern, and eventually a decision is spit out. According to Kim Whitler, a former global marketing executive and now an MBA professor: "In China, marketing executives speak disparagingly about 'strategy' [by which] they. . . . mean the painstaking, bureaucratic, process- [and tool-] heavy planning that takes place in firms."[42] The *Tao Te Ching* addresses the concept most directly, proclaiming that "the Tao moves by returning in endless cycles."[43] In Buddhism, there is no expectation of flawlessly following the path of *dhamma*. Instead, progress occurs when the practitioner strays from the path and exerts the effort to return to it, therefore building the muscle of mindfulness.

Principle summary: If today looks like an extension of yesterday, don't expect the future to follow suit. In fact, those who expect reversion to the mean but accept that they cannot predict when it will happen are more likely to go with the flow of water, bend with the wind, receive calamities with equanimity, and open themselves to new insights.

PRINCIPLE 9. SELF-DISCIPLINE VERSUS SELF AS AN ILLUSION

A cow, a hen, a meadow. Which two go together? According to social psychologist Richard Nisbett's experiments, Westerners tend to find the most in common between the cow and the hen—both are animals. Easterners, by contrast, more frequently pair the cow with the meadow—the meadow nurtures the cow, and the cow returns nutrients to the meadow. This mental process is not one of categorizing, as Westerners tend to do, but of seeing relationships. Extending this principle, the self exists only in relationship to other human beings, to the community, to the world at large.

Indeed, as Nisbett points out, Western mothers are likely to ask their toddlers questions about objects and supply information about them: "The banana tastes good." "The fork fell." "Your brother is big." Mothers in Eastern cultures, on the other hand, are likely to express feelings and relationships: "The farmer feels bad if you did not eat everything your mom cooked for you."[44] American babies learn nouns—mom, food, shoes. Chinese babies more often first learn verbs—feel, cry, throw. Nouns are categorical, whereas verbs have no meaning without an object and a subject—in other words, a relationship.

In the more individualistic cultures of the West, particularly in the United States, a cult of self-reliance tends to glorify the individual. As a result, in America's business culture contributors are often expected to view themselves as responsible for reaching the goals set for them specifically and celebrated for those individual achievements.

The Eastern philosophers we have explored, particularly Confucius and Musashi, stressed the importance of discipline as a gateway to achieving success both in battle and in spiritual awakening, but that discipline does not transform into a glorification of the individual. Discipline is viewed as a prerequisite that can help armies win in battle, a samurai defeat his opponent, or a seeker reach enlightenment. However, each of these individual accomplishments is worth pursuing only because of its service to a greater, relational whole. A just ruler's conquest or a master samurai's victory implies that the world moves closer to a social and political order aligned with the universal law. Enlightenment unlocks for the individual a recognition of her connection to and oneness with the universe. These philosophers preached the importance of practicing self-discipline not in service of achieving individual goals or glorifying the self, but of letting go of attachment to the self and self-perception.

Principle summary: To varying degrees, the teachings described in this book emphasize the notion of shifting focus away from the individual as a separate entity and toward a recognition of a broader fabric of the universe connecting all of us. By letting go of the preexisting views of our organizations, our subordinates, our managers, and ourselves, we can better optimize a strategy to achieve success while remaining resilient in the face of obstacles that the strategy will encounter.

Action Directive IV: Take Action

PRINCIPLE 10. RESOLVE IS FUNDAMENTAL TO MOBILIZATION

Jack Welch's first act as CEO of GE was to disband the proliferating strategic planning departments and fire all external consultants. As he explained in an address to Duke's graduating MBA class, strategic planning had become a ritual, "like a rain dance. You know, 'I know it didn't rain. But, gee, didn't you like the dance?'"[45]

Resolution. Action. Execution. Determination. All are fundamental to strategic success. Clausewitz's fourth step was resolution: After filling the shelves of the brain with histories, clearing one's mind, and experiencing coup d'oeil, all is for naught without ignition, action, energy. The Buddha was similarly clear: Once enlightenment has been achieved and the flash of insight received, the successful leader must follow through. As spelled out in the Gita, leaders act because they now know their dharma, and "it is better to strive in one's own dharma than to succeed in the dharma of another. Nothing is ever lost in following one's dharma."[46] Leaders act "because they have the right to work."[47] They act because good leaders are also good people and, as the Buddha taught, "good people . . . carry out tasks."[48]

Of course, resolve does not mean attempting to carry out every task on one's own. Just as important is decisive action in designating responsibility. As L. J. B., the CEO of Esso Brasil, explained when asked how he kept a centered demeanor in the midst of economic and political chaos: "I merely hire the best engineers, accountants, marketers, and so on. Each of them knows their field far better than I do. And, many of them are smarter than I. My job is to work with them to figure out where to go. Then I set them loose. They are so good at what they do, I am confident that they will take any obstacles in stride and adapt appropriately to circumstances as they arise. Consequently, I sleep well at night." Like the leaders described in chapter 8 on the Tao, L. J. B. got out of his direct reports' way.

Charlottesville, Virginia, 2004

Having just taken office, Virginia's new secretary of transportation assembled his top forty executives to plan a strategy for the coming four-year term. During the process of developing a purpose statement, the Virginia Department of Transportation (VDOT) executives were taken with the image of drivers in convertibles cruising through the Blue Ridge Mountains under blue skies. With this in mind, they proudly came up with the statement: "VDOT brings Virginians the American Dream."

If the intent of a purpose statement is to "grab the soul" of every organizational member, as advised by Collins and Porras in *Built to Last*,[49] it should be tested with a broad employee base. To that end, the department surveyed workers in the field.

Picture a crew of burly men laying asphalt to repair a highway. Hot, sticky, smelly work. Tar permeates their pores and their clothes. The work is usually done in the summer, when ambient temperatures on the tarmac can reach more than 90 degrees Fahrenheit. Now imagine the workers are on break, leaning against a truck with water cups in their hands, wiping sweat from their necks and brows. A car approaches, and a young, enthusiastic, white-shirted government bureaucrat gets out and greets the men with a smile.

In his hand is a poster with the words "We bring Virginians the American Dream!" He says, "What do you think, guys?" The results of the survey were predictably uninspiring. (The workers' actual answers are unprintable.)

Back in Charlottesville, the chastened VDOT executives met again. But this time they included a foreman and a repairman. They exited the meeting with "We keep Virginia on the move." Simple, powerful, and providing meaning to VDOT managers, field workers, office personnel, and administrators across the state.

If you give your team a sense of purpose and general direction, trust them to figure out the details of execution. After all, to quote an Australian aphorism, they are the ones "close to the coal face," and they know their tools. They will look to you for direction, inspiration, and core values. But they know the terrain—the machines, the customers, the suppliers, the employees.

As Lao Tzu tells us: "When the Master governs, the people are hardly aware that he exists. . . . The Master doesn't talk, he acts. When his work is done, the people say, 'Amazing: we did it, all by ourselves!'"[50] "The Master leads by . . . toughening [people's] resolve. . . . Practice not-doing, and everything will fall into place."[51]

Confucius taught that achieving the abstract notion of happiness requires material, concrete action. Positive outcomes can be realized only by living a life centered on universal principles. The flash of insight we might experience is not enough. We must have the resolve to carry through.

Principle summary: Effective strategy is crucial, but its value can be captured only through determined, effective execution. Of course, strategists and decision makers must in their own behavior prioritize a resolute commitment. Just as important, in their management, delegation, and the organizational culture they inspire, leaders must position their teams to pursue committed effort. In this way, the organization can benefit from the working-level expertise of those responsible for execution.

PRINCIPLE 11. TIMING IS EVERYTHING

Manhattan, New York, 1998

Metromedia founder John Kluge, listed by *Forbes* as the sixth-wealthiest man in the United States in 1988, retired to Charlottesville, Virginia, in 1980. Informal dinner parties at his Morven Farm were a weekly event. At one, the senior author noted the calm and equanimity with which Kluge carried himself. The author asked: "John, is this your calm in retirement, or were you always this centered? And if the latter, how did you keep an even keel in the buzzing confusion of deal-making when you were active?" Kluge responded:

> I was always in a hurry. But one afternoon, while hosting a Columbia University classmate, the son of a senior Chinese government official, we left for dinner and went down to catch the subway. As a train was about to close its doors, I broke into a sprint. My friend put his hand on my arm before I got very far and asked, "When is the next train?" My answer, "In about three minutes." He looked at me and tilted his head. I got it. I took a deep breath and slowed to a walk.
>
> Not long after, I studied Buddhism, which I practice to this day. Very few things—actions, decisions, impetuous sprinting about—benefit from urgency, or fail to benefit from patience. This has been one of my operating principles since.[52]

Bangkok, Thailand, June 2018

Mint Namasondhi guided Jay Bourgeois into the Tiger God Shrine, a small, ancient Taoist temple.[53] In the back, next to a small altar, were bamboo cylinders holding wooden sticks. Unlike in Hong Kong's Man Mo Temple more than thirty years earlier, these cylinders held forty-eight sticks instead of a hundred. And the instructions for the ritual were different. Before shaking the cylinder, you had to ask a question relevant to your life that needed resolution. This was no passive see-what-fortune-you-have-in-store exercise. It required serious introspection to find a worthy query. Next, you shook the cylinder until a stick fell out, then cast two painted blocks on the floor. If both blocks fell painted-side up or down, it meant that the chosen stick would not answer your question, and you had to repeat the procedure. Jay's blocks fell into opposite positions, meaning *this was it.*

Jay's daughter Marie, the young artist we encountered earlier, had been widowed four years previously and left with three small children. Fortunately, she had formed a new relationship with Pat, who also was widowed with three children. It was clear that they wanted to marry, but they were constantly postponing, waiting for the "right" time for the children. It had been two years, and the couple's parents were getting restless. Jay's question for the ritual was simple: When should Pat and Marie "get off the pot" and close the deal? More pointedly, "Should I say something to Pat?"

He shook the cylinder and a stick fell out. Jay and Mint took the stick to the waiting monk, who, after silent deliberation, said, "Patience is a virtue."

Damn! That was not the answer Jay wanted to hear. He wanted permission to take action. But he resolved to hold his tongue when he got back to Charlottesville.

Four weeks later, Pat invited Jay to lunch. After a leisurely meal with conversation centered on sports, they ordered coffee. Pat took a sip or two then put down his cup. He looked Jay in the eye and said, "I plan to propose to your daughter, and wanted you to know beforehand."

The Western instinct is to act. Now. Among the winning characteristics that Tom Peters had unearthed in his study of excellent companies, one of the most prominent was a bias for action. This is echoed in Nike's famous motto, "Just do it."

Similarly, despite such famous commands as Captain Prescott's "Don't fire until you see the whites of their eyes" at the Battle of Bunker Hill during the Revolutionary War, Americans tend to encourage heroic and daring action.

Compare this to the Tao: "Do you have the patience to wait till your mud settles and the water is clear? Can you remain unmoving till the right action arises itself?"[54] Sometimes specific problems can be solved by time alone, and trying to rush things causes a problem to become more difficult. Despite wanting to drive the result through action, often it is inaction that creates a harmonious solution. Knowing when to let things go means walking a fine line, yet the Tao implies those situations occur more frequently than we realize. It is our job to know when things are best left to simmer, instead of adding more heat and causing them to boil over.[55]

Earlier, we saw Ravi Menon, Sumeth Laomoraporn, and Naresh Kumra avoid intemperate impulses when confronted with crises by, first, meditating, and next, figuring out how to buy time.

Sometimes there is value in maintaining the status quo, or the action of inaction. It could be argued that some of the Eastern philosophies discussed in this book were originally developed to help maintain the social status quo and preserve the ancient monarchies prevailing when the texts were written. However, there is an important lesson underlying this principle: Our inaction, or the absence of taking a visible course of action, is also an action by omission. What in the West could be seen as indecisive is for Eastern philosophers a powerful act. This is especially true for both Sun Tzu and Confucius—well-timed inaction signals the wisdom of a leader. By so (not) doing, the leader signals his imperviousness to impulse or others' judgment.

Modern business leaders faced with mounting pressure from investors, customers, and other stakeholders are often expected to make quick judgment calls. Even when backed by data and sound analysis, hasty decisions frequently create undue stress for the organization. The high-pressure environment of corporate mergers and acquisitions serves as a particularly powerful example of this dynamic. As anyone who has participated in an acquisition bidding war knows, a pressure cooker environment and the decisions it inspires too often serve as a recipe for overpaying.[56]

As the *Tao Te Ching* teaches: "Rushing into action, you fail. . . . Forcing a project to completion, you ruin what was almost ripe. Therefore the Master takes action by letting things take their course."[57]

Principle summary: Exercising patience may seem obvious in theory, but it often is brutally challenging to put into practice. Even the best decision makers are flawed human beings with unconscious biases, navigating through a sea of shifting currents. To engage with this principle, then, requires training. More than an attitude or a personality trait, Eastern philosophies view the capacity for patience as a skill to be cultivated through focused practice. The capacity for nonreactivity is a core reason for many Eastern philosophers' emphasis on the power of meditation.[58]

PRINCIPLE 12. GOOD STRATEGY IS ABOUT BALANCE, THE MIDDLE WAY, AND MODERATION

Lao Tzu noted that "for governing a country well, there is nothing better than moderation."[59] In recent years, the notions of a BHAG ("big, hairy, audacious goal")[60] and of proclaiming one's strategic intent—a declaration of a future for which current capabilities are potentially inadequate—have become particularly fashionable among Western strategy gurus.[61] Their popularity is understandable; such goal statements are inspiring and exciting.

Bacardi Ltd., ranking eighth in the spirits business in sales in 1993, declared a mission to become No. 5 by the year 2000. According to Jim Collins, a good mission has both a destination and a timeline. This one had both.[62]

Two years later, Bacardi acquired Martini and Rossi, a major competitor. The acquisition catapulted Bacardi into the ranks of the world's top five spirits producers well ahead of schedule. "What now?" company leaders asked the senior author. He answered that their task going forward from 1993 had been to make their mission obsolete, and they had succeeded in doing so. Now, they needed to reset and declare a new mission.

Bacardi's management met again for an off-site strategy meeting. Early in the day, the CEO and his six direct reports came to the assembled thirty executives with a new mission: to, by 2001, "remain in the top five." The collective shoulder slump was palpable. Effectively reading the room, the seven leaders retreated to their private conference space to reconsider. By the end of the day, they returned with a new mission: "to triple sales in six years and become Number 1 in the industry." The Bacardi Cubans and the Martini Italians jumped to their feet and cheered.

How do we reconcile such inspiring grasps beyond our reach with our philosophers' restraint in the pursuit of moderation and balance?

It is a matter of emphasis. BHAGs and strategic intents point to destinations. Eastern philosophies, on the other hand, show us how to undertake the journey.

A common theme across our philosophers' teachings is the importance of achieving balance, especially internally. That is what differentiates great leaders from individuals who simply hold positions of authority. Eastern philosophies teach us how to control our minds and direct our thoughts toward a deeper purpose, a purpose that centers on finding balance while on our path.

Principle summary: Strategists must not interpret Eastern philosophy's emphasis on moderation as a proscription against ambitious targets. From the Buddha's search for nibbana to Musashi's mastery of samurai combat, the Eastern sages showed little reluctance to take on a challenge. What's more, their teachings are not short on examples of intense, committed action, from the persistence with which Zen students pursue the answer to a koan to the Buddha's long meditation under the bodhi tree until he achieved enlightenment. A Westerner might see these as parables for unrelenting hard work. Yet, they are not in conflict with the focus on moderation. Moderation here refers to a quality of openness through which we are well positioned to remain fluid, present, and ready to receive coup d'oeil when insight strikes.

These twelve principles conclude our exploration of Eastern philosophy and how it informs Western strategists and the search for strategic insights. Where do we go from here?

AFTERWORD

Singapore, January 2020

Looking out toward Marina Bay, Ravi Menon reflected on how he had handled the crisis of Global Horizons's 38 percent sales plummet in 2018.

Ravi had found himself trapped in the linear loop of building a foundation—arming himself with business and industry knowledge, reports on market trends and customer behaviors, and so on. But he had forgotten that his mind must also be able to entertain openness and detachment. In short, he forgot to prepare beginner's mind. His commitment to planning thoroughly and driving impressive results, combined with his previous achievements, had gradually taken over his mindset. Now, unexpected market forces had upended his planned strategy, and he found himself struggling to navigate not only the crisis, but also his mental, emotional, and physical reactions.

Ravi was grateful to his boss, Henry, for giving him another chance and encouraging him to navigate the challenge. At their meeting at his office in Zurich, Henry suggested that he first seek the advice of those he was entrusted to lead. He invited Ravi to create an inventory of his most capable subordinates on the Asia region management team, while he did the same. After they compared lists, Henry pointed to the names appearing on both and advised Ravi: "When you get back to Singapore, listen to them for counsel."

Ravi spent the next several days meeting with the managers Henry had identified. The conversations were fruitful in more ways than one. Talking with his team members—whose thinking reflected their upbringing in Asian cultures, and whose perspectives were informed by their work managing the day-to-day operations of markets across the continent—helped him better understand the key issues plaguing performance. Just as important, as he met with the managers Ravi felt himself reengage the Eastern mindset with which he had grown up.

Leaning on the Taoist principles he had learned, as well as insights inspired by the team members' various traditions, Ravi and his colleagues soon developed a range of clever solutions to the challenges facing the business. While they continued to use traditional analytic and strategic tools to better understand the situation, novel approaches inspired by Eastern philosophical traditions also played a vital role in plotting a future course.

Over several months, Ravi led the business in reimagining its relationships with retailers, consumers, employees, and other stakeholders. Within the year, the business had returned to its market-leading position and revenues had returned to precrisis levels.

As he reflected on his decision-making, Ravi noted:

> Even with my engineering and MBA training, there is an irrational side to me that I have not lost. . . . Our Eastern minds accept the nonrational, which explains our resilience. The need for facts is lower for me—I can work from the gut. I am not a big fan of speed, either. But I am not making decisions with fewer facts—I am making decisions with more than facts.
>
> My decision-making is circular rather than linear. [He made a circling gesture with his finger.] My mind is spiraling around, and to an observer it looks like I'm making no progress. But eventually, a good decision emerges.
>
> I think of my mind as a candle in a cave—trying to see in the cave where and what others cannot.

Lighting Your Candle in the Cave

The themes in this book are by and large parables, lessons, and tactics designed to help us momentarily let go of our analytical focus and interpret the world, process information, and draw conclusions in new ways. Unlike Western business practices, these themes are not an exercise in pattern recognition or studies of historical trends in order to develop specific targets and strategies. We are not suggesting that the philosophers covered in this book argued for abandoning this traditional method of strategy development. Instead, we believe that engaging with Eastern philosophies will push strategists to expand their armory by incorporating a broader array of thought processes and approaches.

Where to Now?

By applying Eastern principles—and having built a foundation, prepared our minds, adjusted our lenses, and taken action—the question now is, how do we reconcile these pragmatic instructions with our Western tendencies and training?

As strategy practitioners, all three authors believe heartily in the value of Western-style strategy development. Linear and logical strategic thinking has multiple benefits. It is relatively easy to use, it can be communicated effectively from person to person, and in the Western world we have cultivated effective tools to support this approach. However, we believe Eastern approaches also play a significant role. They serve as a stress test to check our strategies for flaws and sensitivities and identify key assumptions that drive them and will determine their success or failure.

In this book we have sampled several classic Eastern philosophies and glimpsed the philosophical cornerstones of many societies. In contrast to much of the traditional strategy subject matter covered in chapter 1, Eastern philosophy leaves us with more questions than answers, a state that better reflects the vagueness of contemporary and future business competition. It is ultimately the strategic leader's role to acknowledge this challenge and to lead the organization through the uncertainty.

For some readers, consuming Eastern philosophy is like learning a language—it takes time to sink in. It must be practiced. It must be treated as a journey. Along your journey, we encourage you to try out some widely available activities, such as aikido, the game of Go, Tai Chi, meditation and mindfulness, and yoga.

Above all, continue reading, exploring, and filling the shelves of your brain. And occasionally practice one of the contemplative arts—pause, take a breath. As with all effective strategic theories and tools, the key is finding a balance that fits your organization and its external environment.

APPENDIX 1

EXECUTIVES AND ORGANIZATIONS PROFILED

(in order of appearance)

Introduction

Ravi Menon, regional VP, Global Horizons, Singapore
Cheng Gang, professor of philosophy, Tsinghua University, Shanghai
Bacardi C-Suite, Bermuda
Tom Thorsen, CFO, General Electric, Fairfield, Connecticut

1. Strategy, Insight, and Competitive Advantage

Clay Cox, CMO, Dominion Analytics, Herndon, Virginia
Jay Bourgeois, associate dean and director, Darden Center for Global Initiatives, Charlottesville, Virginia
Steve Jobs, CEO, Apple Computer, Mountain View, California

2. Warfare in Eastern Philosophy

Ulrich Bez, CEO, Aston Martin Lagonda, Gaydon, United Kingdom
ICI Australia C-Suite, Melbourne

3. Competitive Dynamics and the Chinese Game of Go

China Steel C-Suite, Taipei
Seaver Solutions, New York City
Seth Winogrond, CEO, Aggregate Materials Industries, Albany, Georgia
Steve Hansel, president, Hibernia Bank, New Orleans

4. Dharma and the Bhagavad Gita

Naresh Kumra, CEO, Jmatek, Hong Kong
L. J. B., CEO, Esso Brasil, Rio de Janeiro
Narayana Murthy, CEO, Infosys, Bangalore

5. The Buddha and His Teaching

Sumeth Laomoraporn, CEO (several divisions), CP Group, Bangkok
Nok Anulomsombut, CEO, Sea Ltd., Bangkok

6. The Buddha and Mindfulness

Lou C., senior VP, Rodale Press, Emmaus, Pennsylvania
Maria Rodale, CEO, Rodale Press
Patchara (Pat) Taveechaiwattana, CMO, Allianz Ayudhya, Bangkok
Fifi Mak, CEO, Dong Rong Electronics, Hong Kong
Kyle Guy, guard, 2018 UVA championship basketball team

8. The *Tao Te Ching*

Seabees lieutenant in charge, personal communication
Adam Westerfeld, VP production, ICI Australia, commodity chemicals division, Melbourne

9. Energy as a Strategic Force

Joyce Bolger, MD and acupuncturist, Charlottesville, Virginia
Cal Turner, CEO, Dollar General Corp., Nashville
Aston Martin, factory workers, Gaydon, United Kingdom
Standard & Poor's Global Ratings, senior executives, New York City
Tom Storrs, VP strategy, Takata Corporation, Tokyo
Juhani Laine, VP strategy, Amer Group, Helsinki
Christo Klaasen, VP strategy, EdCon, Johannesburg
Jennifer Jasinski, insurance executive, Liberty Mutual, Hartford, Connecticut
Joe Ruggiano, division head, Disney Development Corporation, Los Angeles

10. Confucius

Andy Palmer, CEO, Aston Martin Lagonda, Gaydon, United Kingdom
Houlder Offshore, author personal involvement, London
IBM, author personal involvement, Atlanta
Australia Department of Agriculture C-Suite, Canberra
Luke Robinson, VP human resources, Dole Foods, La Ceiba, Honduras
Rod Granger, CEO, Southeast Paper, Macon, Georgia
Tevin Vongvanich, CEO, PTT Group, Bangkok

11. Strategy as a Call to (in)Action

Scott McNealy, CEO, Sun Microsystems, Mountain View, California
Bill Joy, VP research and development, Sun Microsystems
L. J. B., CEO, Esso Brasil, Rio de Janeiro

Virginia Department of Transportation, personal involvement, Richmond
John Kluge, CEO, Metromedia, New York City
Kingsley Liu, CEO, Casey Companies, Hong Kong
Bacardi C-Suite, Miami

Afterword

Ravi Menon, VP Asia region, Global Horizons, Singapore (new title reflects promotion since first mention)

Note: Names of some persons and institutions are disguised in order to preserve confidentiality and privacy.

APPENDIX 2

THE CONTENTS OF *THE ART OF WAR*

The Art of War consists of thirteen short chapters. Their titles and selected statements are below, with direct quotes italicized. Page numbers refer to the 1983 James Clavell translation.

I. Laying Plans (9–11)
All principles and plans are to be modified when circumstances change.

All warfare is based on deception. (11) Feign disorder and weakness; use surprise.

A comparison of two opposing armies on the following dimensions will predict victory or defeat. (10)

1. Which of the two follows the Moral Law?
2. Which general has the most ability?
3. Which army gains advantage from Heaven and Earth conditions?
4. Which side enforces discipline most rigorously?
5. Which army is stronger?
6. In which army are the officers and men most trained?
7. Which army is more certain of merit reward and misdeed punishment?

Note that six of the seven predictors focus on capabilities and leadership, not on numbers or position-based advantages.

II. On Waging War (12–14)
The value of time . . . has counted for more than either numerical superiority or the nicest calculations. (13)

In all history, there is no instance of a country having benefited from prolonged warfare. (13)

In order to kill the enemy, our men must be roused to anger. (14)

III. The Sheathed Sword (15–18)
Win without fighting by leveraging flexibility and deploying individuals according to their strengths and predispositions.

Supreme excellence consists [not in winning all battles fought, but] in breaking the enemy's resistance without fighting. (15)

The skillful employer of men will employ the wise man, the brave man, the covetous man, and the stupid man. For the wise man delights in establishing his merit, the brave man likes to show his courage in action, the covetous man is quick at seizing advantages, and the stupid man has no fear of death. (17)

The most quoted passage in the annals of strategy and war: *If you know the enemy and know yourself, you will need not fear the result of a hundred battles.* (18)

IV. Tactics (19–20)
Wait, be patient, and the enemy will provide opportunities for your success.

To secure ourselves against defeat lies in our own hands, but the opportunity of defeating the enemy is provided by the enemy himself. (19)

The acme of excellence [is not to] fight and conquer and the whole empire says, "Well done!" True excellence is to plan secretly, to move surreptitiously, to foil the enemy's intentions and balk his schemes, so that at last the day may be won without shedding a drop of blood. (20)

V. Energy (21–24)
Energy comes from a combination of resources and indirect tactics.

Use turmoil and tumult, disorder, confusion, and chaos of battle to cloak your underlying discipline, courage, strength, and latent energy.

Energy may be likened to the bending of a crossbow; decision, to the releasing of the trigger. The onset of troops is like the rush of a torrent that will even roll stones along in its course. (22)

VI. Weak Points and Strong (25–29)
Maneuver against an opponent, avoiding his strengths and staying flexible.

VII. Maneuvering (30–36)

One of the most quoted passages appears in this chapter: *We are not fit to lead an army on the march unless we are familiar with the face of the country—its mountains and forests, its pitfalls and precipices, its marshes and swamps.* (32)

Do not interfere with an army that is returning home because a man whose heart is set on returning home will fight to the death against any attempt to bar his way. . . . When you surround an army, leave an outlet free. (35)

VIII. Variation of Tactics (37–40)

There are armies that must not be attacked, positions that must not be contested, and commands of the sovereign that must not be obeyed. (38)

There are five dangerous faults that may affect a general:

1. *Recklessness, which leads to destruction*
2. *Cowardice, which leads to capture*
3. *Delicacy of honor, which is sensitive to shame*
4. *A hasty temper, which can be provoked by insults*
5. *Over-solicitude for his men, which exposes him to worry and trouble . . . [and thus] the prolongation of the war* (39–40)

IX. The Army on the March (41–49)

He who exercises no forethought but makes light of his opponents is sure to be captured by them. (41)

Recognize enemy movements by, for example, using the sudden rise of birds or columns of dust.

In terms of discipline, be humane but ruthless in enforcing rules, consistently and at appropriate levels: *Vacillation and fussiness are the surest means of sapping the confidence of an army.* (49)

X. Terrain (50–55)

Calamities can befall an army by fault of the general:

Flight, when attacking a force ten times greater
Insubordination, when the soldiers are strong and the officers weak
Collapse, when the officers are too strong and the soldiers weak
Ruin, when officers feel resentment or anger
Disorganization, when the general is weak

XI. The Nine Situations (56–72)
Rapidity is the essence of war. (58)

Throw your soldiers into positions whence there is no escape, and they will prefer death to flight. (61)

Soldiers in desperate straits lose the sense of fear. (62)

XII. Attack by Fire (73–76)
To win in battle, use fire to destroy the enemy's resources:

1. In their camp (burn the soldiers)
2. Burn their stores
3. Burn their baggage trains
4. Burn arsenals and magazines
5. Hurl dropping fire on them

To succeed, lead with discipline:

1. Do not move unless you see an advantage
2. Don't fight merely to gratify your ego
3. Don't fight out of anger

XIII. The Use of Spies (77–82)
What enables the . . . good general to strike and conquer . . . is foreknowledge. Now this foreknowledge cannot be elicited from spirits; it cannot be obtained inductively from experience, nor by any deductive calculation. . . . Knowledge of the enemy's dispositions can only be obtained from other men . . . through spies and spies alone. (78)

There are four types of spies:

1. *Inward spies* are officials of the enemy: demoted men, punished criminals, greedy favorite concubines, or fickle turncoats.
2. *Converted spies* are the enemy's spies who are turned by bribes, promises, or false information.
3. *Doomed spies* are your own turncoats who have been fed false information that they will share with the enemy.
4. *Surviving spies* are the ordinary spies who bring back news from the enemy's camp.

Spies are a most important element in war, because upon them depends an army's ability to move. (82; last sentence in the book)

APPENDIX 3

THE FOUR THEMES OF THE *TAO TE CHING*

The purpose of this outline is to allow the reader to locate (by page number listed below) and turn to individual passages or "chapters" according to the theme of interest. The entries are very condensed summaries of the contents of each chapter.

The Tao (33 chapters)

1. Unnamable, untellable.
4. Void. Well that is never used up.
5. Don't take sides (good vs. bad or the sin vs. the sinner).
6. The Great Mother. Empty but inexhaustible.
7. Infinite; eternal.
11. Empty pot. Wood house—inner space makes livable.
12. Trust your inner vision (versus senses).
14. Look and it can't be seen.
16. Empty your mind. Tao is the source of serenity.
18. When Tao is forgotten, goodness appears.
21. Since before time, Tao is.
25. Tao: Serene, empty, infinite.
26. Don't flit about like a fool. Heavy is root of the light.
28. Yin/yang.
32. Tao < electron (can't see it). If all did Tao, world = paradise.
34. Flows everywhere.
35. Is inexhaustible.
36. Soft > hard; slow > fast.
37. When there is no desire, world is at peace.
39. [If] in harmony with Tao, all is beautiful.
40. Being is born of nonbeing.
41. The path to light seems dark.
42. Tao gives birth to one, one gives birth to two, etc.
43. Gentle overcomes hard.
51. Every being in the universe is an expression of the Tao.

52. "In the beginning was the Tao." (See John 1:1 and 1:3.)
54. Let the Tao be present in your life and you will be genuine.
62. New leader: Don't offer your money, offer to teach the Tao.
67. My teaching is nonsense. Three things to teach: Simplicity, patience, compassion.
70. To understand my teaching, you need to put it into practice.
72. When people lose their sense of awe, they turn to religion.
73. The Tao is always at ease. It accomplishes without a plan.
77. Like a bent bow. Acts without expectations.

***Wu Wei* (21 chapters)**

2. Act but don't expect. Have but don't possess.
10. Lead without trying to control.
15. Patience to wait until your mud settles and water is clear.
19. Stay centered and let things take their course.
22. Because the master has no goal in mind, everything he does succeeds.
23. Open yourself to the Tao and everything will fall into place.
24. Tiptoe, clinging—just do your job, then let go.
27. A good traveler has no fixed plans.
29. Stop trying to control. "There is a season."
38. The master does nothing, yet leaves nothing undone.
45. Allow things to happen, then shape as they come.
47. The more you know, the less you understand.
48. True mastery is a function of letting things go their own way.
50. Give things up. Know you're going to die.
55. If you never expect results, you will never be disappointed.
63. Act without doing. Confront the difficult while it is still easy.
64. Rushing into action, you fail.
65. Teach not-knowing. When people think they know the answer, they are difficult to guide.
68. Virtue of noncompetition.
71. Not knowing is true knowledge.
74. All things change. If you're not afraid of dying, there's nothing you can't achieve.

Leadership (13 chapters)

3. Lead by *wu wei*.
8. KISS. Don't compare yourself.
9. Bowl/brim. Money/unclench. Approval/prisoner.
17. "We did it all by ourselves."
30. Don't try to force issues.

49. Treat people as if your children.
57. Stop trying to control.
58. Serve as an example. Don't impose your will.
59. Govern with moderation. Moderate = free from your own ideas.
60. Governing = like frying a small fish.
61. Great men admit mistakes. Critic = teacher.
69. All streams lead to the sea.
81. Don't force. No need to prove your point.

Philosophy (14 chapters)

13. Success as dangerous as failure.
20. Others are better than I (bright/dark; sharp/dull).
31. Weapons are tools of violence.
33. If you realize you have enough, you are truly rich.
44. Look to others for fulfillment. Fame versus integrity.
46. If you see through (the illusion of) fear, you are always safe.
53. Class and economic status differences—not in keeping with the Tao.
56. Basically: Shut up.
66. Prevent trouble before it arises.
75. High taxes lead to hunger; trust and "leave them alone."
76. Men are born soft and supple, die stiff and hard.
78. Water soft and yielding; soft > hard.
79. Failure = opportunity to blame someone else.
80. Wise government = content people (who won't travel far away).

NOTES

Introduction

1. Oster, *Modern Competitive Analysis.*
2. Hamel and Prahalad, "Strategic Intent."
3. C-Suite is shorthand for the chief executive's team of direct reports, often with such titles as chief operating officer, chief financial officer, and chief learning officer.
4. Clausewitz, *On War,* trans. Howard and Paret.
5. Stanford MBA class, October 1984.

1. Strategy, Insight, and Competitive Advantage

1. At the time, the CGI was called the Taloe-Murphy International Institute. It has since been renamed the Center for Global Initiatives.
2. Personal communication.
3. Jenny Craddock, L. J. Bourgeois, Yiorgos Allayanis, Morela Hernandez, and Luca Cian, "Aston Martin: The Crossover Conundrum," UVA-S-0298, Darden Business Publishing, 2018.
4. Porter, "How Competitive Forces Shape Strategy." The Five Forces describe the pressures on an industry that reduce its profitability. A profitable industry, for example, attracts new entrants, so (1) if barriers to entry are low, newcomers can enter easily; (2) suppliers will raise prices (and therefore costs) to the industry; (3) buyers might negotiate prices down; (4) viable substitutes might supplant the industry's offerings; and (5) the intensity of competition—usually price—among players may increase.
5. Antoine Jomini, *Summary of the Art of War,* Military Service Publishing, 1947.
6. Duggan, *Strategic Intuition,* 60.
7. Henry Mintzberg, "Patterns of Strategy Formation," *Management Science* (May 24, 1978), 934–48.
8. This section is based on Geoff Lewis, Andre Markel, and Graham Hubbard, *Australian Strategic Management,* Prentice-Hall, 1993, 28–30.
9. Jay B. Barney, "Organizational Culture: Can It Be a Source of Sustained Competitive Advantage?" *Academy of Management Review,* vol. 2, no. 3 (1986): 656–65.
10. Personal communication from a PARC architect.
11. Oster, *Modern Competitive Analysis;* Porter, "How Competitive Forces Shape Strategy"; Kim and Mauborgne, *Blue Ocean Strategy;* Collis and Montgomery, "Competing on Resources"; Beihnocker, "Robust Adaptive Strategies"; Williamson, "Strategy as Options on the Future"; L. J. Bourgeois, "Note on Portfolio Techniques for Corporate Strategic Planning," UVA-BP-0292, Darden Business Publishing, 1988, rev. February 1997.

12. Bourgeois and Brodwin, "Strategy Implementation: Five Approaches to an Elusive Phenomenon."
13. Duggan, *Strategic Intuition,* 2.
14. Duggan, *Strategic Intuition,* 7.
15. Ghyczy, Oetinger, and Bassford, *Clausewitz on Strategy.*

2. Warfare in Eastern Philosophy

1. EUR = Euros; one euro = about USD1.39 in 2009.
2. "Lagonda: Revival of a Luxury Brand," Aston Martin press release, 2009.
3. GBP = British pounds; one pound = USD1.60 in 2009.
4. Chris Hedges, *War Is a Force That Gives Us Meaning,* Public Affairs, 2002, 13.
5. Amazon lists more than forty thousand books related to the term "military," while Barnes & Noble offers more than thirty-seven hundred titles in the category of military strategy.
6. Several Westerners, such as Mark McNeilly, Donald Kraus, and Gerald Michelson, have noted the *Art of War*'s application to business.
7. Sun Tzu, *The Art of War,* trans. Griffith, 18.
8. Sun Tzu, 16.
9. Sun Tzu, *The Art of War,* trans. Clavell, 26.
10. "James Has a Notion of Where Blame Belongs," *Los Angeles Times,* August 8, 1987, Sports, 2.
11. Norman A. Berg, "Polaroid-Kodak," Case 376–266, Harvard Business Publishing, 1976.
12. Sun Tzu, *The Art of War,* trans. Griffith, 22.
13. Sun Tzu, *The Art of War,* trans. Clavell, 11.
14. Sun Tzu, 29.
15. Sun Tzu, 11.
16. Sun Tzu, *The Art of War,* trans. Griffith, 32.
17. Sun Tzu, 26.
18. Because the bulk of Musashi's book focuses on individual, hand-to-hand battle with long and short swords, we advise readers to pay less attention to the sections devoted to details of foot placement, eye movement, exchanging blows, stabbing different parts of the enemy's body, and so on. Instead, we direct readers to the following in W. S. Wilson's translation: Read all of the "Introduction," "Earth," and "Emptiness" chapters. In "Water," read only the opening section ("the frame of mind for the martial arts") and chapter ending; and only the openings and endings of the "Fire" and "Wind" chapters. (One may wish to skim pages 44–55 in "Water" for "how to kill," and pages 74–87 in "Fire" for examples of how to overcome the enemy.)
19. We should note that Musashi was explicit in "neither borrowing the ancient words of Buddhism or Confucianism" in his instruction in the Way of the Martial Arts. Musashi, *The Book of Five Rings,* trans. Wilson, 4.
20. Quotes in this section are from Musashi, 11–15.

21. Musashi, 5.
22. Musashi, 21.
23. Musashi, *The Book of Five Rings*, 14. https://www.holybooks.com/wp-content/uploads/The-Book-of-Five-Rings-by-Musashi-Miyamoto.pdf.
24. Musashi, trans. Wilson, 17.
25. Musashi, *The Book of Five Rings*, 9. https://www.holybooks.com/wp-content/uploads/The-Book-of-Five-Rings-by-Musashi-Miyamoto.pdf.

3. Competitive Dynamics and the Chinese Game of Go

1. Robert Reinhold, "Maoist Strategy Likened to Complex Game of Go," *New York Times*, March 6, 1971.
2. Modern chess originated as *chaturanga* in India in the seventh century AD.
3. W. A. C. Adia, "Chinese Strategic Thinking under Mao Tze-Tung," *Canberra Papers in Strategy and Defense No. 13*, Australian National University Press, 1972, 2.
4. Emma Young, "Chess! What Is It Good For?" *Science*, March 3, 2004.
5. Because doing is often a better teacher than telling, we have our MBA students engage in a Go tournament as part of our Strategic Intuition and Eastern Philosophy elective at the Darden School of Business. The contest is led by Professor Dewey Cornell, an avid Go player who teaches at UVA's Curry School of Education.
6. Reinhold, "Maoist Strategy," 3. In fact, Sun Tzu derived many of his *On War* principles from Go. (See chapter 3, "Competitive Dynamics and the Chinese Game of Go.")
7. *Mao's Selected Military Writings*, 96–97.
8. This comparison was widely employed in the early 2000s within the American military establishment to better understand China's rise as a major potential geopolitical competitor. Published in 2004, David Lai's *Learning from the Stones* stands as a well-executed example of this type of analysis.
9. The strategies used by IBM engineers to program Deep Blue's algorithms were not limited to effective patterns of movement for the pieces on the board. The engineers also programmed the computer to employ certain behavioral tactics (such as extensive delays that Kasparov might interpret as Deep Blue's experiencing problems in calculating a move) that sought to play on human psychology to develop an advantage.
10. Early moves in many Go games focus on the corners of the board because a player needs to encircle territory on only two sides. (Two edges of the board serve as automatic boundaries.) Mao's encirclement of the KMT is a classic example of occupying a corner (Nanking) and moving corner-to-corner in subsequent "moves" (Nanking, to Canton, to Chonqing, to Sichang, to Chengdu).
11. Senior author's personal communication.
12. Srinivasa Rangan and Chris Bartlett, "Caterpillar Tractor Company," Case 9-385-276, Harvard Business Publishing, 1988.
13. In 2019 U.S. dollars.
14. Srinivasa Rangan and Chris Bartlett, "Komatsu Limited," Case 9-385-277, Harvard Business Publishing, 1988.

Part II. The Inner Mind, overview

1. Herbert A. Simon, *Administrative Behavior,* MacMillan, 1947.
2. Barrett, *Zen Buddhism,* 71.

4. Dharma and the Bhagavad Gita

1. "Sears, Once Retail Colossus, Enters Painful New Era," *Wall Street Journal,* October 16, 2018, A1.
2. While the beauty of the Gita is worth appreciating in its entirety, for readers without a background in Hinduism we recommend focusing on chapters 1–6 and 18.
3. Hinduism also differs dramatically from Christianity by positing original goodness rather than original sin.
4. See the afterword in Barbara Stoler Miller's translation of the Bhagavad Gita: "Why Did Henry David Thoreau Take the *Bhagavad Gita* to Walden Pond?"
5. This chapter relies on the following translations of the Gita: Barbara Stoler Miller; Eknath Easwaran; Laurie Patton, Penguin Classics, 2008; Gavin Flood and Charles Martin, W. W. Norton, 2012; and Graham Schweig, HarperOne, 2007.
6. Easwaran, trans., The Bhagavad Gita, 80.
7. Easwaran, 81.
8. Easwaran, 88.
9. Easwaran, 97.
10. Easwaran, 107.
11. Easwaran, 105.
12. Nair, *A Higher Standard of Leadership,* 3.
13. Nair, 68.
14. Nair, 94.
15. Nair, 117–18.
16. Miller, trans., The Bhagavad Gita, 147.
17. Ralph Waldo Emerson, *The Conduct of Life,* Houghton, Mifflin, 1888.
18. Easwaran, trans., The Bhagavad Gita, 54.
19. Easwaran, 118–19.
20. Easwaran, 144.
21. Austin Carr and Dina Bass, "The Most Valuable Company (for Now) Is Having a Nadellaissance," *Bloomberg Business Week,* May 2, 2019, 2.
22. Carr and Bass, 3.
23. Carr and Bass, 4.
24. "Walt Disney Productions (A)," UVA-BP-0332, Darden Business Publishing, 1992.
25. "Honda (B)," 9-384-050, Harvard Business Publishing, 1984.
26. Facebook livestream: https://www.facebook.com/DardenMBA/videos/10154200644141315/.
27. Naresh Kumra's address to the senior author's Strategic Intuition and Eastern Philosophy MBA class, October 2018.
28. Naresh Kumra's address.

5. The Buddha and His Teaching

1. "Billionaires: The Richest People in the World," *Forbes*, March 5, 2019.
2. Perhaps the most common English reference to the Buddha is "Siddhartha Gautama," a transliteration from Sanskrit, the high-caste language spoken primarily by Northern India's religious elite. Although the Buddha was from a high caste and familiar with Sanskrit, he taught in Pali, a simpler language of the masses, in order to make his teaching accessible to the majority. In this chapter, we will refer to him as Siddhattha Gotama, and in describing other Buddhist principles we will use transliterations of Pali terms whenever possible. To ground this chapter's Pali words in terms familiar to many readers, here we point out some Sanskrit/Pali contrasts of familiar words: dharma/*dhamma*, karma/*kamma*, and nirvana/*nibbana*.
3. Our goal here is to present how these principles can inform readers' capacity to leverage strategic insight. Other writings draw connections between Buddhist traditions and general business best practices. For example, see Roach, *The Diamond Cutter;* Dalai Lama and Field, *Business and the Buddha;* and Dalai Lama and Muyzenberg, *The Leader's Way.*
4. Armstrong, *Buddha.*
5. Armstrong, 11.
6. Given the lack of highly verifiable sources regarding the Buddha's biography, the description offered here focuses on details that are believed to be the most likely version of events by a consensus of modern-day scholars.
7. Armstrong, *Buddha*, 89.
8. Easwaran, trans., The Dhammapada, 56.
9. Logan, *The Alphabet Effect.*
10. Walshe, trans., *The Long Discourses of the Buddha*, 344.
11. Walshe, 346.
12. Walshe, 347.
13. Pascale and Athos, *The Art of Japanese Management.*
14. Walshe, trans., *The Long Discourses of the Buddha*, 25.
15. Easwaran, trans., The Dhammapada, 44.
16. Easwaran, 45.
17. Epstein, *Advice Not Given*, 85.
18. Epstein, 105.

6. The Buddha and Mindfulness

1. Kristyna Zapletal, "Neuroscience of Mindfulness: What Happens to Your Brain When You Meditate," *Observer*, June 26, 2017.
2. Recent research indicates that yogic and mindful practices increase levels of hormones and neurotransmitters such as serotonin, dopamine, oxytocin, melatonin, and bradykinin. The positive effects include feelings of social connectedness, relaxation, and lower blood pressure and stress. Neuroplasticity allows the increase of gray matter and cortical thickness, which improves attention, cognitive flexibility, planning and prob-

lem solving, and emotion regulation. Ina Stevens, "Stress Physiology and Mindfulness Practices," presentation to White Hall Meditation, Crozet, Virginia, February 26, 2020.
3. Talbot-Zorn and Edgette, "Mindfulness Can Improve Strategy, Too."
4. Viktor E. Frankl, *Man's Search for Meaning,* Simon & Schuster, 1984, 75.
5. Christian Greiser and Jan-Philipp Martini, "Unleashing the Power of Mindfulness in Corporations," Boston Consulting Group, April 26, 2018.
6. The number of mindfulness academic research publications has soared, from 4 in 1995 to 21 in 2005, 596 in 2015, and 692 in 2017. Leslie Hubbard, "Contemplation and Contemplative Sciences," presentation to Darden MBA class, October 22, 2019. One of these publications notes that there are 80 to 100 billion neurons in the human brain, allowing hundreds of trillions of synapses between them. Neuroscientists are only now beginning to understand our ability to control some of these synapses through meditation and how we can influence our own brain's development because of its neuroplasticity. See Zapletal, "Neuroscience of Mindfulness."
7. Goldstein, *Mindfulness,* 391–95.
8. Walshe, trans., *The Long Discourses of the Buddha,* 270.
9. Nhat Hanh, *Silence,* 154.
10. Walshe, trans., *The Long Discourses of the Buddha,* 348–49.
11. Walshe, 335.
12. Walshe, 336.
13. Goldstein, *Mindfulness,* 101.
14. Walshe, trans., *The Long Discourses of the Buddha,* 340.
15. Analayo, *Satipatthana,* 182–86.
16. Walshe, trans., *The Long Discourses of the Buddha,* 341–50.
17. Walshe, 349.
18. Epstein, *Advice Not Given,* 177.
19. Personal communication.
20. Dalio, *Principles,* 219.
21. Courtney Cronin, "Controversy? Yes. But Kyle Guy Still Had to Hit the Free Throws," ESPN, April 6, 2019.

7. Zen

1. "Steve Jobs Keynote Macworld 2007 SF," YouTube video, 1:43:27, posted by "Steve Jobs Video," December 29, 2014, accessed October 16, 2019.
2. Parmy Olson, "BlackBerry's Famous Last Words at 2007 iPhone Launch: 'We'll Be Fine,'" *Forbes,* May 26, 2015.
3. Joel Hruska, "Ballmer: iPhone Has 'No Chance' of Gaining Significant Market Share," *Ars Technica,* April 30, 2007.
4. "Bloomberg writer: Apple iPhone Won't Make Long-Term Mark; Will Only Appeal to a Few Gadget Freaks," *MacDailyNews,* January 15, 2007.
5. Roland Lazenby, *Michael Jordan: The Life,* Little, Brown, 2014.
6. Sam Smith, "Phil Jackson Gets the Chicago Bulls Coaching Job in 1989," *Chicago Tribune,* July 10, 1989.

7. "Chan Buddhism," *Stanford Encyclopedia of Philosophy,* March 2, 2019.
8. Barrett, *Zen Buddhism,* 61.
9. D. T. Suzuki, a twentieth-century Japanese Buddhist scholar and leading ambassador of Zen to modern Western audiences, described Huineng as "the real Chinese founder of Zen Buddhism." Barrett, 82.
10. Barrett, 82.
11. Attributed to eighteenth-century monk Hakuin. C. B. Liddell, "Hakuin: The Sight of One Hand Clapping," *Japan Times,* January 17, 2013.
12. Delehanty and Jackson, *Eleven Rings,* 13.
13. Delehanty and Jackson, 18.
14. Michael Jordan, as told to Rick Telander, "Michael Jordan on Phil Jackson, Jerry Krause and the One NBA Player He Couldn't Stand the Most," ESPN, April 19, 2020.
15. Farhad Manjoo, "'It Smelled Something like Pizza': New Documents Reveal How Apple Really Invented the iPhone," *Slate,* September 10, 2012.
16. Delehanty and Jackson, *Eleven Rings,* 21.
17. Sam Anderson, "Why Basketball Won't Leave Phil Jackson Alone," *New York Times Magazine,* May 16, 2013.
18. Delehanty and Jackson, *Eleven Rings,* 21.
19. Manjoo, "It Smelled Something like Pizza."
20. Manjoo.
21. Barrett, *Zen Buddhism,* 98.
22. Delehanty and Jackson, *Eleven Rings,* 14.
23. Our readers are warned that for most Western practitioners unused to sitting in bent knee postures on the floor, the lotus position will initially prove extremely challenging. A teacher will be able to offer a wide range of alternatives to readers interested in experimenting with *zazen* but unable to assume the lotus position.
24. Charles Duhigg and Keith Bradsher, "How the U.S. Lost Out on iPhone Work," *New York Times,* January 21, 2012.

Part III. Relationships, overview

1. This notion was first introduced in the West by Chester Barnard in 1938 in *The Functions of the Executive.*

8. The *Tao Te Ching*

1. Seabee officer's personal story shared with the senior author.
2. Morgan, *The Best Guide to Eastern Philosophy,* 226.
3. Smith, *The World's Religions,* 198.
4. Gupta, student paper.
5. Cher Yi Tan, "Explaining the Curious Chinese Paradigm," *Medium,* June 22, 2018.
6. Frenchman Julian Alaphilippe told the Associated Press how he was able to plunge his bicycle down the Alps through hairpin turns at 55 mph to win his thirteenth stage in the Tour de France. *Daily Progress,* July 26, 2019, B5.

7. Puett and Gross-Loh, *The Path,* 103.
8. Smith, *The World's Religions,* 212, emphasis added.
9. Smith, 213.
10. Smith, 14.
11. Tara Brach, "Awakening from the Trance of Unworthiness," *Inquiring Mind,* vol. 17, no. 2 (Spring 2001): 4.
12. Lila MacLellan, "The Best Strategies for Self-Assessment, According to Buddhist and Stoic Philosophy," *Quartz,* April 18, 2017.
13. Jim Collins, "Level 5 Leadership," jimcollins.com.
14. Morgan, *The Best Guide to Eastern Philosophy,* 227.
15. Michael Ordona, "Review: ESPN's Latest Doc 'Be Water' Puts Bruce Lee in Cultural Context," *Los Angeles Times,* June 4, 2020.

9. Energy as a Strategic Force

1. The remainder of this chapter is based on Jonathan Doner and L. J. Bourgeois III, "Universal Mind in a Practical World," UVA-S-0286, Darden Business Publishing, 2016. Doner is *yondan* (fourth *dan,* or level) in *Ki-Aikido* and *joden* (upper tier) in *Shin Tōitsu Aikido.*
2. Sōhō, *The Unfettered Mind.*
3. Sōhō.
4. Musashi Miyamoto, *Gorin no sho.* Annotated by Nakamura Naokatsu, Kodansha, 1970.
5. "Aikido," Wikipedia.
6. John Stevens, *Abundant Peace,* Shambhala, 1987.
7. John Stevens, *Aikido: The Way of Harmony,* Shambhala, 1984.
8. Stevens.
9. Reed, *A Road Anyone Can Walk.*
10. Reed.
11. William Reed, *Ki: A Practical Guide for Westerners,* Japan Publications, 1986.
12. Reed, *Ki.*
13. Reed, *A Road Anyone Can Walk.*
14. Sōhō, *The Unfettered Mind.*
15. Personal communication.
16. Tōhei, *Ki Sayings.*
17. Personal communication.
18. Tōhei, *Ki Sayings.*
19. Tōhei.
20. Personal communication.
21. Adele Westbrook and Oscar Ratti, *Aikido and the Dynamic Sphere: An Illustrated Introduction,* Tuttle Publishing, 1970.
22. Ueshiba, *The Art of Peace.*
23. Tōhei, *Ki Sayings.*

24. Oh and Gummeson, student paper.
25. Lai, *Learning from the Stones*, 29.

10. Confucius

1. Andrew Cave, "Culture Eats Strategy for Breakfast. So What's for Lunch?" *Forbes*, November 9, 2017.
2. There is some debate about whether Drucker ever actually said this. While the exact phrase cannot be found in any of his published works, his writing often emphasized that for any strategy to succeed it must be aligned with organizational structure and culture.
3. Cleary, *The Essential Confucius*, 9.
4. Ronnie L. Littlejohn, "The World into Which Confucius Came," in *Confucianism: An Introduction*, I. B. Tauris, 2011.
5. *The Analects* is traditionally considered a leading primary source of Confucius's teachings as recorded by his students in the years after his death. Over the last several centuries, a variety of scholars have translated *The Analects* into English.
6. Muller, trans., *The Analects of Confucius*.
7. Senior author's personal experience.
8. Smith, *The World's Religions*, 162.
9. Personal communication.
10. Personal involvement.
11. Nair, *A Higher Standard of Leadership*, 15.
12. Personal involvement.

11. Strategy as a Call to (in)Action

1. Sun Tzu, *The Art of War*, trans. Clavell, 11.
2. See L. J. Bourgeois and K. M. Eisenhardt, "Strategic Decision Processes in High Velocity Environments: Four Cases in the Microcomputer Industry," *Management Science*, vol. 34, no. 7 (July 1988): 816–35.
3. IBM was known as Big Blue because of its blue logo.
4. David Gilles, "Indra Nooyi: 'I'm Not Here to Tell You What to Eat,'" *New York Times*, March 24, 2019, 3.
5. As mentioned elsewhere, this book's origins can be traced to the Strategic Intuition and Eastern Philosophy course taught to Darden MBA students at the University of Virginia. A key part of the course is reflections written by the students regarding the philosophical texts they encountered and the connection between these materials and the lessons of their broader MBA education. Here and in chapters 8 and 9, we quote from some of those reflections.
6. Danielson, student paper.
7. Reardon and Hoang-Le, student paper.
8. Reardon and Hoang-Le.

9. David Gray, "Wanted: Chief Ignorance Officer," *Harvard Business Review* (November 2003): 1.
10. Reardon and Hoang-Le, student paper.
11. Ahmad and Heywood, student paper.
12. Personal communication.
13. David Brooks, "Longing for an Internet Cleanse: A Small Rebellion against the Quickening of Time," *New York Times,* March 28, 2019, 1.
14. Brooks, 2.
15. Shankar, student paper.
16. Walter Isaacson, *Steve Jobs,* Simon & Schuster, 2001, 49.
17. Mulchandani, student paper.
18. Lila MacLellan, "The One 'Fascinating' Mind-Training Exercise Microsoft CEO Satya Nadella Practices Every Day," *Quartz,* May 25, 2018. We are indebted to Christina Gonsalves, MBA 2019, for this reference.
19. Joann S. Lublin, "Meditation Brings Calm to CEOs," *Wall Street Journal,* November 29, 2017.
20. Colton, student paper.
21. Easwaran, trans., The Bhagavad Gita, 18–20.
22. Easwaran, 94.
23. Mitchell, trans., *The Tao Te Ching,* 9.
24. Colton, student paper.
25. Ron Counts, "Mendenhall Deal Details Released," *Daily Progress,* June 12, 2019, B1.
26. "Steve Job's Best Quotes," *Wall Street Journal,* August 28, 2011.
27. Derrick A. Paulo, "How a Buddhist Monk Turned CEO Revived Japan Airlines from Bankruptcy," Channel News Asia, December 15, 2018.
28. Tyagi, student paper.
29. Mitchell, trans., *The Tao Te Ching,* 27.
30. Clave, student paper.
31. Mitchell, trans., *The Tao Te Ching,* 78.
32. Hannah Yasharoff, "ESPN's New Bruce Lee Documentary, 'Be Water,' Is a 'Must-Watch' Look at Racism in Hollywood, Critics Say," *USA Today,* June 7, 2020.
33. Mitchell, 76.
34. Tom Peters and Robert Waterman, *In Search of Excellence,* HarperCollins, 1982, sold more than 3 million copies. James C. Collins and Jerry L. Porras, *Built to Last: Successful Habits of Visionary Companies,* Harper Business, 1994.
35. Yoon, student paper.
36. Nisbett, *The Geography of Thought,* 13.
37. Nisbett, 177.
38. For example, see Epstein, *Advice Not Given,* where chapters 1 through 8 are each dedicated to one of the steps in the Eightfold Path. To be fair, this writer provides one of the clearest maps available to Western readers.
39. Personal communication.
40. Clausewitz, *On War,* trans. Howard and Paret, 108.
41. Williamson, "Strategy as Options on the Future."

42. Kimberly A. Whitler, "What Western Marketers Can Learn from China," *Harvard Business Review* (May–June 2019), 82.
43. Trans. unknown, *The Tao Te Ching,* chapter 40.
44. Nisbett, *The Geography of Thought,* 59.
45. As recounted by a Duke colleague.
46. Easwaran, trans., The Bhagavad Gita, 108.
47. Easwaran, 94.
48. Armstrong, *Buddha,* 128.
49. Collins and Porras, *Built to Last.*
50. In chapter 17.
51. In chapter 3.
52. Personal communication.
53. Tiger God Shrine was erected in 1834 and moved to the current location in 1870. In the past, the shrine was famous among Teochew Chinese immigrants in Thailand. Recently it has become popular among Thai people in general and has been included in the Tourism Authority of Thailand's "Respect to the Nine Temples" campaign.
54. Mitchell, trans., *The Tao Te Ching,* chapter 15.
55. Grusky, student paper.
56. Lira, student paper.
57. Mitchell, trans., *The Tao Te Ching,* 64.
58. Lira, student paper.
59. Mitchell, trans., *The Tao Te Ching,* 59.
60. Collins and Porras, *Built to Last.*
61. Hamel and Prahalad, "Strategic Intent."
62. Collins and Porras, *Built to Last.*

BIBLIOGRAPHY

Strategy

Beihnocker, Eric D., "Robust Adaptive Strategies," *Sloan Management Review* (Spring 1999): 95–106.

Bourgeois, L. J., and David R. Brodwin, "Strategy Implementation: Five Approaches to an Elusive Phenomenon," *Strategic Management Journal*, vol. 5, no. 3 (July–September 1984): 241–64.

Collis, David, and Cynthia Montgomery, "Competing on Resources," *Harvard Business Review* (July–August 1995), 118–28.

Duggan, William, *Strategic Intuition*. New York: Columbia Business School Publishing, 2007.

Ghyczy, Tiha von, Bolko Oetinger, and Christopher Bassford, eds., *Clausewitz on Strategy*. New York: John Wiley & Sons, 2001.

Hamel, Gary, and C. K. Prahalad, "Strategic Intent," *Harvard Business Review* (July–August 1989).

Kim, W. Chan, and Renee Mauborgne, *Blue Ocean Strategy*. Boston: Harvard Business School Press, 2005.

Oster, Sharon M., *Modern Competitive Analysis*, 3rd ed. Oxford: Oxford University Press, 1999.

Porter, Michael, "How Competitive Forces Shape Strategy," *Harvard Business Review* (March–April 1979), 137–45.

Pugh, Jonathan, and L. J. Bourgeois, "Doing Strategy," *Journal of Strategy and Management*, vol. 4, no. 2 (2011), 172–79.

Sarasvathy, Saras D., *Effectuation: Elements of Entrepreneurial Expertise*. Cheltenham, United Kingdom: Edward Elgar Publishing, 2008.

Williamson, Peter J., "Strategy as Options on the Future," *Sloan Management Review* (Spring 1999): 117–26.

Philosophy of War

Clausewitz, Carl von, *On War* (translated by Anatol Rappaport). New York: Penguin, 1968.

———. *On War* (edited and translated by Michael Howard and Peter Paret). Princeton: Princeton University Press, 1976.

Lai, David, *Learning from the Stones: A Go Approach to Mastering China's Strategic Concept, Shi*. Carlisle, Pennsylvania: U.S. Army War College Press, 2004.

Mao's Selected Military Writings. Peking: Foreign Language Press, 1963.

This compilation was widely employed in the early 2000s within the American military establishment to better understand China's rise as a major potential geopolitical competitor.

Musashi, Miyamoto, *The Book of Five Rings* (translated by W. S. Wilson). Boulder, Colorado: Shambhala, 2012.

Sun Tzu, *The Art of War* (translated by James Clavell). New York: Delacorte Press, 1983.

——, *The Art of War* (translated by Samuel B. Griffith). Oxford: Oxford University Press, 1963.

Taylor, Peter, *The Thirty-Six Stratagems*. Oxford: Infinite Ideas, 2013.

A compilation of Chinese essays from approximately three hundred years ago, the book contains a series of stratagems used in politics, war, and civilian life, often through unorthodox means.

Hinduism

Doniger, Wendy, *The Hindus: An Alternative History*. New York: Penguin, 2009.

Easwaran, Eknath, trans., The Bhagavad Gita. Tomales, California: Nilgiri Press, 2007.

Miller, Barbara Stoler, trans., *The Bhagavad Gita: Krishna's Counsel in Time of War*. New York: Bantam Classics, 2004.

Buddhism

Armstrong, Karen, *Buddha*. New York: Penguin Books, 2001.

Conze, Edward, trans., *Buddhist Scriptures*. New York: Penguin, 1959.

Essentially Armstrong's *Buddha* in more detail, this book provides a more solid grounding about the Buddha, Buddhist teaching, and Buddhism.

Easwaran, Eknath, trans., The Dhammapada. Tomales, California: Nilgiri Press, 2007.

Epstein, Mark, *Advice Not Given*. New York: Penguin, 2018.

Hallisey, Charles, trans., *Therigatha: Poems of the First Buddhist Women*. Boston: Harvard University Press, 2015.

Osho, *Buddha Said . . . : Meeting the Challenge of Life's Difficulties*. London: Watkins Press, 2007.

The book quotes and explains key sutras.

Thera, Nyanaponika, and Hellmuth Hecker, *Great Disciples of the Buddha: Their Lives, Their Works, Their Legacy*. Somerville, Massachusetts: Wisdom Publications, 2003.

This book provides a different lens through which to learn about Buddhism—not stories of the Buddha but of the Buddha's key disciples. Practitioners can relate to some of the disciples' experiences.

Walshe, Maurice, trans., *The Long Discourses of the Buddha: A Translation of the Digha Nikaya (The Teachings of the Buddha)*. New York: Wisdom Publications, 2012.

A pure translation of the important Theravada teachings.

Mindfulness

Analayo. *Satipatthana: The Direct Path to Realization*. Chiang Mai, Thailand: Silkworm Books, 2003.

Goldstein, Joseph, *Mindfulness: A Practical Guide to Awakening.* Louisville, Colorado: Sounds True, 2013.

Kabbat-Zin, Jon, *Wherever You Go, There You Are: Mindfulness Meditation in Everyday Life.* New York: Hyperion, 2004.

Nhat Hanh, Thich, *Be Free Where You Are.* Berkeley, California: Parallax Press, 2002.

This short (fifty-six pages) book was originally intended for prisoners. A compendium of Nhat Hanh's core teaching, it is based on a talk given at the Maryland Correctional Institution.

———, *The Miracle of Mindfulness: A Manual on Meditation.* Boston: Beacon Press, 1975.

———, *Silence.* New York: HarperCollins, 2016.

Zapletal, Kristyna, "Neuroscience of Mindfulness: What Exactly Happens to Your Brain When You Meditate," *Mindful Entrepreneurship,* May 18, 2017.

Zen Buddhism

Barrett, William, ed., *Zen Buddhism: Selected Writings of D. T. Suzuki.* Los Angeles: Three Leaves Press, 2006.

Delehanty, Hugh, and Phil Jackson, *Eleven Rings: The Soul of Success.* New York: Penguin, 2013.

Pine, Red, trans., *The Zen Teaching of Bodhidharma.* New York: North Point, 1989.

This book is about the events happening before the *Sutra of Hui Neng* and provides sufficient background on Zen Buddhism.

Price, A. F., and Wong Mou-lam, *The Diamond Sutra and the Sutra of Hui Neng.* Boulder, Colorado: Shambhala Classics, 2005.

A thin Zen Buddhism book that you will spend time with to pause and think about each sentence. From our coauthor Mint Namasondhi: "I read it several times, going from a 50 percent understanding after my first reading to a higher level of understanding. The moment I thought I understood the meaning, I was so mesmerized that I felt my arm hairs stand up with fascination—like an 'aha!' moment."

The Tao

Hoff, Benjamin, *The Tao of Pooh.* New York: Penguin, 1982.

Many Western students will recognize Winnie-the-Pooh from their childhoods. He was actually a Daoist.

Mitchell, Stephen, trans., *The Tao Te Ching.* New York: Harper Perennial, 1992.

Energy

Reed, William, *A Road Anyone Can Walk: Ki.* Tokyo: Japan Publications, 1992.

Sōhō, Takuan, *The Unfettered Mind.* Tokyo: Kodansha International, 1986.

Tōhei, Kōichi, *Ki Sayings.* Tokyo: Ki No Kenkyukai H.Q., 2003.

Ueshiba, Morihei, *The Art of Peace.* Boston: Shambhala, 1992.

Confucius

Cleary, Thomas, trans., *The Essential Confucius.* New York: HarperOne, 1992.

Lau, D. C., trans., *Confucius: The Analects.* New York: Penguin Books, 1979.

Muller, A. Charles, trans., *The Analects of Confucius.* Tokyo: Resources for East Asian Language and Thought, Musashino University, December 4, 2018.

Additional Resources

CULTURAL DIFFERENCES

Logan, Robert, *The Alphabet Effect: The Impact of the Phonetic Alphabet on the Development of Western Civilization.* New York: William Morrow, 1986.

See chapter 3, "A comparison of Eastern and Western writing systems and their impact on cultural patterns." See also 38–44, from "The introduction of vowels in alphabetic writing" to "Why the Chinese never developed an alphabet."

Morrison, Terri, and Wayne Conway, *Kiss, Bow, or Shake Hands*, 2nd ed. New York: Simon & Schuster, 2006.

This guide to doing business in sixty-two countries covers such topics as culture, business protocol, decision-making styles (individualistic versus collectivistic), sources of anxiety reduction, and negotiations. You may find that the most interesting chapter is the one on your own country.

Nisbett, Richard, *The Geography of Thought: How Asians and Westerners Think Differently . . . and Why.* New York: Free Press, 2003.

EASTERN PHILOSOPHY AS APPLIED TO BUSINESS PRACTICE

Dalai Lama and Lloyd Field, *Business and the Buddha: Doing Well by Doing Good.* Boston: Wisdom Publications, 2007.

———and Laurens van den Muyzenberg, *The Leader's Way: The Art of Making the Right Decisions in Our Careers, Our Companies, and the World at Large.* New York: Crown Business, 2009.

Dalio, Ray, *Principles.* New York: Simon & Schuster, 2017.

Hougaard, Rasmus, and Jacqueline Carter, "How to Practice Mindfulness throughout Your Work Day," *Harvard Business Review,* March 2016.

Koyen, Gary, Becca O'Connor, and John Maurer, *The Warrior and the Monk: The Journey to Wise Leadership and Market Dominance.* Guilford, Connecticut: Meridian Consulting Group, 1999.

Malloch, Theodore Roosevelt, *Practical Wisdom in Management: Business across Spiritual Traditions.* Oxford, United Kingdom: Taylor & Francis, 2015.

Nair, Keshavan, *A Higher Standard of Leadership: Lessons from the Life of Gandhi.* San Francisco: Berrett-Koehler, 1994.

Pascale, Richard T., and Anthony G. Athos, *The Art of Japanese Management.* New York: Simon & Schuster, 1981.

Roach, Michael, *The Diamond Cutter: The Buddha on Managing Your Business and Your Life.* New York: Rand McNally, 2009.

Talbot-Zorn, Justin, and Frieda Edgette, "Mindfulness Can Improve Strategy, Too," *Harvard Business Review* (May 2016).

Tan, Chade-Meng, *Search Inside Yourself.* New York: HarperOne, 2012.

GENERAL REFERENCES TO EASTERN PHILOSOPHIES

Morgan, Diane, *The Best Guide to Eastern Philosophy and Religion.* Los Angeles: Renaissance Books, 2001.

Puett, Michael, and Christine Gross-Loh, *The Path: What Chinese Philosophers Can Teach Us About the Good Life.* New York: Simon & Schuster, 2016.

Smith, Huston, *The World's Religions.* New York: HarperOne, 1991.

IMPERMANENCE

Rovelli, Carlo, *The Order of Time.* New York: Penguin, 2017.

Taleb, Nassim Nicholas, *Fooled by Randomness: The Hidden Role of Chance in Life and in Markets.* New York: Random House, 2004.

INDEX

Page numbers in italics refer to figures and tables.

ABOUT THE AUTHORS

L. J. Bourgeois III is Emeritus Professor of Strategy and senior fellow at the Darden Center for Global Initiatives, University of Virginia. He is a former Tayloe Murphy Professor of Strategy at the Darden Graduate School of Business, Associate Dean for International Affairs and Director of the Darden Center for Global Initiatives. He was also an associate of the Boston Consulting Group Institute and a member of the Charlottesville Committee on Foreign Relations.

He taught at the Stanford Business School, where he was the director of the Strategic Management Program. Author of 3 books and 95 cases and articles, Bourgeois' research is required reading in leading doctoral programs on strategy in the US and Europe. He has coached CEOs and consulted with more than 100 firms, governments and non-profits around the world on strategy and post-merger integration. *Journal of Management* has recognized him as one of the top 150 management scholars out of 25,000 worldwide.

Serge Eygenson is a management consultant for a global consulting firm, where his work focuses on supporting organizational leaders on strategic questions related to growth, profitability, digital transformation and operating model design. Serge grew up in Moscow, Chicago and London and is a graduate of Tufts University and the University of Virginia Darden School of Business. He is passionate about organizational strategy, mindfulness, travel, fitness and crafting the perfect music playlist of early 2000s hits.

Based in Bangkok, **Kanokrat 'Mint' Namasondhi** is a consultant at a global management consulting firm and a CFA charterholder. Mint is a Thai–Chinese–Japanese Buddhist. She studied in a Catholic school before earning a bachelor's degree in English literature from Chulalongkorn University, Thailand. Mint pursued her MBA at the University of Virginia Darden School of Business, where her journey toward a passion for the integration of Buddhism, Eastern Philosophy and Western management began. At Darden, Mint also received the Faculty Award for Academic Excellence and was selected as part of the Tri-Sector Leadership Fellows Program.